T0265765

Running Effective Meetings

by Joseph A. Allen and Karin M. Reed

A Wiley Brand

Running Effective Meetings For Dummies®

Published by: **John Wiley & Sons, Inc.**, 111 River Street, Hoboken, NJ 07030-5774, www.wiley.com

Copyright © 2023 by John Wiley & Sons, Inc., Hoboken, New Jersey

Published simultaneously in Canada

Includes text used with permission from *Suddenly Virtual: Making Remote Meetings Work* (John Wiley & Sons, Inc., 2021) and *Suddenly Hybrid: Managing the Modern Meeting* (John Wiley & Sons, Inc., 2022), authored by Joseph A. Allen and Karin M. Reed.

For general information on our other products and services, please contact our Customer Care Department within the U.S. at 877-762-2974, outside the U.S. at 317-572-3993, or fax 317-572-4002. For technical support, please visit www.wiley.com/techsupport.

Wiley publishes in a variety of print and electronic formats and by print-on-demand. Some material included with standard print versions of this book may not be included in e-books or in print-on-demand. If this book refers to media such as a CD or DVD that is not included in the version you purchased, you may download this material at http://booksupport.wiley.com. For more information about Wiley products, visit www.wiley.com.

Library of Congress Control Number: 2022943107

ISBN: 978-1-119-87570-3 (pbk); ISBN: 978-1-119-87571-0 (epdf); ISBN: 978-1-119-87572-7 (epub)

Contents at a Glance

Table of Contents

Introduction

"Yay! Another meeting!"

We would bet big money that these words have never been said, except perhaps by Joe who has been studying meetings for decades. In fact, meetings have been maligned from practically the dawn of meetings themselves. But meetings, on their own, aren't bad. We would suggest it's the meeting leaders who are bad at running them (and the meeting attendees who are bad at contributing within them) . . . and that's why we are thrilled you are reading this book.

Whether you've never run a meeting before in your career or curse the hours you've spent running what you'd objectively consider rotten meetings, think of this book as your ultimate guide. You will discover all you need to know about running an effective meeting, one where you actually get stuff done, move business forward, and perhaps even have fun along the way.

But even if you don't run many meetings, you'll still find value in giving this book a read. There are nuggets of insight throughout the book on how you can be a better meeting attendee and support your meeting leaders in their efforts to make their sessions worthwhile. Heck, you might even find yourself coaching up your supervisor or boss on better meeting management. That would make our day and likely your future in meetings just a little bit brighter!

About This Book

If you are a manager, much of your workday will be devoted to meetings. Some you will lead and some you may just attend. We focus in this book on the former. We've loosely organized the book in sequential order, sharing best practices for what to do before, during, and after a meeting.

Some of what we include may not be news to you. In fact, many meeting best practices are common sense but uncommonly practiced. Even if you read something that seems elementary to you, pause to put it into context. You may know that "starting on time" is a good idea, but do you really hold yourself to that standard? Everything included in this book is designed to build a strong foundation for a meeting that is both productive and satisfying for all involved.

To make the content more accessible, we've divided it into five parts:

» **Part 1: Understanding the Role of Meetings in Business.** This is a great place to start to get a solid overview of how meetings are incorporated and conducted across the corporate landscape. We also include some specific considerations related to video use and global participants.

» **Part 2: Setting Up for Success — What to do Before a Meeting.** How effective your meeting will be is often dictated before you even enter the meeting room, whether it's a physical or virtual one. In this part, we talk about the critical steps you should take prior to your meeting.

» **Part 3: Facilitating an Effective Meeting — What to do During a Meeting.** It's showtime! This part is devoted to ensuring you orchestrate a meeting that accomplishes its goal. We focus primarily on promoting full participation and tamping down bad meeting behavior while spending some time on best practices in delivering presentations within a meeting.

» **Part 4: Making a Meeting Worthwhile — What to do After a Meeting.** Don't let all of your hard work be for naught. What you do once the official meeting adjourns is just as important as what you do prior to and during your session. In this part, we lay out the actions you need to take once everyone has left the meeting room.

» **Part 5: The Part of Tens.** Looking for some quick inspiration? The chapters in this part are our top ten lists offering you specific strategies for amping up participation, jump-starting a stalled dialogue, and rethinking where a meeting should take place.

Foolish Assumptions

In this book, we assume that you fall into one of two categories:

» You are a new manager with either no or very limited experience in leading a meeting.

» You are a not-so-new manager who is dissatisfied with how you're leading your meetings.

Either way, you will find a lot of valuable information that will help you to either create good habits from the get-go or break bad habits and replace them with better ones.

We also assume that you are relatively tech savvy or are willing to learn how to incorporate technology into your meetings. Given the proliferation of virtual and hybrid meetings, you will have at least some familiarity with online meeting platforms.

Icons Used in This Book

Throughout this book, icons in the margins highlight certain types of valuable information that call out for your attention. Here are the icons you'll encounter and a brief description of each:

TIP

The Tip icon marks tips and shortcuts that you can use to make running your meetings easier. They're very practical in nature and include specific actions we recommend you take to improve the meeting experience for you and your attendees.

REMEMBER

Remember icons mark the information that's especially important to know. To siphon off the most important information in each chapter, just skim through these icons.

TECHNICAL STUFF

The Technical Stuff icon marks information of a highly technical nature that you can normally skip over. However, if you are looking for the "why" behind the "what" for some of the best practices we mention, feel free to read on. Joe, as a meeting scientist, would be especially delighted when reading text marked with this icon.

WARNING

The Warning icon tells you to watch out! It marks important information that may save you headaches, when you are plotting out your strategy for planning, running, and following up on your meetings.

Beyond the Book

In addition to the abundance of information and guidance related to meetings that we provide in this book, you get access to even more help and information online at *Dummies.com*. Check out this book's online Cheat Sheet. Just go to www.dummies.com and search for "Running Effective Meetings For Dummies Cheat Sheet."

Where to Go from Here

If you are new to this meeting leader thing, you may want to flip open the front cover and keep flipping the pages until you reach the back cover, reading all of the chapters in the sequence shown. That works!

If you are simply looking to improve your current meeting process, you may only need a bit more insight here, a bit more intel there. The choice is yours. For example, if you're interested in making the discussion in your meetings more effective and enjoyable, flick through to Chapter 3. Or if differences in people's culture and how it impacts their behavior in meetings is something you've always wanted to find out more about (but were afraid to ask), check out Chapter 6. And if you're looking for a general overview to explain why running meetings well is important (whether for yourself or to explain to others), turn the page and start with Chapter 1.

If you want to devour the entire thing in chronological order, go for it. If you want to hop in and out of chapters, based upon what you need to know, that works too. Each section stands alone, but we will let you know if you are reading a section on a certain topic which is discussed elsewhere in the book.

Meetings matter. Run them poorly, and they gum up the works of any business. Run them well and they'll be like a well-oiled machine that keeps business chugging along. Time to start the journey!

1

Understanding the Role of Meeting in Business

You might be asking yourself, "Why do meetings matter?"

It's a fair question, but we are going to assume that if you bought this book, you have more than just an inkling that your ability to run them well may be a key component to your success. Considering how much of your time as a manager is spent conducting meetings, you're spot on! However, knowing how to facilitate and manage a meeting is a lot more complex than you might imagine.

In this part, you will discover why meetings are so important to business. You will learn about the full meeting continuum, things to do before, during, and after a meeting. We'll also explain the key decision points around how to meet, including face-to-face, virtual, and hybrid.

Chapter **1**

Making Meetings More Effective

S o be honest with us: Were you given this book as a gag gift by your team who thought it would be hilarious to give you a book about running *effective* meetings . . . for *dummies*?

When we first heard the proposed title, we thought it might lend itself to that kind of purchase. No worries, regardless of how this book made its way to you, we're glad you're here, and we think you will be too. Why? Because when it comes to running meetings well, there's a lot to learn whether you are a newbie to the task or have been leading meetings for decades.

Some meetings are well run and result in employees and team members being inspired, encouraged, and ready to perform at a high level. Many meetings are not run so well. They suffer from a lack of focus, a constraining of participation, and result in people leaving confused, misdirected, or simply just annoyed.

Our promise to you is that following the guidance in this book will make the meetings you lead be well run. The tips and tricks, the best practices, and the prioritized processes contained herein are tried and true. In other words, they are science-based practice. What does that mean?

Science-based practice means that every recommendation we make and tip we give you has emerged from the scientific community that studies workplace meetings. In fact, the vast majority of these recommendations come directly from the science of meetings that Joe studies and the practice of meetings that Karin leads. You can proceed to implement any of the things we suggest with complete confidence that they will indeed change your meeting experiences for the better.

Gone are the days where you lead a meeting and leave it feeling like you didn't accomplish the goals you had for the meeting. Follow the steps in this book and you can enjoy countless good meetings, and get this . . . even see some free time open up on your calendar. How is this possible?

Our data tells us one bad meeting results in three more meetings, meetings that are needed to clean up the mess of the original one. Think about it this way, if you have fewer bad meetings, you'll have fewer meetings overall!

And if that's not reason enough to read this book, let's give you just one more reason. You don't have to run meetings to use many of the tips and recommendations provided in this book. In fact, a good meeting attendee has a powerful influence on the effectiveness of the meetings they attend. Sure, you may not be able to replace the meeting leader, but you can help replace the bad behavior that sometimes permeates the meetings you attend. (If you want more detail, check out Chapter 14 that provides ways to stifle those bad behaviors.)

There's indeed hope for a brighter meeting future and we're here to help you achieve it.

Understanding Why Meetings are Important

This is the ages-old question that Joe tries to answer in every paper or book he writes, "Who cares?". More specifically, why should we care about meetings? We all have them. They are kind of "meh," and they do essentially all that we need them to do, albeit not as well as we might generally like.

Well, let's review a few facts:

>> According to some amazing survey work by Elise Keith at Lucid Meetings, there were at least 55 million meetings per day in the United States in 2015. But that was before COVID-19 hit, and there was an explosion in the number

of meetings that we were having. In fact, it's estimated that the number of meetings increased by 252 percent during the pandemic and have not come back down. So, doing a little math here, that means we're at somewhere around 139 million meetings a day. That's a lot of meetings.

» Fifty-one percent of meetings in the U.S. are rated as poor. Not so-so. Not okay. Poor! That means more than half of those 139 million meetings are just plain lousy. They're awful, uninspiring, time-sucks that drain the energy and life out of people. It's no wonder that we commiserate at the water cooler after a long day of meetings (or more likely the pub on Fridays).

» In larger organizations, managers spend 75 percent of their time on meeting-related activities. That is, the vast majority of their time is spent preparing for, attending, and leading meetings. If you're a manager in a larger organization, you're probably yelling at the book right now. We hear you and we feel your pain! We've lived that painful narrative ourselves, and that's why the science and practice of meetings is coming together to give you this book.

REMEMBER

Meetings are everywhere. They fill up our calendars. But, they do not have to be terrible. They can and should be better and we can help!

Now, just because we do something a lot doesn't make it important. So, we repeat, "Who cares?" Well, where are all the important business decisions made? How are scarce resources in an organization divided up? Where do we both bond with our colleagues and lend them support at the same time? Where are strategies for the future born? Where are products moved from idea to reality? We could go on, but the answer is meetings. For more on the many purposes of meetings, flick through to Chapter 7.

Meetings are a highly customizable and adaptable collaboration environment where three or more people come together to discuss something. They are typically more formal than a quick chat, but less formal than an organized lecture or convention. Meetings are where people make many of the decisions that manage organizational life and are also where communities, cultures, and social connections are initiated, maintained, and sometimes ended.

In sum, meetings are everywhere and they can do many things. But, the people in them are just people. We all make mistakes. We all have flaws. And we carry those issues with us into our collaborative environments. Good meeting practices are intuitive and can help us collaborate effectively regardless of our mistakes, flaws, and issues. But, we have to choose to do follow them.

Discovering Why Better Meetings Benefit Everyone

We all have a ton of meetings and they can do a lot of good things for us, but will it really benefit you if you put more effort into each one? Yes! And there's really good scientific evidence to back up this emphatic claim.

TECHNICAL STUFF

In 2008, Joe started working with his mentor Steven Rogelberg on a study looking at how meetings might relate to job satisfaction. Specifically, we were trying to provide evidence that human resources managers and others should care about meetings, how they are run, and how they impact employees. Steven's idea around this was to see if meeting satisfaction related to job satisfaction. In the first study, we decided to statistically control for the facets of job satisfaction. These include satisfaction with one's pay, coworkers, the work itself, promotion opportunities, and the boss. Once you account for those five things, there's not a whole lot left that could relate to job satisfaction. In fact, what are meetings? Gatherings of coworkers and often the boss. Our hope was that meetings are more than just being around coworkers and the boss, but something more core to employees' ability to do their work. To our surprise and wonder, meeting satisfaction still related to job satisfaction even after we accounted for all five of these things! That meant that there's something interesting about meetings that's more than just wrapped up in our relationship with and satisfaction with our coworkers and bosses.

This led to a series of studies looking at the positive impact and negative impact of meetings, including how meetings can help or hurt overall employee health and well-being. Here's what we concluded:

>> Good meetings positively relate to overall employee satisfaction with their job, their level of employee engagement, and their performance on the job. In other words, good meetings make for happier, harder working employees that actually get the job done.

>> Bad meetings lead to more dissatisfaction, disengagement, and lower job performance. However, it doesn't stop there. Bad meetings also relate to employee stress, reductions in overall health, and increases in burnout. In other words, bad meetings actually make people less well and are a major driver of burnout and turnover in organizations.

And maybe we shouldn't be all that surprised. Given how prevalent they are, for a lot of people, meetings are their work. We know from a long history of workforce research that when people are happy in their jobs, they are generally happy with life. If your meetings are miserable and you have a lot of meetings, you probably aren't that happy with your job. To find out more on how to evaluate your meetings, check out Chapter 16.

REMEMBER

Good meetings lead to good outcomes. Bad meetings lead to bad outcomes. And we are all about helping you and everyone else have more good meetings, and fewer bad meetings.

Knowing What Kind of Meetings this Book is About

Given the range and flexibility of meetings, it may come as no surprise that there are a number of different meeting types:

>> There are small meetings among team members.

>> There are large meetings, such as conferences and conventions where hundreds of people come together.

>> There are even medium-sized meetings such as board meetings or stand-up meetings for a larger workforce in a facility.

But that's all just about size.

You could also put meetings into general categories or meeting types such as:

>> the staff meeting

>> the safety meeting

>> the committee meeting

>> the stand-up meeting

>> the debrief meeting

Meetings can also have a variety of purposes including, but not limited to:

>> Strategy development

>> Product development

>> Human resources decisions

>> Project meetings

>> Agile meetings

>> Meetings to plan other meetings

We could go on and on with these bullet lists, but we think you get the gist.

Joe likes to remind people that humans started holding meetings with each other as soon as there were enough people to call for one. That's a long time ago. Our meeting purposes now are a bit different than they probably were then. Instead of decisions about where to hunt for our next meal, we have meetings about where we want to get lunch for our new client. Wait, that sounds awfully similar!

REMEMBER

Regardless, this book could not be about every single potential meeting type. That would be absurd and would require a whole series of *For Dummies* books (and a new set of bookshelves for you), rather than one book. So, our focus in this particular book is on the small group or team meeting. It just so happens to be the most common form of meeting that fills up our calendars to no end. So, it's a good place to start.

The small group meeting

The *small group meeting* is a gathering of three to around seven individuals as a group to discuss a matter. Yes, two people can have a meeting, but it takes three to be a group. Folks in small group meetings can be from the same team within an organization or they can be from different departments or even different organizations. That is, the meeting can be with *internal stakeholders* (people in the organization) or *external stake holders* (people outside the organization).

The key attribute is that these are relatively small gatherings where a variety of topics may be discussed and decisions are often made. They essentially follow Jeff Bezos' (Amazon CEO) two pizza rule, which states that a meeting shouldn't contain more people than could be fed by two large pizzas. That pretty much caps out small group meetings at around five to seven people, give or take. We talk about this more in Chapter 2.

REMEMBER

The small group meeting is the most common form of meeting from a size perspective, and the kind of meeting that represents the vast majority of meetings on most people's calendars.

The most common meeting types

Within the small group meeting context, there are a number of meeting types. And within those meeting types there are probably 1,000 different purposes that people could identify for hold a meeting. We won't even attempt to get into the purposes of meetings because they are so varied. However, we do provide here the list of the five most common meeting types for small group meetings.

» **Staff meeting:** A recurring, often regularly scheduled, meeting to provide updates, discuss upcoming events, coordinate tasks, and address current problems or challenges.

» **Committee meeting:** A regularly scheduled meeting of a rotating group of organizational members that focus on and discuss a specific topic area.

» **Project team meeting:** A group of employees coming together for a structured meeting based on the project purpose to discuss plans, provide status updates, determine leadership on tasks, and provide a project review.

» **Shift-change meeting:** Also referred to as a handoff meeting, this meeting is between off-going shift members and oncoming shift members to exchange relevant information about the work.

» **Debrief meeting:** A meeting scheduled as needed to discuss a recent work event, review regular operations, and/or discuss recent safety or performance activities with the overt goal of learning and improving effectiveness.

The vast majority of your meetings you have each week would fit into these common types of meetings. However, we would be remiss if we were to claim these are all the meeting types (check out the nearby sidebar for other kinds of meeting). If you want to learn how to align your meeting purposes with your goals, flick through to Chapter 8.

WARNING

MEETINGS THIS BOOK IS NOT ABOUT!

In case you missed it, this book is about running effective small group meetings. That means this book is not about some other common meetings that you'll run across. Some of these already have very good *For Dummies* books of their own. For example, this book is not about conventions and conferences. These are a very different kind of meetings, with different purposes, aims, and criteria. *Meeting and Event Planning For Dummies* by Susan Friedmann (Wiley, 2003) would be a good place to start for doing these kinds of meetings.

Additionally, another meeting type that this book is not about is the one-on-one. This meeting has become more and more common as more people have the option to work remotely. In fact, some recent estimates suggest it is even becoming more common

(continued)

(continued)

than the small group meeting on some people's calendars. Managers often use the one-on-one to touch base with their employees. They are essentially a check-in and can be used for a variety of purposes. However, by definition, they do not constitute a small group, so they don't really fit with the meeting type that this book focuses on.

We will add, however, that these example meeting types that this book is not about could benefit from some of the best practices we describe. For example, we discuss the importance of starting on time and ending on time. That's very relevant for conventions, conferences, and one-on-ones. However, having a written agenda may not be.

With this in mind, exercise caution when attempting to apply our recommendations in this book to meetings that are not within the scope of the small group meeting. You're welcome to experiment with using the tips and tricks here in other contexts, but we cannot vouch for their usefulness in these other meeting situations.

Discovering Why Meetings are So Complex

Meetings have needed a face-lift for some time now. Much of the research on workplace meetings occurred in the last ten years and decidedly showed that we could do better and that we need to do better. However, meetings are decidedly more complex now than ever before. Why is that?

Not so many years ago, economies were country-centric. Most goods and services were created within a given country's borders. For example, "Made in America" stickers and advertising ploys were not really a thing at that time because everything that people used came from a shop or factory within the national borders.

Since that time, organizations and economies have globalized and that means meetings that were once all between individuals in a single organization or with their partners down the street are now between partners across oceans and on different continents. Cultural differences are now part of the dialogue and norms of workplace meetings. For more on the global and cultural aspects of meetings, flip to Chapter 6.

Globalization meant an increase in the complexity of meeting from dealing with cultural differences to time zone challenges to simply speaking the same language. However, probably the biggest change that has made meetings more complex is the different ways that we meet. Part of this is due to this globalization that has occurred, but much of it can be attributed to some abrupt and sudden major disruptions in how we meet overall!

COVID-19: Disrupting the way we meet

Story time! In early March of 2020, Joe and Karin participated in a webinar for a mutual client about the future of meetings. We talked all about how the future of meetings would require more meetings to be video-based meetings. That people would need to learn how to engage more effectively on camera and collaborate across distances. Of course, our predictions were that this would be a slow transition over the course of the next three to five years.

Everything we said in that webinar happened three to five days later. On March 12, 2020, the first major lockdowns due to the COVID-19 pandemic began in the United States. Most employers shut their office doors and told employees to go home and work from there. This meant that every meeting became a virtual meeting. Every meeting was changed from face-to-face to either audio- or video-based communication.

Our electronic calendars exploded with meeting invites because we no longer bumped into colleagues in the office. The casual day-to-day conversations in the hallway, sticking your head into someone's office, or chatting at the watercooler were no more. If it wasn't on the calendar and in a virtual meeting room, then it didn't happen.

The problem was that not everyone was well equipped for this transition, both physically (such as owning a good webcam) and psychologically (mentally being "on camera"). No longer were webcams a nice feature of a good laptop, but they became essential hardware. And they sold out in stores pretty quickly!

But wait! We didn't experience just one major meeting disruption. As offices started to slowly open their doors and in response to overwhelming employee demands, we experienced a second major meeting disruption with the introduction of the hybrid meeting. This format allows participants to join a meeting from wherever they are, whether that is in the office or anywhere else, provided they have a strong internet connection.

REMEMBER

Face-to-face, virtual, hybrid: All of these meetings are regularly conducted across practically every industry now. That requires navigating a more complex communication environment than ever before and calls for a stronger focus on training people like you on how to run any and all of these meetings effectively. Hence the need for the book you are devouring now!

Learning about new ways to meet

For all the reasons previously mentioned, running effective meetings now requires you to be able to manage meetings that are face-to-face, virtual, or hybrid (find out more about these different ways of meeting in Parts 2 and 3 of this book). The pandemic motivated Karin and Joe to write two books:

» *Suddenly Virtual: Making Remote Meetings Work* (John Wiley & Sons, Inc., 2021)

» *Suddenly Hybrid: Managing the Modern Meeting* (John Wiley & Sons, Inc., 2022)

Throughout this book on running effective meetings, we talk about many of the best practices, tips, and tricks contained in those books. That's because we now have to meet in all these formats. Sometimes we're in person and sometimes we aren't. You can't just apply all the same practices in each of these contexts. For example, you don't have to worry about seating in a virtual meeting. That's on the attendees to figure out, but you do in a face-to-face meeting. Likewise, in an all in-person meeting, you don't typically have to worry about if the camera is working or that you have an internet connection with enough bandwidth for five high-definition camera feeds.

REMEMBER

Running effective meetings now requires optimal flexibility and awareness of what the different formats require. You'll find great advice to guide you through designing your meetings for virtual and hybrid contexts in Chapter 8, and on setting expectations for your meetings in these formats in Chapter 9. But, we don't stop there. We have a whole chapter on using video in virtual and hybrid meetings (see Chapter 5) and nearly every chapter thereafter has sections that breakdown the implications of every single tip recommendation for these different formats! We've got you covered!

Acknowledging the growing role of technology

Sure, technology in a conference room used to be a projector and a cord to connect your computer. Now, that would be a "dumb" conference room. The new "smart" conference room includes a camera or cameras and a means by which one can connect to hold a virtual or hybrid meeting. And there are a lot of conference rooms across the United States and beyond that will be upgrading to become smart conference rooms in the future with even more embedded innovations.

Technology that was once only used in boardrooms or even science fiction are now standard in our workplace conference rooms and meetings. No longer is it sufficient to have a large conference phone in the middle of a big table. No longer is having a single camera facing down a long table the best way to ensure everyone is seen and heard. Individuals and organizations have and will continue to embrace technology. (For more on embracing video in your meetings, check out Chapter 5.)

The faulty assumption is that everyone knows how to use the technology that is now essential in every meeting environment. Yes, most people learned how to turn on their computer and connect to a virtual meeting. But, how to use a smart conference room to connect folks into a hybrid meeting environment is more challenging in a number of ways. Does this intrigue you? If so, check out Chapter 12 for how to get everyone to participate in these new technological charged meeting situations.

TIP

We strongly recommend organizations upgrade their employees software, hardware, and skillware. From a technology perspective, the software and hardware distribution effort is the easy part. And, in many organizations, it's done. The skillware is the hard part. That's the "how to." How do you use this stuff? How do I make hybrid meetings work? How do I make sure everyone gets a chance to participate and contribute? Flip to Chapters 11 and 12 for guidance on how to both enable and expect participation that improves meeting equity.

We tackle the skillware challenge, and if that's what you are looking for, you've come to the right place. *Running Effective Meetings For Dummies* provides the essential guide to do just that!

Yes, meeting technology is here to stay and we need to ensure everyone knows how to use it. Yes, meeting room setups need to change to accommodate hybrid meetings. No, we're not going to be the definitive guide in either of those areas. If you are looking for a deep dive into the technology that supports many of the meeting formats we use today, you won't find it here. But there are plenty of *For Dummies* books well suited for the job: think of your technology of choice and look it up on dummies.com . . . you're sure to find many useful titles there.

Running an Effective Group or Team

For those who may still have doubts about whether running effective meetings really matters, we provide one more important bit of information here. Many meetings are between groups or teams that have to collaborate effectively to accomplish their work. Organizations are made or broken by whether the teams that comprise them can function well. Where are all the decisions and collaboration process occurring for these teams that are so key to organizational success? Meetings!

REMEMBER

Basically, the final argument for taking a bit of time to permanently enhance your meetings is the long-term improvement in your teams' effectiveness, performance, and overall well-being. Meetings are a window into how a team is operating. Meetings put leadership on display, for good or ill, and how you lead your team is observable for everyone in the room. If the meetings are going well, the you and your team are probably performing well. If the meetings are going poorly, the team is probably performing poorly. Running effective meetings means running an effective group or team.

Our guess is that most teams are "achieving expectations." Remember that option on the standard performance appraisal tool that basically says you're doing enough to keep your job and get your annual cost-of-living raise? It's the "meh" button. It's the performance result that says, "We did it and it's okay." Are you happy with that? If you are reading this book, we think your answer is a resounding "no."

REMEMBER

If you want to lead a highly functioning team, then you need to run highly functional team meetings, and that requires intention and effort across the entire meeting continuum. Your meeting success isn't resting solely upon what you do during the meeting itself. Make no mistake, you can really mess it up by not doing the right things before and after the session too. Take heart, dear reader. We are here to guide you along the entire meeting journey. So long "meh" meetings. Say hello to meetings that move the needle — for you, for your team, and for your organization as a whole.

Chapter **2**

Matching the Meeting Style with the Meeting Goal

H ave you ever been in a meeting where the agenda didn't fit the length of the meeting? Maybe the meeting was scheduled to last 30 minutes, but you knew it would probably take 90 minutes to cover every topic listed. Or maybe the communication approach was unrealistic based on the time allotted. The meeting leader wanted to take a round robin approach, allowing everyone to comment, but there are ten people in the meeting. If everyone shared their five-minute thought, there'd be no time for discussion or decision making.

In both of these cases, the meeting style did not match the meeting goal.

Even those with the best intentions can fail in execution, as Joe experienced in a recent meeting. The meeting leader created a well-designed agenda with a clearly defined goal. He even assigned individuals to present each item. But when he walked into the room, he took one look at the agenda and said, "Okay, so which of these items should we discuss first?". Within the first ten seconds of the meeting, he completely blew up the agenda structure, and proceeded to haphazardly work through some, not all, of the topics. His style for running the meeting and the espoused goal, as indicated on the agenda, did not match!

WARNING

Don't get us wrong. That approach might work, but there's a mismatch here. Don't create an agenda with names, time stamps, and a planned flow, and then not use it! Doing so negates any benefit of all the work that went into the agenda in the first place.

REMEMBER

Successful meetings match the meeting communication style with the meeting goal.

In this chapter, we discuss the importance of picking a communication style or approach when running a meeting. More importantly, how we communicate in our meetings makes it possible to accomplish our goals. We also address the idea that some meetings require more formality than others. A casual meeting that takes place when you pop into someone's office may work to get quick clarification on something but if you need to make a major decision, you need to take a more formal approach. We wrap up our discussion of matching meeting styles and goals by talking about an organization's meeting culture and norms and how you manage expectations within them.

Picking a Meeting Communication Style

For any good meeting, you have to first figure out the purpose for the meeting. It may seem like an easy enough thing to do, but it may be more complex than you imagine.

The number of different purposes for which meetings are called is quite astounding. Here's a sampling of common meeting purposes:

>> Brainstorming ideas

>> Identifying problems and solutions

>> Strategizing for the future

>> Updating on projects

>> Information sharing or status updates

>> Decision making

>> Performing a needs assessment

TIP

Always pick your purpose and set your goal/agenda before you decide how to achieve it.

Identifying the main structures of meeting communication

Once a purpose is identified, it's time to pick a meeting communication style or approach that helps you to achieve your goal, but this is where you may run into trouble.

Let's look at an example. Say the purpose of the meeting is to brainstorm ideas, but the meeting leader just talks the whole time. If the meeting leader is the only person speaking, very few ideas are likely to be generated. The presentation-style approach is a mismatch with the goal.

Is a presentation communication style always the wrong approach? No, not necessarily. In fact, there are a number of different approaches that can be taken and none of them are inherently good or bad, so long as they match the purpose. When they mismatch, terrible meetings occur with results that fall short of their goals.

Let's take a look at some of the most common meeting communication styles.

Using the round-robin approach

The most common type or structure for meeting communication is the *round-robin approach*. In this approach, a topic is presented or a question is posed and then everyone in the meeting is given an opportunity to share their thoughts. You often see this approach used regularly in a typical staff meeting where status updates are shared. In fact, the most common form of meeting is the information-sharing meeting, and in those meetings, the round-robin approach is often deployed.

Now, if we stopped there, and told you to just use the round-robin approach to ensure participation by everyone in every meeting, we would be doing you a great disservice. Sadly, it's a disservice that is repeated often in books that provide tips on making meetings better. The reality is, the round-robin approach is overused and abused! For example, in a team of five people, a standing weekly meeting with this approach could be done in 30 minutes with everyone remaining awake and engaged. However, in a team of 20 people, if everyone takes five minutes, that's 100 minutes. Ever fallen asleep during a standup meeting? Joe has, and it's because the communication style didn't match the goal.

In these larger standing meetings, where you have many people in the room, a traditional round-robin approach isn't appropriate. Instead, we advocate using a critical information approach. In this approach, you have two options:

>> You can identify ahead of time the individuals who have critical updates to share and calls upon them by name during the meeting.

>> You can kick off the meeting by asking, "Who has a critical update or need that we need to address today?" By opening it up to the floor, you create a natural filter among the participants.

Your communication style and approach needs to match your goal.

Leveraging the creative problem-solving approach

Let's say your goal is to discuss an issue and identify solutions. You may run into a problem with the round-robin approach. If everyone is allowed to weigh in on the problem, you could end up in a complaining cycle where everybody complains but no solution is presented. It would bog down the meeting.

Instead, you should structure the problem and solution process by first collaboratively defining the problem, making sure all the implications of the problem are discussed. Then you should transition to identifying potential solutions, allowing for elaboration and discussion of each potential solution. Ultimately, you will want to guide the process to resolution by jointly selecting the one solution that the team agrees has the greatest likelihood of success. In other words, you should follow these steps:

1. **Identify the problem.**
2. **Elaborate upon the problem.**
3. **Identify potential solutions.**
4. **Elaborate on each potential solution.**
5. **Select from the solution options.**

We call this communication approach the *creative problem-solving approach*. This approach is rather flexible and could be applied to a number of different meeting purposes.

Groups don't necessarily need to do each step in the order shown here, but rather can go from 1 to 2 then back to 1 and so on.

Knowing when to use the collaborative communication style

A final communication style in your armory is the *collaborative communication approach*. This is often the most flexible application and can be adapted to nearly any purpose. This communication approach is based on two assumptions:

>> The purpose of the meeting has been identified.

>> The people invited to the meeting are there because they likely have something meaningful to share in relation to that purpose.

Under these two assumptions, you want to ensure everyone has the opportunity to participate, to have a voice in the decision making, and to engage.

What does this look like? Here's a real-world example. In a recent meeting that Joe led, he followed the collaborative communication style because he knew the agenda had a number of items on it that required input from the majority of people in the meeting. Since these people had not met together before, he started by telling everyone to be prepared to share their thoughts and ideas on the topics on the agenda. He then presented the item, or asked someone with key knowledge about it, to lead things off. As the discussion unfolded, he made note of who had not participated, and called them by name. But he made it clear that saying "I have nothing to add" is an appropriate response as well. The meeting proceeded, and like a good meeting scientist he anonymously sought feedback on how the meeting went after the session. The results? Some of the highest scores for participation and engagement he's ever seen!

In other words, the approach works and here are the steps:

1. **Inform the group you are taking a collaborative approach to the meeting.**

2. **Let them know you expect their participation.**

3. **Let them know you might call people by name.**

4. **Make sure they know that "having nothing to add" is an appropriate response to being called upon.**

5. **Encourage participation and discussion throughout.**

WARNING

We would be remiss if we didn't acknowledge that we've deliberately shared three very broad communication styles. One of these three will likely fit the vast majority of meeting purposes. However, some meeting purposes might require innovative approaches. Be flexible and be willing to try new approaches to communication in your meetings.

Choosing the right communication structure

So, which approach should you choose? That depends upon the purpose:

>> If the purpose of the meeting is to share information with everyone and get feedback at the end, then we'd recommend a presentation followed by a swift round robin. By swift round robin, instead of five minute updates, you adapt and make it 30 second reactions. See, the round robin is flexible!

>> If the purpose is to talk through a number of discussion items, then the collaborative approach is ideal. Meeting purposes such as decision making, strategy development, and performing a needs assessment fit this approach. The key question is: "So you need people to collaboratively discuss and build upon each other's ideas?" If yes, the collaborative approach works quite well.

>> If the purpose is to resolve any number of problems, the creative problem solving approach is best. Honestly, this approach is probably best for complex problems.

Simple problems with minimal options for solutions likely do not need the comprehensive approach. In those cases, we recommend abbreviating the steps to:

1. **Identify the problem.**
2. **Identify the solutions.**
3. **Pick the solution.**

This ensures the complex problem and solution are fully fleshed out so unintended consequences are not overlooked.

Managing the Meeting's Formality

We've all done it. Walked into a room, looked around, and realized we were underdressed. The same thing happens in meetings. Some meetings are very formal. Sometimes, that formality can be outwardly visible in what people are wearing, but there are plenty of times when that formality may be only understood by observing how people are talking to each other. Not only must the level of formality reflect the purpose and goals of the meeting, but it also is impacted by who is in the meeting, why it is being called, and the implications of the outcomes.

MEETING FORMALITY

So what do we mean by meeting formality? *Meeting formality* refers to the how closely a given meeting or interaction follows typical meeting and professional etiquette. For example, a board meeting for a large corporation is typically a formal affair. Participants are dressed in business formal attire. The agenda is developed and established ahead of time. They may even follow a standardized protocol for participating in the dialogue of the meeting like parliamentary procedure. By contrast, have you ever stuck your head in someone's office to ask a question and a meeting ensued? More than likely that kind of interaction is not nearly as formal as the board room meeting. You must use the cues around you to help know how formal the interaction is. The more formal, the more thought should go into your inputs into the meeting. As a meeting leader, you have to also recognize that formality can equate to more filtering by participants. You might get less of what they really think and more of what they think you (or the boss) really want.

Matching the formality of the meeting to its purpose is essential for meeting success.

There are two key takeaways to remember when it comes to meeting formality:

>> Choose the formality level of your scheduled meetings.

>> Read the room for the formality level of the meeting; this is essential to meeting success.

Choosing the right level of meeting formality

Let's assume you are considering calling a meeting, or at a minimum, have a question that you need answered. At that moment, you can decide how formal you want the interaction to be that provides the answer to your question. If the question is, to your understanding, a quick one, then popping by someone's office or even calling them up on the phone for a quick chat is sufficient. Be mindful that you and the person you talk to might label the interaction a meeting. Even just labeling a chat a meeting increases the formality, particularly as other team members learn about the conversation.

However, you might decide that the question you have or the thing you want to discuss requires the input of a number of different people. Sure, you could chase them all down one by one and ask their thoughts, or you could call a meeting and give them an opportunity to weigh in all at once.

If you decide to call a meeting, you now have several choices relative to formality.

>> Is this an in-person, virtual, or hybrid meeting?

>> As this will be a scheduled meeting, when should it occur?

>> Where should it occur?

>> How long should the meeting be?

>> Who should be in the room?

Answers to each of these questions impacts the formality and consequence of the meeting. For example, including your boss automatically elevates the formality due to the formal reporting relationship. By the same token, holding the meeting in a conference room and requiring in-person participation creates a heightened sense of formality that perhaps didn't exist before the adoption of virtual and hybrid meetings.

TIP

Keep this one guiding principle in mind when it comes to the level of formality of a meeting: Make the meeting as formal as it needs to be to legitimize the decision being made, the question being answered, or the input being shared.

In other words, a formal meeting where a decision is made carries greater weight within most organizations than a "bump into Bob" moment. After all, when you say, "Hey, I just bumped into Bob and he said I should do this," it's not nearly as meaningful as stating, "I was given this assignment in our recent team meeting." What's the difference, particularly if Bob is the boss? The formality of the meeting where the assignment took place.

Planning for collaboration

The most important aspect of meeting formality is the way in each it enables collaboration. A formal meeting with invited participants, an agenda, in a conference room (perhaps with remote attendees) should be more collaborative than calling a single person on the phone, or catching them at the water cooler. It's hard to have a collaborative water cooler chat, but building upon each other's ideas and thoughts is a big benefit to getting a bunch of people together in the same room.

Planning for collaboration means that as a meeting leader, you prepare for people to engage and encourage it to occur, in a formal and expected manner. In most cases, this means letting go of some of the control as to how the communication flows during the meeting. But, it also means that you might get more help doing that thing. For example, if you take a problem-solving approach to a meeting, those who contribute to elaborating on the solution could easily be the subgroup charged with collaboratively enacting the solution. By not dominating the conversation, you create a group of willing helpers in carrying out the solution.

REMEMBER

Collaboration doesn't just happen. It has to be planned. If you want that to happen, you have to formalize the meeting. Here are the steps to making a meeting more formal by planning for collaboration:

1. **Make it a scheduled meeting.**

2. **Invite participants who are relevant to the purpose.**

3. **Select a communication approach (for example, creative problem solving).**

4. **Identify a more formal location (for example, tech-enabled conference room).**

5. **Encourage participation throughout the meeting.**

By following these steps, the meeting will be more formal, the collaboration will be planned, and the scope of the outcome will fit with the efforts required to accomplish the desired goal.

Meshing with Meeting Culture Norms in Your Company

Every organization has a meeting culture, and the meeting culture is often a reflection of the culture of the organization overall. We've worked with companies where it is perfectly acceptable for the boss, often the meeting leader, to arrive 10 to 15 minutes late. No one is bothered by it because it's "just how things are done around here." We've also had clients who valued punctuality, almost above all else. If you were a minute late to the meeting, you missed a minute of content because no one was about to wait for you to arrive. The thing is . . . that didn't happen very often because everyone in the organization knew that was the standard operating procedure: We start on time.

And that's what meeting culture is. It's "how we meet around here." It's what is considered normal, okay, accepted, and expected as it pertains to meeting in a given team, group, or organization. They are not necessarily inherently good or bad. They just are. Every organization has somewhat of a pattern of behaviors surrounding their meetings. They vary from organization to organization, and it's generally okay.

However, in some cases, the meeting culture may begin to violate best practices. Take the first example we offered where arriving ten minutes late is basically considered "on time." In reality, starting a meeting late is a huge problem if you listen to meeting science (see Chapter 1 for more about this science). In fact, meeting lateness is universally a problem and one that has a dramatic negative impact on the behaviors during the meeting and people's motivation to work after the meeting. Sadly, many organizations embrace norms about meetings that are not good, while thankfully, others embrace norms about meetings that are quite useful.

REMEMBER

Meeting culture norms in your organization exist and have the potential to help or hurt your meetings

Normalizing lateness is one example of potentially hurtful meeting practices. Here's another common one that spawns from FOMO. *FOMO* refers to "fear of missing out" and it manifests in meetings with an overly long invite list. You may want to have your meeting be as inclusive as possible. It's certainly an admirable goal, especially if it's from the perspective of diversity, equity, and inclusion. But often, you may want to be inclusive in a different way, by inviting anyone who might want to know what happens in this meeting, and perhaps even a few that don't. As meeting size grows, the ability to contain, control, and succeed in the meeting decreases.

TIP

Here's a way you can combat FOMO from bloating your meeting size. Use the "two pizza rule" that many organizations, including Amazon, have adopted. The *two pizza rule* for meetings states that every meeting should be small enough that attendees could eat two large pizzas and be full. In practice this translates to five to seven people in every meeting. For nearly every meeting purpose that we've heard of, five to seven people is the optimal size. Most that go beyond that size become difficult to manage or have a purpose that includes essentially information sharing with minimal to no interaction, like presentations at a conference.

Understanding communication, participation, and efficiency patterns

When considering organizational meeting culture, there are at least three areas where norms often emerge:

>> Communication

>> Participation

>> Efficiency

For communication, organizations and groups therein often default into a particular communication style for their meetings. Probably the most common is the round-robin style (described earlier in this chapter), which can be useful, but should not be the only style used. If you need to accomplish something other than reporting out or brainstorming ideas, other communication styles may be more appropriate. In fact, we would advise not allowing your group or organization to adopt just one style, but should embrace the notion of flexibility and experimentation with different communication approaches like round robin, creative problem solving, and collaborative communication. By matching the style to the goal of the meeting, the communication process unlocks the meeting potential rather than constraining goal achievement. For more information on aligning your meeting purpose, goals, and agenda, check out Chapter 8.

For participation, norms often emerge around who can and should participate, and who is marginalized. Unfortunately, some of these norms have included the marginalization of women and minorities in the meeting environment. The data is clear and Joe, as a meeting scientist, has confirmed repeatedly that in most organizations, women and minorities speak the least in meetings across all industries and verticals. The good news is, like any organizational norm, groups within organizations are often different, and your group can be different if you engage in more appropriate participation norms.

TIP

Set an inclusion rule around participation in your meetings to ensure that everyone who wants to participate is encouraged to do so.

Too many great ideas go unsaid and unheard because of negative norms and even stereotypes around who can and should participate in meetings. Interestingly, during the sudden onset of virtual meetings caused by the COVID-19 pandemic, equality in talk time emerged in meetings. One reason for people's desire to continue with hybrid work environments is the hope that participation in meetings remains more equal, particularly for women and minorities.

REMEMBER

Societal norms and stereotypes about women and minorities continue to influence meeting behavior inside our organizations, but we should actively avoid embracing those norms.

Efficiency patterns of meetings within organizations are often dictated not by the people running them but rather the technology used to create them. Organizations often let their calendaring system determine how long a meeting should be, even when the length of a meeting could be more efficiently scoped and sized. Simply because a company uses a calendaring system that has 30 minute and 60 minute defaults when scheduling meetings, doesn't mean every meeting should be 30 or 60 minutes. In fact, most meetings, when properly managed, can and should be shorter than they are.

What typically happens is that humans tend to fill the time allotted to them, even if they don't need the time. How often have you been in a meeting where the agenda was accomplished in 40 minutes and then the floor is opened up for other topics not on the agenda? Personally, we don't like the "open forum" item on the standard agenda because it usually results in back filling the meeting and can even result in meetings running long.

Instead, embrace the idea that you can define the length of your meeting. You can control the flow of communication. You can formalize the meeting, if desired, and make your meetings more efficient.

TIP

Don't let your calendar decide the length of your meeting. Instead, decide based on the scope of your agenda and purpose. Embrace the 42 minute meeting . . . or the 12 minute one . . . or the 27 minute one!

Recognizing and developing your team's meeting culture

We've spent a good deal of time talking about how organizations have a meeting culture. But, so do groups and teams. That's right, you may have noticed a pattern to how your team interacts in meetings.

The question you have to ask yourself is, "Are you happy with your team's meeting culture?" If you are, then that's wonderful. If you are not, that's more typical.

Our advice is to take a moment to recognize your team's meeting culture and perhaps even schedule a meeting to discuss it with your team. Decide if you are okay with how your meetings operate in general. Does everyone feel they are seen and heard adequately? Does participation flow? Are the decisions made and solutions leveraged in an effective way?

As you go through this book, take note of the best practices we discuss and then explore the norms around the behaviors in your meetings. What might be considered "just how we do things" may be doing more harm than good. Maybe your meetings are known to have a lot of joking around in them. But does that joviality create camaraderie or hurt feelings?

Meeting culture is multi-faceted and there's no one-size-fits-all. This book will give you a lot to consider when it comes to making your meeting culture positive one that allows you to make the most of them. The main thing is to never be satisfied with mediocrity. Just because the majority of your company's meetings run over doesn't mean yours have to. Nor do you have to adopt the weekly standup that has no set goal, purpose, or agenda that usually just gobbles up time on everyone's calendar.

Work to develop a positive, effective, efficient team meeting culture. Work to develop a culture that rewards, supports, and encourages good meeting practices. Doing so will set the stage for success in all your team meetings.

TIP

Don't let your organization's meeting culture define your meetings for you. You decide how you want them to go and make it happen!

Chapter **3**

Understanding the Full Meeting Continuum

You may think of meetings as an event, and you wouldn't be wrong. A *meeting* is a gathering that occurs at a specific time on a specific day and in a specific place, including physical or digital environments. But if you want your meeting to be effective and worthy of the calendar slot it occupies, you need to think beyond the event itself and consider what we call the full meeting continuum.

REMEMBER

The *full meeting continuum* includes what should happen before, during, and after the meeting. The full meeting continuum must be carefully considered in order for a meeting to be successful.

Good meetings have good things that happen before, during, and after the meeting. Bad meetings have bad things that happen before, during, and after the meeting. Most meetings are sort of "meh" (to put it in highly technical terms). They have "meh" things that happen before, during, and after the meeting. They aren't great. But, they aren't bad. They sort of accomplish some or part of the things the meeting intended to accomplish, but don't truly meet their goals. It's like leaving a restaurant and feeling full, but not satisfied. Most meetings leave us full, but not satisfied, because some things that were supposed to happen before, during, or after the meeting didn't happen.

Try thinking of meetings this way: Meeting are like birthday parties. Before the party, someone has to identify who should attend. Then they have to figure out the food. Will the cake be chocolate or vanilla and will there be ice cream served alongside? They have to figure out decorations, and if it is a surprise party, determine how to keep it that way and get all these things done before the party. Now at the party, they have to make sure the most important guest, the person whose birthday it is, is happy and satisfied. They also have to make sure everyone gets a chance to interact with the birthday person, and they orchestrate the upholding of traditions of this particular group, like the singing of "Happy Birthday" and the customary blowing out of candles on the cake. In other words, they make sure the processes of a birthday party happen. Once the party concludes, their work isn't done. After the party, they make sure everyone leaves. Perhaps they even check on a few guests to make sure they made it home okay, and lead the cleanup efforts of the party space. A good birthday party, like a good meeting, is a result of the right things, the good things, happening before, during, and after the event.

In this chapter, we discuss the full continuum of meetings. That is, we discuss things that should happen before the meeting, things that need to happen during the meeting, and things that need to happen after the meeting. We even mention a few things that shouldn't happen. The aim of this chapter is to provide a bit of a surface level overview of the meeting continuum with later sections and chapters digging deeply into how to do many of the described best practices.

Being the Architect of Your Meeting Design

Just as an architect designs a home or a building, meeting leaders and organizers need to design their meetings. Joe likes to refer to meeting design as *meeting scaffolding*. From architectural design and building perspectives, scaffolding serves the purpose of both supporting the building as it is built, as well as getting the workers to the right spots to work on the building. It would be impossible for buildings, particular larger buildings, to be built without some form of scaffolding around it to allow for workers, designers, and so forth to interact with the building, from foundation to roof top.

The same thing can be said for meetings. If the meeting scaffolding is not curated by the meeting leader or organizer, then the meeting will not hold up. There will be missing components and ultimately, the meeting could come crashing down in a glorious implosion. We've all been there. A meeting that had so much potential that didn't rise to the level it was intended. Perhaps the agenda never showed up, so the purpose wasn't clearly defined. Perhaps a key attendee was not invited, making it impossible or even inappropriate to make a decision.

Take a moment to think through each meeting you lead or organize, and make sure the meeting is designed properly including purpose, people, and potential outcomes. This chapter shows you how.

Designing for before the meeting

Meeting leaders, organizers, and attendees have a number of things they should do or consider doing before their meetings. These rather simple tasks set the stage for a meaningful, useful, and productive meeting. In fact, some of these things will sound so simple, you'll probably scratch your head and wonder, "Who on earth would not do something like that?"

Believe us, there are tasks that some people just do not do when it comes to their meetings. As we like to say, some best practices may seem like common sense, but they are uncommonly practiced.

Here's the list of things to consider and act upon before the meeting:

>> Define the meeting purpose

>> Prepare an agenda (even a short one)

>> Share the agenda beforehand

>> Distribute any needed documents prior to the meeting that need to be reviewed in advance

>> Identify the best time for the meeting (considering yours and others schedules, workflow, and location)

>> Invite only attendees essential to the accomplishment of the meeting's purpose

>> Schedule the meeting for the appropriate length (right size to the purpose and agenda)

>> Determine the appropriate modality (face-to-face, virtual, or hybrid)

>> Ensure the room, virtual or otherwise, is prepared to receive the attendees

>> Provide refreshments for longer meetings

>> Arrive before the start time

>> Engage in pre-meeting small talk

>> Start on time

You may have noticed that this list seems targeted to meeting leaders and organizers. That's because it is. However, most of these things intersect with the attendees and require their buy-in and support of the design of the meeting. For example, you as the meeting leader might really appreciate your potential attendees keeping their calendars up to date. In a world where our electronic calendars often govern our days, if they are not accurate, it's easy to double-book people without even realizing it.

You also want to encourage attendees to be responsive to before-meeting requests. Ask them to review agenda items, look over any documents to be discussed in the meeting, and provide feedback on the agenda if possible. You can also create a culture where arriving early, or at least on time, is expected, by demonstrating that yourself.

WARNING

If you schedule back-to-back meetings, you are actually making it harder for meeting leaders and attendees to carry out many of these before-meeting behaviors. And it also becomes harder to start the next meeting on time, as it's likely people won't be able to transition quickly enough between meetings. Then, some meetings will go overtime, exacerbating the issue. Consider scheduling time between meetings for recovery from the previous meeting and preparation for the next.

Designing for during the meeting

Not only should your meeting design include items that should be done before the meeting, but you should also think about creating a framework that allows you to get the most out of the meeting once it is underway.

REMEMBER

Having a meeting purpose and agenda, and a carefully curated invite list, will help set you up for success. These are before-the-meeting tasks that are essential for an effective during-meeting experience. But there are still other actions that should take place before the meeting that shape the meeting flow itself. Here's our list things to help design your meetings:

>> Assign someone to record minutes for later distribution.

>> Plan to monitor time in order to keep the meeting on track.

>> Practice with the meeting technology.

>> Learn how to use procedural communication.

>> Have a plan for switching speakers throughout the meeting.

>> Be prepared to intervene when dysfunctional behaviors occur.

>> Ensure everyone can access the virtual meeting space (if applicable).

>> Provide training on the meeting software, if necessary.

Many of these are, once again, no brainers. Obviously, you'll want someone to take notes for later distribution. Yes, you'll need a way to transition from one person to another in the flow of the conversation. But, some of these come from meeting science and need more explanation, such as procedural communication.

WARNING

Procedural communication sometimes requires interrupting others. It's normative in many groups, organizations, and cultures not to interrupt others when they are talking. With this in mind, take care when implementing this and consider establishing the ground rule that the meeting leader may interrupt folks if they get outside the topics of the meeting. Check out Chapter 11 for more advice on the use of procedural communication.

TECHNICAL STUFF

PROCEDURAL COMMUNICATION

Procedural communication is a form of communication that helps ensure the meeting can move forward smoothly towards its defined goal. It can be a useful intervention when someone engages in dysfunctional behavior. For example, you can use procedural communication when you interrupt someone who is monologuing on their favorite unrelated topic. You know them. They have an issue they like to talk about and no matter the purpose of the meeting, they go off on it as soon as they find an opening.

Monologuing on unrelated topics is a counterproductive behavior and procedural communication is the polite way to deal with it. Here's an example. Let's say Joe is talking ad nauseum about the lack of healthy food options in the vending machine, but you meeting's purpose has nothing to do with that pet peeve of his. You could say, "Thank you Joe for your comments on that. However, we're talking about the product launch next week. Do you have anything to add on that topic?" It's okay if they then take a minute to respond to the item at hand, but the key is you've used procedural communication to pull them back to the planned discussion and gotten the meeting back on the rails.

Facilitating a Productive Discussion

The most important thing that happens in most meetings is discussion and collaboration. In fact, we would argue that if you don't plan on discussing or collaborating, then you don't need to meet at all. However, knowing that you need to or want to discuss something doesn't mean that it will be a productive discussion. Have you ever gone into a meeting with a plan to discuss one thing and ended up discussing something else? Or even worse, have you ever gone into a meeting, planning to discuss something with others, and ended up listening to a lecture by the boss or another person with a strong opinion about the discussion topic? If you're not yelling "Yes" at the book right now, we'd be very surprised.

Unfortunately, most meetings struggle to have productive discussions and collaboration sessions. Sometimes this is due to a lack of planning before the meeting. However, many times, even with the best meeting design and scaffolding in place, the discussion just does not work out, go as planned, or even happen in the meeting.

TIP

If you do not plan how you are going to facilitate discussion in your meetings, you leave discussion and collaboration to chance. Consider how best to ensure everyone gets an opportunity to engage in the conversation.

Building a process for turn taking

Several years ago, Joe was flown to New York City by a large enterprise organization to observe several different teams as they held their weekly meetings. Most of these meetings were staff meetings which were designed to provide project updates and a forum for discussion about those updates. Several of the team meetings took a round-robin approach, going from person to person, allowing each some time to share an update. But there was one team meeting, he'll never forget . . . check out the sidebar for the full story!

REMEMBER

One of the keys to facilitating a productive discussion is to have a clearly defined way to contribute. In Joe's example described in the sidebar, they all knew how to get the stick. They all knew what to do when they got the stick. They all adhered to the procedure without fault.

There are a number of different ways you can facilitate a meeting. Sure, you could use a talking stick, or even a conversation stapler, since you're in an office. However, our recommendation is to have a plan for facilitating the meeting. Make sure everyone knows what that plan is, and proceed to follow that plan.

JOE'S STICKY MEETING

"I walked into the meeting as everyone gathered together. I stayed in the back and off to the side to avoid interrupting. I was introduced and immediately informed them to forget I was even there and to proceed with their meeting. What happened next was as surprising as it was impressive. As the meeting got underway, the meeting leader brought out a stick. The stick appeared to be painted, worn a bit on one end, and about 18 inches long and an inch or so thick. So, not large enough to play baseball with, but longer than a pencil or pen.

The meeting leader continued with announcements and then proceeded to the first discussion item. He then called on one of the others by name and handed them the stick. She commented and as she did so, two other people put their hands up. As she completed her thoughts, she called on one of the two people by name and handed that person the stick. This continued throughout the balance of the meeting: name, stick, comment, name, stick, comment, and so on."

What Joe realized was that this team had deployed the practice of using a "talking stick" as a means for facilitating comments and discussion in their meetings. This turn-taking ritual has been around for centuries but Joe had never seen it used within a business context. However, it worked amazingly well.

This becomes even more important when you consider virtual or hybrid contexts. How do you pass the talking stick to the person on the screen? The simple answer is, you have to establish norms in your group for how people participate. Explicitly state how people can get into the conversation queue and make sure those norms fit the meeting format you will be using. For example, in virtual meetings, most software has a tool, such as the raised hand. For face-to-face meetings, you could use a physical object or pay attention to more subtle cues such as leaning in or eye contact. For hybrid, you will likely need a combination of both.

TIP

Make sure you have a way for people to join the conversation queue regardless of how they are connected to the meeting.

For fully remote teams, you might suggest people raise their emoji hand or their physical hand if they have something they want to say. For hybrid teams, you'll likely want to incorporate the use of chat as another way to jump into the dialogue. Sometimes, it can be tough for virtual attendees of a hybrid meeting to insert themselves because in-person attendees can more easily dominate the conversation. Using chat (and actually attending to it) gives remote attendees one more tool to help level the playing field. But it's up to you as the meeting leader to verbalize the comments and even invite the originator of them to elaborate on them out loud.

If the participation in your meetings is lacking, you might need to take a more proactive approach. We call it *cold calling with good intention* where you ask someone by name to offer their input even though they haven't indicated they would like to speak.

Here's an example. Let's say you know Jane has a lot of experience with the topic being discussed, but she hasn't said one word. As the meeting leader, you can call on Jane to weigh in by saying, "Jane, I know you've been in this situation many times before and I think your opinion would be very valuable. What's your take on this?" Notice how this is phrased. You aren't intending to put Jane on the spot. Rather you are truly interested in what she has to say because she has a unique perspective.

WARNING

Beware of creating performance pressure. If you are going to engage in cold-calling with good intention (and we hope you do, especially in virtual or hybrid meetings where it's harder to read the room) you want to establish that it is perfectly okay to say, "I don't have anything to add."

Setting ground rules for participation

One of the best ways to ensure participation by everyone in a meeting is to set ground rules. Just as sports have rules that must be followed in order for the game to be played, groups and teams should set rules pertaining to how people participate in their meetings.

Setting ground rules is not something that should be done unilaterally. That is, the meeting leader, often the boss, should not come in and say, "From now on, if you want to participate, you have to wait until I call you by name." Most groups will may find such directive behavior problematic, annoying, and a reason to fight against such rules.

TIP

Set your ground rules together. Collaboratively. Doing so provides buy-in from each member of the group and ensures the rule is more likely to be followed.

Unless someone has a chisel and a flat stone handy, ground rules should not be set in stone. In other words, as you collaboratively make your ground rules, make sure the team knows you're trying out a rule, and if it works you'll keep doing it. If it doesn't, you'll work together to change it.

For example, let's say you decided to use a physical object as a means to facilitate participation in your team meetings. Seemed like a fantastic idea . . . before the global COVID-19 pandemic. What do you do now? You cannot physically pass the baton to the next person. You may not even be in the same space any more, and if you are, passing the baton may mean tossing it across the room if you're socially distant. It's a meeting, not a physical education class. Instead, you'll have to enable participation in a non-physical manner, such as calling on each person by name.

REMEMBER

Situations and circumstances for the group will change. When they do, the rules may have to change. Allow for that flexibility in your turn-taking policy.

You'll notice we have not said, "Here are the ground rule for you." Well, that's because groups and teams have meetings in varying circumstances, situations, environments, and conditions. Joe once had a meeting beside railroad tracks. Given the context, one ground rule for participation that they added was: If a train comes by while someone is talking, they keep the floor after the train passes.

REMEMBER

The bottom line: The rules for participation must fit the group or team, its situation and context, and how collaboration and discussion can occur best for them.

Holding People (Including Yourself) Accountable

Have you ever walked into a meeting and heard "So, what did we talk about last time we met?"

Or, even worse, have you ever spent the first 15 minutes of a 30 minute meeting figuring out what was decided during the last meeting together, seeing if anyone did anything they were asked to do, and then determining what you should even talk about? We sure have. Too many times. That might be why we are so motivated to share with you suggestions on how to avoid such experiences. (And no, we aren't going to tell you to cancel all the meetings on your calendar, or even ghost your staff meeting.) What we are going to focus on is the final stop on the meeting continuum, what happens after the meeting. If you mess up here, all of the hard work you put in before and during the meeting will be for naught, so follow the advice written here.

TIP

We strongly recommend you hold people, including yourself, accountable for the decisions made in your meetings together. If you don't, your efforts before and during the meeting will have been wasted.

Basically, we've talked about what needs to happen before a meeting. We've introduced some ideas about what ought to be happening during the meeting to facilitate participation. Now, we need to end the meeting well. As the meeting ends, you need to do the following:

>> Summarize any decisions that were made.

>> Create an action plan.

>> Delegate responsibilities for each action item to specific individuals.

>> Ensure that people agree to carry out their assigned tasks.

>> Follow up with individuals on their action items before the next meeting.

Following these steps will ensure that the meeting ends well and the next meeting starts well. If your next meeting begins by people asking what happened in the last meeting, you know you missed the mark.

Additionally, don't fall into the trap that all those things in that list are the meeting leader's job to make happen. You can make it a shared responsibility with meeting attendees beyond just delegating specific tasks. As the meeting leader, discuss with your team that everyone is responsible for meeting success, and the team's overall success. Reminding them of the shared responsibility will help them be more comfortable taking the initiative during the meeting to make things better, including their own behavior.

TIP

As the meeting ends, work together with your team to create and record the action plan. In fact, consider interjecting during the meeting with "Who's going to do that?" when a decision is made. That way each decision includes an assigned person to carryout whatever was decided.

Defining expectations and consequences

REMEMBER

When a meeting is coming to a close, before everyone runs back to their office, turns off their virtual meeting software, or begins transitioning to their next task, action items need to be identified and assigned. As that process unfolds, it's extremely important that the meeting leader and attendees define expectations.

TIP

When you ask someone to do something, give them some expectations of what you want done or delivered. That way they have an idea of how to fulfill the assignment to your satisfaction.

Action items refer to something that needs to be done by an assigned person. If you've done your job well, everyone in the meeting knows what that action is and who is responsible for doing it. However, don't assume that the person assigning the action item and the person doing the action item are on the same page. When an action item is given, be sure to ask clarifying questions. For example, if you are the one assigning the task, ask things such as "Do you understand what you need to do?" or perhaps, "Do you know how you plan to get started?"

By the same token, make sure you empower and encourage any action item receiver to ask their own clarifying questions. For example, if the receiver isn't sure what to do, they should feel comfortable enough to ask, "How would you recommend I get started on this?" (And what they might really be thinking is . . . "I don't have a clue what I'm supposed to do.") Believe us, we've been clueless before too and you probably have as well. Make sure you give people agency to ask those questions. Let them know that taking the cluelessness with them and carrying it all the way back to the next team meeting is far worse than asking for clarification now.

WARNING

It can be psychologically damaging for people to admit, in front of their peers, that they don't know how to do something. That's why following up is crucial. It gives people a chance to admit they need help and then you get the opportunity to enable them to do good work.

As uncomfortable as it may seem, you also want to create consequences for individuals who take on an action item and fail to do it. Often times simple embarrassment at the next meeting can be a powerful psychological tool to motivate them to figure things out. No one likes to be called out for not getting their work done, even if they didn't know how to get started. So, instead of public embarrassment, lean into following up with people outside the meeting and in private. This helps remove the embarrassment and motivates them to ask when they don't know how to get started.

You may want to also include other consequences, or at least voice the potential for them. For example, many action items are not independent; often one can't be accomplished without the other being done first. For those interdependent tasks, make everyone aware of that correlation in the meeting itself. Let people know the relationship between each action item and indicate the importance of the timing of their completion. For example, you can say, "Hey, this action item needs to be done first, today or tomorrow. The other items on the list can't be addressed until we get the results of the first one. Then the rest of you can jump in and do yours." The consequence in this case is pretty clear for the person with action item number one: Any delay in their actions will hold up everyone else's progress.

REMEMBER

Determining action items and assigning responsibility is one of the least-followed best practices for successful meetings. Just doing this one thing and doing it well has the potential to dramatically improve individual, team, and organizational performance.

Letting follow-up and action items drive the business

Most organizations depend heavily upon groups and teams to collaboratively solve problems and ensure the organization performs well. However, many groups and teams do not meet well. And sadly, too many meetings don't end well.

But, there's hope still. When meeting leaders and attendees conclude their meetings with action items and they follow-up with (and encourage) one another, they can unlock performance gains.

Imagine if all those meetings where you spent time figuring out what happened at the last meeting just started with an update of everyone's completed action items. That could be followed with a discussion of next steps, considerations of problems or challenges, and the assignment of new tasks for each team member.

TIP

Organize your meetings across the full continuum, considering what to do before, during, and after the meeting, and your team will quickly outperform every other team in your organization. Under these conditions, the meetings become the driver of the business because the meetings drive the actions and the followup inspires performance.

Chapter **4**

Choosing How You Should Meet

For decades upon decades, the way we held meetings didn't change much. If you were having a meeting, you were meeting face to face. You selected a day and time, reserved a conference room perhaps, and then made sure everyone could gather at the right spot and at the right time.

As technology advanced, our ability to meet using other formats started to change. We were able to do teleconference meetings starting with some of the early speaker phones originally patented in 1935. It took another 70 years for video to become common enough for people to start having virtual meetings. However, these forms of meeting represented only about 10 percent of meetings in October 2019.

Then COVID-19 hit and those in-person interactions became off limits. Our standard operating procedures were sidelined for the safety of ourselves and our coworkers. What took the place of all those face-to-face meetings? Video meetings, by and large, which became the go-to for the vast majority of knowledge workers. What may have seemed like a temporary fix, though, actually became a viable and important option for meeting.

The mass "return to the office" did not play out the way most people anticipated. It turns out that most people appear to prefer a *hybrid work* model, spending some days in the office and some days somewhere else. Even if you decide Tuesdays are your day to meet in person in the office, you can't control when every single meeting needs to take place. Ad hoc meetings happen and you need a way for your team to gather. Video conferencing platforms provide the communication connective tissue for a global workforce that prioritizes flexible work, often above all else.

Given the options you have today, figuring out the best way to meet is much more complex than it has ever been, with much more to consider. Do you need everyone to be in the same room because what you are discussing is so sensitive that it demands it (see Chapter 5 for more details)? Are attendees so far flung that it would be nearly impossible to get everyone in the same location at the same time? Is time so much of the essence that you need to meet right now?

In this chapter, we help you determine the best meeting format to fit your meeting purpose. Once you determine your format, we talk about what to look for in a meeting room, whether it's a physical one or a virtual one. We wrap up the chapter by talking about how long your meeting should be based on the format you've chosen.

Picking the Best Meeting Format

Choosing the proper format for your meeting is no longer straightforward because we have more ways to meet than ever before. Face to face, virtual, hybrid . . . they all are used within most organizations with varying degrees of success and effectiveness. The menu of meeting formats has forever changed and even if one format doesn't look as appealing as another, you might have to eat a bit of broccoli every now and then anyway.

REMEMBER

Figuring out what format is best for any particular meeting is a product of multiple factors, including:

>> The purpose of the meeting

>> The location of the attendees

>> The urgency of the meeting

Let's take a look at each of these factors within the context of the most common meeting formats that you will see today.

Meeting in-person

Face-to-face meetings were long considered the only way to meet and dominated the meeting landscape for as long as meetings were a thing. Face-to-face meetings also were a reflection of the historically dominant work model where practically everyone was in the office full-time. For some, face-to-face meetings will continue to be the most common form of meeting.

Now that the way we meet has shifted with a wider array of meeting formats available, in-person meetings often have a different role. For example, in hybrid working situations, in-person meetings are often reserved for those meetings that truly demand it, giving them a certain level of gravitas that they didn't have before. Popping into a conference room in pre-pandemic times may have been a regular occurrence for you. Now, meeting in the same room with a bunch of people may feel like a bigger deal — even with a higher calling. And if you've opted for a face-to-face meeting, it should feel like that — because in-person meetings need to reflect a compelling purpose.

Identifying purposes that call for face-to-face meetings

Not all in-person meetings need to have a lofty goal or involve a discussion of something truly complex. However, often they do have that purpose. Why?

REMEMBER

In-person interactions allow for the fullest form of communication possible and when the topic of conversation is challenging, emotional, or difficult to grasp, you need every communication tool in your arsenal to tackle it.

The key here is that in meetings that have these attributes (such as complex ideas, emotions, or challenging conversations), you need the meeting format that has the fullest communication format possible. Any reduction in the ability to hear, see, and understand others in the meeting can become a disaster in these more serious meetings.

Here are a few examples of meeting purposes that best match an in-person format:

>> Performance reviews (especially when they are negative)

>> Complex product development discussions

>> Promotional decisions

>> Long-term strategy

>> HR decisions (such as hiring or firing someone)

TIP

Not all in-person meetings need to have a weighty purpose. In fact, some meetings that are best done face to face are more about developing team cohesion and building relationships. When you share the same space with others, you are able to create a different kind of energy in the group than you do when people are spread out across different mediums.

Even organizations that are primarily remote or heavily hybrid often plan out in-person meetings that are more social in nature than productive. Feeling like you are part of team leads to better engagement, better job satisfaction, and ultimately better business outcomes.

Addressing the location logistics of attendees

If your entire team is located in the same place, it is easier to call in-person meetings. Under these circumstances, you may have to account for someone traveling or being out sick or on vacation, but for the most part, you won't encounter too many barriers to getting people together in the same room.

The challenge comes when your team is dispersed across offices, time zones, or even countries. Or when you want to give your team more flexibility, greater work-family balance, more possibility for inclusion, or avoid commuting for sustainability reasons. If this is the case, you will have to carefully consider how important it is to have everyone sharing the same physical space. Does the purpose of the meeting justify the travel expenses for all of the attendees? Are you going to be able to coordinate everyone's schedules to find a day that works for everyone to be in one place? Do you even have time to figure that out?

Determining if the urgency of the meeting allows for in-person

If you plan team-building meetings in-person on a quarterly basis, you can easily schedule those in advance and make sure everyone has those dates blocked out on their calendars. The meeting isn't urgent but it is important. The regular cadence of them, though, allows plenty of time for planning in advance for a face-to-face meeting that will be a valuable opportunity for your team.

WARNING

What might throw you for a loop, though, is when a crisis occurs that calls for a meeting of key stakeholders as quickly as possible. If everyone is in the office, it's a no-brainer. Call that in-person meeting and call it soon. But what if Cheryl is on-site with a client for the week and John and Emily are working out of a satellite office on an interim basis? Ask yourself if your meeting can wait whatever period of time it will take to bring everyone back from remote work. If the answer is no, and you absolutely need your entire team to be present and accounted for, then an in-person meeting format is not your best option. The urgency of the meeting trumps your desire to have the richest meeting platform possible. Call the meeting, but opt for a different way of gathering.

Meeting virtually

Thanks to the wonders of technology, you can hold an effective meeting regardless of the location of your meeting attendees. Video collaboration platforms have broken down the geographic barriers and allow you to meet virtually at any time and any place, provided you have a strong enough internet connection.

REMEMBER

During the COVID-19 pandemic, virtual meetings became the primary if not only option for bringing people together. Now, you may choose to meet virtually for a number of reasons. While you may exercise this option for immediate health reasons (no need to come into the office when you have the sniffles and risk spreading around your germs) the key drivers for picking the virtual meeting format are efficiency and flexibility.

As with any meeting format, though, you want to be mindful of the purpose of the meeting, the location of the participants and how timely your discussion will be. Let's look at those three factors related to virtual meetings.

Identifying purposes that lend themselves to virtual meetings

To figure out what purpose matches best with the virtual meeting format, you first need to know what purpose it does *not* serve well. Virtual meetings are not well suited to building team ties, especially when they have no agenda and are loosely formatted. If you've attended one of those virtual happy hours, you know what we're talking about. The "forced fun" component usually involves stilted conversation and awkward pauses. Isn't eating and drinking on camera taboo anyway?

By contrast, virtual meetings are most effective when they are strategic, purpose-driven towards a particular goal or outcome. If you need to come to a decision, determine next steps or create a plan of action, a virtual meeting format might work well. In order to accomplish your goal, though, you as the meeting leader will need to guide the group towards it. A virtual meeting requires proactive facilitation and as the meeting leader, that means you will likely need to take charge of that.

Here are a few examples of meeting purposes that best match with a virtual format:

- Quarterly business reviews
- Quick project update and next-step discussion
- Staff meeting
- Targeted brainstorming session
- One-on-ones

Just because the purpose of a meeting is to result in action doesn't mean a virtual format is always the right option. You also need to consider the emotional weight of the decision being made. If the topic requires a full accounting of everyone's responses, both verbal and nonverbal, then you may need to back away from the virtual format and lean into the in-person one. A second thing to consider is the norms of your group concerning virtual meetings. If the norm is to leave the camera off, then instead of having both verbal and nonverbal communication, you're really only getting verbal inputs. Again, if the topic or purpose is sensitive in any way, virtual with the cameras off is not the right way to go.

Allowing attendees to join from anywhere

Virtual meetings are location agnostic. Your participants can log in from wherever they happen to be, provided they are able to connect to the internet. With the popularity of remote work, virtual meetings provide a portal for everyone to connect and feel connected to the team. Yes, it is okay to meet from the park, or the coffee shop, or your car, so long as your internet connection is adequate and the norms for your organization allow for such flexible meeting locations.

However, the ability to meet at any time from anywhere doesn't mean you should. One of the danger zones of remote work is the bleeding over of work into your personal life. The boundaries are blurred more than ever before and as a leader, you need to be on the lookout for ways you might violate the separation that should happen between your teams' personal and professional lives. The balance between work and life needs to be top of mind for both the meeting leaders and the attendees.

Think about what times of day may be challenging for your team to meet. If you know one of your team members has carpool every day at 3 p.m., shift your meeting so that it falls either before or after that. It's also easy to fall into the time zone trap. In the United States, what might be a great time for your east coasters may be before the crack of dawn for your west coast cohort.

Leveraging the last-minute nature of virtual meetings

A distinct advantage of the virtual meeting is the ease at which you can schedule it. With a few clicks, you can send a calendar invite winging its way to the inboxes of all your attendees. This is nearly as effective as picking up the phone used to be, particularly between office workers.

If you need to meet quickly, virtual meetings are usually your best bet, especially if not everyone is physically in the same location.

You may find it empowering to be able to call a virtual meeting so easily, but you want to make sure not to abuse that functionality. Meetings should only be called when they have a specific purpose that requires collaboration. Don't clog calendars with meetings that should not be meetings in the first place. And don't expect people to have had time to prepare for these last-minute meetings. If you don't give preparation time, don't expect people to be prepared. That has to be a consideration when identifying the purpose. Check out Chapter 7 for more on identifying your meeting's purpose.

Meeting in a hybrid environment

Given the popularity of the flexible work model, you may need to opt for one of the most challenging meeting formats available — the hybrid meeting. *Hybrid meetings* are meetings that use at least two different modalities for connecting, including some face-to-face, as well as some connected through technological means. The good news is a hybrid meeting promises to be the most inclusive of any meeting type because it allows people to potentially choose how they work best. Some people on your team may love the hum of the office, 9 to 5. Others prefer to ditch the commute and do their best work from home. Most probably want a combination of both.

That's why a hybrid meeting can be the best way to get the most out of your team. Let's talk about a hybrid meeting within the context of the meeting purpose, participant location, and urgency.

Knowing what meeting purpose matches a hybrid format

Hybrid meetings combine the best of both worlds — the energy generated by the in-person experience with the efficiency of a virtual gathering that can be called quickly. Those who are in the office at the time can get together in the designated conference room and click on the meeting link to join their remote colleagues. Seems simple, right? If it were only so!

Hybrid meetings can be hard, especially if the technology isn't in place to create an equitable participation and sharing experience for everyone. In order for the hybrid meeting to work, everyone in the meeting, regardless of location, needs to be seen and heard by everyone else. In-room attendees need to be able to easily see and hear their virtual counterparts. Virtual attendees need to feel like they are as close to the in-room action as possible with high-quality conference room cameras and audio systems.

Unfortunately, all these challenges unique to the hybrid meeting may have you thinking, "Maybe I should just run back to my office and stick with virtual meetings only, unless everyone can be present." That would be a mistake.

Consider this. Humans are social beings. We like and need to be in the presence of others. Even if only a portion of your team can share the same space, there is still huge value in that — value that spills over to the remote attendees as well, provided that they are encouraged to be part of the conversation and not just spectators.

Remote attendees can feed off that in-room energy and add to the ideas being generated if everyone in the meeting makes an effort to be inclusive of all participants. In-room bias is only natural and you, as a leader, need to constantly push back against it by creating policies that allow for participation equity. We'll talk more about what kind of strategies you can employ in Chapter 12.

Don't forget the bias that existed between remote workers and in-person workers in 2019 (and before). Remember how we used to joke about the people working from home in their pajamas, eating bonbons and relaxing, while we at the office did all the work? Post COVID-19 pandemic, we all know just how wrong that was. You can work from home and it is still very much work.

Given the inherent challenges with hybrid meetings, though, you want to reserve them for those meeting that require a higher level of collaboration and discussion than perhaps a daily stand up. Maybe you keep daily meetings in the virtual format but have a weekly team meeting in a hybrid format to capture that unique energy and foster team relationships.

Normally, this is where we would list a few examples of topics and meeting purposes that fit well with this format of meeting. However, that's the interesting thing about hybrid meetings. They have the potential to handle all the easy and difficult meetings we have. When done correctly, in a way that everyone is seen and heard, the hybrid meeting format can match with any purpose, no matter how complex or emotional it may be. For hybrid meetings, it comes down to a bit of extra effort on the part of the leader and the attendees. The main driver for choosing hybrid over virtual or face to face is likely the location of the attendees, where flexible work allows for people to be in the office or remote, or getting everyone together for a face-to-face meeting can't be done within a reasonable time frame or cost structure.

Creating the best of both virtual and in-person worlds

If your meeting's purpose would normally dictate an in-person meeting but the location of your attendees won't allow it, opt for a hybrid approach over a virtual one. Hybrid meetings provide middle ground that allows you to leverage those in-person connections while allowing for remote attendees to be present and participate.

Face-to-face meetings allow for the most nuanced and full communication possible. If your meeting calls for that but logistics won't allow it, harness as much of that nuance as you can by at least allowing some people to be located in the same room. Just be careful to ensure that the remote attendees are included, seen, and heard.

Giving yourself time to plan for a hybrid meeting

Don't go into a hybrid meeting without some planning and an intentional approach. This format is not suited for a free-for-all of ideas and a loose agenda. In-person attendees are in a position where they can hijack the conversation and direction of the meeting because they have more "presence" than their virtual counterparts. Unless you plan ways for the remote attendees to be active participants throughout, they will check out and you will lose all of their valuable insights. When remote, if you aren't included, there are too many distractions to pull attendees away. Help them by including them.

Before a hybrid meeting, you need to carefully plan out your agenda and determine how and where you plan to insert opportunities for engagement. You also may want to assign roles to team members, such as a tech lead, minutes taker, or time keeper, to create even greater and broader investment in the meeting's success.

You will need more time to prepare for a hybrid meeting to make it worthwhile, and that's why you shouldn't have it as the default format for every meeting for your team. Like the face-to-face format, you want to use the hybrid format for when it matters most — when the decisions being made are consequential or call for everyone's input. And you must be strategic and plan if you want full participation by all attendees.

Choosing the Meeting Space

Once you've chosen how you are going to meet, you need to figure out where you are going to meet. It's not just a matter of picking a conference room or selecting a video-conferencing platform. Here are some things you should consider based on the format you are using.

Selecting the physical room

There are two meeting formats that require a physical meeting room — face-to-face and hybrid. Both need the room to be big enough to accommodate the people who will be gathering in it. Both need the room to be comfortable with either adequate heat or air conditioning. But beyond the basics, you need to keep some format-specific needs in mind for face-to-face and hybrid meetings.

Designing the room for a face-to-face meeting

A face-to-face room begins with adequate seating and table design. There are a host of options that can be seen in any number of conference rooms around the world.

REMEMBER

We recommend tables that don't immediately indicate who is in charge simply by where they sit like the table head. There's a reason King Arthur's table was round. Barring a round table option (and a host of knights at your beck and call), the conference room needs a large enough table for attendees to be comfortably spaced and the seating should be comfortable enough for longer meetings, when necessary. Nothing worse than a 2 hour (or longer) meeting with chairs that get uncomfortable in 10 minutes.

Beyond the table, here are some additional design elements to consider:

>> **Room acoustics:** You want to account for soft-spoken members of the team and have sound proofing for privacy.

>> **Lighting:** You need adequate lighting for visibility.

>> **Refreshments:** You don't want your team's energy to flag because they are hungry or thirsty. For longer meetings, refreshments are a must.

>> **Adequate A/V (audio/visual) system:** If you want to share slides or screens, you need the equipment that allows for that.

TECHNICAL STUFF

WE HAVE THE TECHNOLOGY, WE HAVE THE CAPABILITY

If you're using an A/V system, make sure you know how to use it and that it is set up and ready to go. Don't just take someone else's word for it, check it out yourself before the meeting.

It's very common for organizations to have a hodge-podge of system configurations across the enterprise as hardware is taken out of service and new devices are installed. You might find it good practice to have someone from the IT department on speed dial just in case you show up at your meeting room and find the "improvements" made to the system are impossible to figure out.

Designing the room for a hybrid meeting

When it comes to planning out the physical room for a hybrid meeting, the biggest factor in the design of the space are the virtual attendees. Yes, many of the previous thoughts in this chapter on face-to-face meetings still apply. However, you want to ensure presence for all. That means your space allows remote attendees to see and hear everyone in the meeting room and your in-room attendees can clearly see and hear virtual participants. This may require a different design or setup to the typical conference rooms we often see in corporate offices.

For a hybrid meeting to work, the physical meeting room needs a high-quality camera that captures everyone on screen. If it's a smaller room, a static shot may be adequate to capture a limited number of people within the frame. If it's a larger room, though, you may need to invest in a camera that has auto-zooming that will tighten up the shot to frame the person who is speaking.

WARNING

Be careful of the bowling alley look in the conference room. A single camera looking right down the table means that people could be hidden by the people they are sitting next to, making it hard for remote attendees to see all the in-person attendees.

REMEMBER

For remote attendees to feel like they can read the room, they need to be able to see everyone clearly. If they can barely make out the faces of people seated at the far end of the table, they will miss out on critical nonverbal cues and feel marginalized.

Also, be conscious of how the chairs are arranged. Ideally, you want them to be situated in a semi-circle with the camera (or cameras) occupying one side of the table and the in-person attendees making up the other side. Make sure no one is hiding behind someone else, either on purpose or by accident.

While high-quality video is important, excellent audio fidelity is even more so. After all, you can still have a meeting without video. If you have no sound, you have no meeting. The key to in-room audio is a system that picks up the voices of every person seated at the table. Don't just assume that the one microphone at the far end of the room has a wide enough range to pick up the voices of the people at the other end of the room.

If the remote attendees can't hear what's going on, they will be frustrated and feel like they are on the outside looking in. Get feedback from your remote attendees on how clearly they could hear the conversations in the room. If there are deficiencies, take it up with the appropriate department and ask them to address them.

Lastly, be mindful of your monitor size. It is easy for in-room participants to forget about their virtual colleagues. One way to constantly remind them of their presence is to make sure they are visually represented adequately. You want your virtual attendees to be as large as possible in gallery view and that means using a monitor with plenty of real estate.

TECHNICAL STUFF

High-speed internet connections are essential for hybrid meetings to even be possible. Ideally the high-speed connection is on both ends, the office and the remote colleagues locations. No, you probably don't need to run down to IT and demand gigabit internet, but whatever is considered a high-speed connection to your IT team should be the type of connection in your meeting rooms. This is the side of the hybrid meeting that you have greater control over and so you should make it as good as possible. If you're on the remote end, get to a location with the best internet connection that you can find. Joe had to upgrade his connection speed at his home during the COVID-19 pandemic and continues to pay that extra fee as he continues to use virtual and hybrid meetings all the time.

Setting up the virtual space

Most organizations have a favored video conferencing platform. You may or may not like it, but using a different one may be more trouble than it's worth. When the world first went fully virtual, the virtual meeting space felt like the Wild West. Most people just used whatever they could download in the moment to get business done, but the lack of standardization drove IT departments crazy and caused a lot of anxiety over potential security breaches. By now, most organizations have streamlined their meeting tech stack and are loathe to have other applications added by individuals. We suggest you don't try to swim upstream and instead try to make the best of the platform that has been selected for the enterprise as a whole.

Within that context, you do want to make sure all of your attendees know how to use the technology and feel comfortable with all of its functionalities. Don't just assume people will figure it out on their own. They may not have the time or the ability to do so. You may want to ask for someone from the IT department to do a quick tutorial for your team, showing them the basics as well as some more advanced capabilities. A little training goes a long way. A 20-minute session could mean the difference between someone not knowing how to share their screen and someone wowing during a presentation for a potential client.

TIP

If you plan to use any more advanced technology tools (like virtual whiteboards or external polling apps) give attendees a heads up in the calendar invite. Include a quick introduction of the tool and then provide a link to either a video or text tutorial that explains how to use it. You want everyone to enter the meeting room (physical and virtual) with a base level of knowledge that will allow them to participate equally.

Timing it Right

How long should meetings last? You might say the shorter the better and most would probably agree. However, how long a meeting should be is a product of a variety of factors including the meeting format and the structure of the agenda.

The length of the meeting should coincide with the amount of time need to accomplish its purpose, and no longer.

Right-sizing the meeting duration

Time spent in a virtual meeting feels different than time spent during an in-person meeting. Often, a meeting spent on screen can feel much more draining than a meeting of the same length in person. Researchers have thrown out all sorts of reasons for this — a lack of mobility when attending a virtual meeting; the hyper focus that is required to try to read the body language of all of those people on gallery view at one time; the pain of having to watch yourself, up close and personal, on screen for way too long.

Whatever the reason, what is important for you to understand is there is not a one-to-one ratio between time spent in a face-to-face meeting and time spent in a virtual meeting. Don't assume that an in-person meeting that normally lasts four hours will translate to a four-hour virtual meeting that is effective. Trust us, it won't be.

In general, the science is clear: Virtual meetings need to be shorter than in-person meetings to account for digital exhaustion. That means you need to adjust your agendas accordingly. Don't try to fit two hours of content into an hour-long block. Instead break up your agenda into manageable pieces. Sure you may need to have several shorter meetings rather than one long one, but you will get much more out of the process.

When Karin moved her training from in-person to virtual, she found that her typical full-day schedule was too much for her remote participants to stay engaged. What did she do? She restructured her training from an eight hour day to four, two-hour days with plenty of breaks during all of the sessions.

The same rules about meeting length hold true for hybrid meeting as well. Even though your in-room attendees may be totally fine with a longer agenda, you need to prioritize the limits of attention and endurance of your remote attendees. In short, keep those hybrid meetings shorter too — even though your in-room attendees might be able to handle a longer meeting.

Building in buffers between meetings

Did you ever look at your schedule for the day and wonder, "How am I even going to go to the bathroom?" If you are like most us, your day is made up of meetings that appear in clumps on your calendar. What you probably don't see are spaces between those meeting chunks, and that's a problem. One-time, Joe had eight-hours of back-to-back meetings with no breaks. Knowing what he knows about meeting science, he looked at his calendar and decided which meeting he could get away with arriving late to.

REMEMBER

If the meeting organizers don't provide time, you may just have to find some yourself. Everyone needs time between meetings.

After a meeting, you need time to process what just happened. Maybe you need to immediately address some action items you were assigned or you need to at least catalog them. Maybe you need to take a bio break, grab a bite to eat, or simply stretch your legs.

You also need time before a meeting to prepare. That could be as simple as going over the agenda so you can give at least a little thought to the topics of discussion. Maybe you are presenting and you want to flip through your slides one more time.

TECHNICAL
STUFF

From a cognitive psychology perspective, humans need time to transition from topic to topic. This is so well understood, we integrate it into how we train our children in secondary schools. Yes, sometimes the passing period includes unnecessary PDA (public displays of affection) between students, but it also helps them cognitively switch from physical education to algebra. The same human need applies to adults and meetings.

If your meetings are primarily in person, this may not be as much of a challenge for you especially if the meetings are in different locations. You probably recognize the commute time and build it into your day. If your meetings are mostly virtual, though, breaks may not be at the top of your mind. There's no real commute time to account for when you are meeting in the same spot, your office chair.

You may think your calendar app is the root of all of your scheduling woes, and you wouldn't be entirely off base. After all, most of them default to hour or half hour blocks. Here's your opportunity to take control. Don't be the default. Don't let the calendar govern your day. Take charge!

TIP

Build in buffers between meetings. Don't let a calendar app determine how long your meeting needs to be. If you can accomplish all you need to do in 45 minutes, schedule the meeting for 45 minutes. It may require a few extra clicks to override the default time that your calendar app chose. But what's a few clicks, when it can save you your sanity? Or 15 minutes? Or at least give you an opportunity to grab a cup of coffee for a stamina boost. Definitely worth the extra clicks!

Chapter 5

Using Video in Virtual or Hybrid Meetings

O ne of the keys to a successful meeting is ensuring everyone can be seen and heard. This is usually a no-brainer for face-to-face meetings where people are showing up in the same physical location. So long as the seating arrangements allow for clear lines of sight and no one mumbles too much, pretty much everyone in the meeting has the potential to be seen and heard.

Not so for a virtual or hybrid meeting. When people attend a meeting remotely, they may have the option to be seen and heard using the tools of the virtual meeting platform, but often they may choose *only* to be heard, opting out of turning on their video.

REMEMBER

You might think keeping your camera off is of little consequence, but in many cases, you would be wrong. Your personal decision to not turn on your camera impacts the effectiveness of the meeting for everyone. In this chapter, we discuss why video is valuable in a virtual or hybrid meeting and the potential problems it wards off. We also help you figure out when having your video on is imperative and when it is not. Lastly, we help you create a video policy with your team, so the choice to keep the camera on or off becomes a team decision, not a personal decision dictated by whether or not it's a "good hair day."

Understanding the Value of Video When Meeting

Do you remember the days of the spider phone at the center of the conference room table? That device — in essence, a speaker phone on steroids — allowed for the early version of the hybrid meeting. The vast majority of meeting attendees would gather in a room in the brick-and-mortar office, and maybe one person would "dial in."

Technology has come a long way since then and has empowered today's virtual and hybrid meetings. Video collaboration tools such as Zoom, Microsoft Teams, and Google Meets allow people to gather together at any time and any place provided they have a good internet connection. Meetings with video at their core have cemented themselves into the communication DNA across every industry.

During the COVID-19 pandemic, video meetings were a lifeline, the closest approximation to the in-person interactions that were not possible due to the threat of spreading the virus. We appreciated seeing the faces of our friends and colleagues and even got used to seeing each other on the screen from the torso up. We also got used to seeing ourselves on camera which many of us found not only distracting but disconcerting ("Do I normally blink that much when I speak?"). Despite our discomfort at times, the technology did allow us to feel connected without being collocated.

At some point, though, there was a shift. People started resenting being on camera for hours and hours at a time. You started hearing the term "Zoom fatigue" as a catch-all phrase for the exhaustion blamed on too many video calls. You also started seeing the gallery view, that used to be full of faces, be populated more and more often by black boxes with names in them. If video was not mandated, people were starting to opt out.

The pushback against using video is understandable due to the meeting explosion that happened during the COVID-19 pandemic. We had more meetings than ever before, that lasted longer than ever before, with barely any time in between to grab a snack, take a stretch, or even go to the bathroom. Additionally, nonstop video calls meant seeing yourself nonstop on camera. It was like walking around with a mirror held up to your face all day. Sometimes you might feel okay about what was staring back at you. Other times, not so much, especially on a bad hair day. Between the schedule and the self-awareness, we became more and more exhausted with the camera-on format. However, they were pointing the finger at the wrong suspect.

Video call fatigue is not the fault of the platform. It's operator error. The bottom line is that we have too many meetings that last too long without enough breaks in between.

While we get why people want to keep their cameras off, we also believe that can be a big mistake in virtual or hybrid meetings, especially when the stakes are high.

REMEMBER

Cameras aren't the cause of bad meetings. Before we used video in meetings all the time, a lot of meetings still weren't good. Cameras aren't the source of bad meetings, but keeping them off can be a contributing factor if the topic of discussion requires complex communication.

Creating a richer meeting experience

Let's say you have some yardwork to do. Lucky for you, you have all of the tools that you need: a shovel, a pickaxe, even a new wheelbarrow. You set off on the task, digging a sizable hole, resulting in a rather large mound of dirt to match. You need to get that dirt to the back of the property line. Now that's where the wheelbarrow comes in. But instead, you decide that you are going to move the dirt to its new destination using only your hands. Can you get the job done? Yes. Is it the most effective way of getting the job done? Of course not. It seems nonsensical because you have a tool that is perfect for the job that you are keeping on the sideline.

When you decide not to use video during a virtual meeting, you choose to keep a powerful tool on the sideline . . . a tool that can make that meeting a much richer experience for everyone involved. Allow us to explain.

When conveying a message, how you share it largely depends upon how complex and emotionally charged it is. Confirming dinner plans ("Pizzeria Mario's at 7 p.m.?") is not complex and is probably not emotionally charged. You can easily deliver that message in a text. But can you imagine conducting a performance review via text thread? If that review is not flattering, would you have that conversation even over the phone? Probably not. Why? Because you want to be able to have as many ways to read the room as possible and all the tools you can muster to communicate your message as fully as possible.

TIP

What we are getting at is something called *media richness theory*. We won't go into all of the specifics but understand this basic premise: the more layered, emotional and challenging the message, the richer the medium you want to use to deliver it. By rich we mean more cues, more information, more ways to understand what the other person is saying or feeling.

Text is great for delivering facts, but not so great at delivering a message with nuance or emotion. It's hard to read the tone of a string of words, no matter how many emojis you include.

When those words are given voice (in a meeting environment, audio), the intent of the message is much easier to read. You can't read sarcasm, but you can certainly hear it when someone sneers as they speak. You also can tell if someone is sounding angry or anxious, happy or hurt, by simply listening to the sound of their voice. As a result, audio is a richer way of conveying a message than any form of text, whether that be an email, a text, or a message in a Teams or Slack channel.

However, there are times when seeing someone's face is critical when communicating. If you are delivering bad news, you want to be able to see how someone is reacting, not just try to imagine it in your head. If you are presenting a big change management initiative, you want to be able to read the room to gauge the immediate response. Maybe someone is nodding along. Maybe someone is looking like they could blow a gasket. If you are just relying upon audio alone, you lack all of those nonverbal cues that can guide your next steps and inform your response.

There's a huge debate about what percentage of a message is delivered through our body language, so we won't wade into the numbers debate. What we will say is our nonverbals provide essential clues that we can use to shape how we communicate.

REMEMBER

If you keep your camera off, you make it harder for people to understand the intent of your message because they don't have the nonverbal cues that paint the entire picture of what you are trying to convey. If you allow others to keep their cameras off, you can't read the impact your message is having on your audience. Their response is a literal and figurative black box that can't be opened. These gaps in understanding make it nearly impossible to build emotional rapport amongst meeting attendees.

Video coupled with audio allows you to communicate more fully and is the richest medium aside from being in-person. Need to schedule a lunch date? Text works. Need to conduct a performance review with a not-so-flattering undertone? If you can't meet in person, use all of the virtual tools you have at your disposal, which means using the richest media possible — audio and video.

Keeping people from multi-tasking

During the onslaught of COVID-19, another pandemic took hold . . . multitasking. With all of the back-to-back meetings, we found it nearly impossible to get all of the action items done that we were assigned, so we did what many of us do when we are short on time — we doubled down on trying to do several things at once.

WARNING

The only problem is multitasking is a myth. It's actually just "tasking" because our brains will only allow us to do one thing at a time. When we multitask, we are attempting to task switch quickly, which impacts how well we accomplish any task. Multitasking during meetings makes those meetings worse and often results in even more meetings to clean up the mess of the previous one.

If you keep your video off while attending a meeting virtually, you are much more likely to just "sort of" attend a meeting. You half-listen to what is being discussed while checking your email, working on your expense report, or doing any number of the action items on your long list of to-do's. It's too easy to simply open up a new tab and do other work while keeping loosely connected to what is going on in the meeting itself.

However, if you are on camera, you have a much higher chance of being engaged in the meeting because it holds you accountable to others on the call. Your fellow attendees can tell when you are checked out and not focused on the action in the meeting, even if you think you are being sly about it.

A meeting, by definition, requires there to be a purpose for it, one that calls for collaboration. Holding a meeting with a bunch of disengaged or partially engaged participants is a waste of everyone's time. If you ask for everyone to keep their cameras on, you substantially raise the chances that all in attendance will actually focus on the meeting agenda and take part in the discussion in a meaningful way. You increase your chances even more if you set a ground rule at the beginning that multitasking is not permitted. Let them know it's in everyone's best interest; a good meeting involves full participation by all, not participation by a select few.

Recognizing the Potential for Video Overload

You may never have imagined your job would require you to be on camera all day, but if you are a manager in a fully remote or hybrid organization, that might be your reality. And if you are like most managers, your day is best described as a string of back-to-back meetings. While video can play a pivotal role in making a meeting worthwhile, you might find a full day of video meetings draining. Why is this the case? Read on!

Diagnosing the downside of being on camera

When you first went fully virtual and conducted most of your meetings on video collaboration platforms, you may have seen yourself communicate in real-time for the first time. Seeing yourself on the screen may have been very distracting and possibly even disconcerting. You may have stared at your image and wondered if you've always had a slightly crooked smile or if your right eye has always been slightly larger than your left eye. It's okay, Joe's nose points the wrong direction and Karin's eyebrows don't match. Maybe you cock your head when concentrating, sort of like your dog (and our editor) does. We all perceive flaws through our camera lens that most people do not see at all.

Watching yourself speak

Being on a video call puts you in an unnatural communication scenario where you are seeing yourself from the outside looking in. It's equivalent to walking around with a mirror to your face. Unless you are a supreme narcissist, that is not something you would enjoy for long periods of time. To make matters worse, when you watch yourself, you are not seeing the "real" you because you have a tendency to try to curate what you do on the screen. When you are both spectator and speaker, you act differently than you normally would, which undercuts a key element of success in video communication.

REMEMBER

The secret to being an effective on-camera communicator is authenticity — just you being you.

TIP

It's hard to be yourself when you are in your own head and judging everything you are saying and doing in real-time. All of that self-evaluation is exhausting, and many of the video collaboration platform vendors have an easy fix built into their interfaces. See if your chosen platform allows you to remove your own image from your screen. The function is often called "hide self-view" and can be clicked on and off easily in the settings in the platform window.

Managing the technology

When you are in person, you don't have to worry too much about the technology. The most challenging tech setup might be figuring out how to project your slides. When you are virtual or hybrid, you need to navigate all sorts of potential technology pitfalls. Does the meeting link work? Can everyone join? Is everyone's internet connection stable? Can you share your slides or your screen?

Technology is fickle, and even if you've practiced and prepared for a possible tech failure, you can still feel stressed about it. The extra layer of worry makes it harder for you to focus on the content of the meeting itself.

TIP

One way to decrease your cognitive burden of leading a meeting and managing the technology is to give the tech job to someone else. Appoint a technology lead for your meeting. Someone who can be the assigned tech troubleshooter. That way, if someone can't connect, for example, that tech lead can work on that problem separately with the person affected while you continue to run the meeting.

Dealing with the distractions

If you are working from a home office, you may have another mental barrier to being on camera — all of the distractions that are very much in your space but off the screen. Your fellow meeting participants might see only what you want them to see in your background, but you could have total chaos going on just out of frame.

You are very aware that your giant dog just knocked over your end table and all of the potting soil from your houseplant is now scattered across your new rug, but you are doing your best to make sure your fellow meeting attendees are none the wiser. Distractions of all shapes and sizes are part and parcel of working from a space that may not be solely designed for work and may even regularly clash with your life outside of work.

Still, you may endeavor to keep life out — at least on screen — which creates an additional cognitive burden that you have to carry around. Essentially, it divides your attention between what is happening on screen and what is happening in your immediate vicinity.This cognitive burden can derail our ability to focus and perform. Karin experienced this first hand when her sweet husband brought her a cup of coffee in the middle of one of her webinars. While she appreciated the gesture, she ended up getting tongue-tied during a section of her presentation that she normally delivers smoothly, all because she was trying to process this additional person just out of frame (bearing gifts no less!) while navigating through the finer points of the appropriate on-camera gestures.

WARNING

When you have a lot of potential disruptions and surefire distractions around you, keeping the camera off can feel like the best and perhaps only option, and honestly, sometimes it is. However, for all of the reasons we mentioned before, you lose much of your ability to exert influence in a meeting when you are not visually represented.

SELECTING YOUR SET

Have you ever gone to a picnic gathering and felt totally outclassed by the feast your friends have brought along? You might have stopped by the local sandwich shop and picked up a bag of chips to share, while others seemily took days to create a magazine-worthy spread, with a delectable array of tasty options, served on china no less.

When it comes to backgrounds on virtual calls, you may suffer from the same sense of inadequacy. Yes, there will be some people who seem to have hired a set designer to create a picture-perfect backdrop behind them. How can you possibly compete? The good news is you don't have to. While that carefully curated background might be a *nice*-to-have, it's not a *need*-to-have, and it shouldn't keep you from turning your video on. The goal is to have a background that is not distracting and professional.

You don't need a ton of space to create an adequate backdrop for your virtual call, just a few feet between you and whatever is behind you to add some depth to your shot. You don't want to sit up against a blank wall because you'll look like you are getting your passport photo taken. Positioning yourself with a corner behind you automatically adds a bit of dimension.

If you are worried about your background being too sterile, try hanging a piece of art-work on the wall behind you, but make sure it's not too busy. That could end up pulling focus away from you as people fixate on the picture and not what you are saying. Try adding a plant for a pop of color in your shot. Place one on top of a table so it's in the frame to your left or right (not directly behind you, coming out of your head).

A lot of people like to personalize their backgrounds by, say, hanging up some sports memorabilia from your favorite team. That's perfectly fine. We would call that a conversation starter. One conversation starter is fine. Ten conversation starters will read as clutter.

If a "real" background is not in the cards (if you share a space and will likely have people walking behind you during your calls) almost all meeting platforms have the option to use virtual backgrounds that allow you to superimpose any image you'd like behind you. (Some companies require you to use preapproved backgrounds, so make sure you follow the rules for your own organization.)

Most platforms also have the option to blur your background, so you are seen clearly but everything else in the frame appears fuzzy and indistinct. Virtual backgrounds can hide a wealth of chaos, but make sure the technology is working correctly in your environment. Sometimes the artificial intelligence used to generate the backgrounds can't tell where you end and your background begins, and you end up with those watery edges that can sometimes eat your hair, for example.

(Karin once had a client try to use a shot of the Northern Lights as her virtual back-ground during a coaching session. Unfortunately, the virtual background layered on her face instead. The only sign of her visage were the frames of her glasses.)

Feeling stuck in one place

During the COVID-19 pandemic, when your commute perhaps went from a walk to the train to seven steps downstairs to the home office, you may have felt like your lifestyle had taken a very sedentary turn. If you were like thousands of people, you tried to add some more movement into your days by using a standing desk with a treadmill underneath. What seemed like a panacea for too much sitting time may have been a total annoyance for your coworkers. It's hard to focus on what is being discussed when your virtual conversation partner is bouncing back and forth while getting their steps in.

Leading or attending a meeting remotely requires you to stay within the frame of your webcam. That means you are pretty much stuck in one spot for as long as the meeting lasts . . . or even longer because with the number of back-to-back meetings that occur, you may not even have time to get up for a quick stretch for a much longer period of time.

It's true. Too much movement when you appear on screen can be very distracting, but the result is you may feel like you are being held captive by the camera lens.

REMEMBER

Sometimes you need to turn that camera off, even if it's simply to deal with biological necessities. The key is knowing when it's okay to turn the camera off and when you should prioritize keeping it on.

Using video when it matters most

When you should have your video on when leading or attending a meeting remotely is largely dependent upon three factors: the purpose of the meeting, the size of the meeting, and your relationship to those in attendance.

Using video for the right purpose

If the purpose of your meeting is to do a brief check-in, to get quick clarification or confirm a fact, having your video on is not imperative. The meeting's purpose isn't too weighty and can likely be accomplished without the necessity for a fully nuanced conversation that audio and video provide. However, if the purpose of the meeting carries some emotional heft or the topic is complex, you want everyone to have their cameras on, so you can read the room and communicate as fully as possible.

Using video for the right meeting size

Some organizations have made it mandatory for everyone to always have their cameras on if they are attending any meeting remotely. While we applaud the intention, it may not be the best option in practice. Consider the town hall meeting where everyone across the entire enterprise is in attendance. Seeing a sea of faces in tiny boxes isn't doing anyone much good. In fact, it can be more of a distraction to see all of those miniature images cluttering the screen.

By contrast, being able to see if someone rolls their eyes or nods their head when you are in a decision-making meeting of perhaps five to seven people is incredibly valuable feedback. It doesn't take too much effort to quickly read the virtual room if the boxes are big enough to be able to reveal the subtleties of the nonverbal cues that can impact the direction of the conversation.

Using video based on relationships

If everyone in the meeting knows each other well, you may be able to get away with not having video on (even though you may still want to have the camera on just to see friendly faces). But even with the camera off, you know when you hear the sarcasm in someone's voice that it is likely supported by a wink-wink because you've seen them do it countless times before. You don't need to see it happen. Your mind fills in the blanks, based upon previous history.

When video becomes essential though is when anyone in the meeting is new to the group. The newcomer doesn't have that history to fall back on and needs all of the nonverbal cues they can gather. That sarcasm might be too subtle for them to understand with just audio inputs. Seeing the body language of people speaking may ward off the chance of miscommunication or misperception.

TIP

Turning video on when someone is new to the group is also just a welcoming thing to do. It's really hard to form a relationship with a disembodied voice. There's a reason why people say, "It's nice to be able to put a name with a face."

Setting a Video Policy for Your Team

One of the worst ways to approach the use of video for virtual or hybrid meetings is to have no policy at all. Leaving it up to individuals to decide when to use video or not opens up the door for inequities. If someone never turns their video on, it may mean they are multitasking and focusing on their own to-do list at the expense of the outcomes of the meeting they are supposed to be fully engaged in. If someone always turns their video on while the majority of others don't, it may give them a louder voice than others in the meeting because leaders, based on human nature, may think to call on them more because they're visually represented.

REMEMBER Coming up with a video policy for your team removes any doubt about what is acceptable and what is not. You want to set expectations right off the bat and then make sure everyone adheres to them.

Determining the video culture of your organization

Every company has its own video culture even if it's not explicitly stated. You can tell simply by observing what common practices are. Do you log into an online meeting with your video on but soon realize your face is the only one on the screen? Or are you horrified when you log into an early morning meeting, hoping to be incognito while eating your cereal, when every other person has their camera on but you?

How organizations handle video use varies from company to company. It's not like one industry is more pro-video than another. We've worked with financial institutions that would never, ever turn on their video on virtual calls. We've worked with banks that have mandated that all virtual attendees have their cameras on, no matter what.

Often, video culture is a product of personal preferences at the top of the enterprise. If senior leadership embraces video, they will usually either make a policy that mandates it is used, or those lower on the corporate ladder will emulate what their bosses do. This trickle down approach does have plenty of exceptions though; Karin has had a C-level executive say, "Video is great for my team, but I don't think it's really necessary for me."

Knowing the video culture of your organization can help inform the video policy for your team. If video is mandated enterprise-wide, you best make sure you abide by that with your team as well. However, if there is no policy at the organizational level, it does give you some wiggle room to create guidelines that make sense for your own team.

WARNING Often the video culture for internal meetings is different to the video culture for meetings with external stakeholders. Even the most ardent video opponents see value in turning it on for meetings with customers and clients. The rub comes though when the customer or client refuses to turn their video on. You may feel like your looming image on the screen may make your customers feel uncomfortable, and you are almost shamed into turning it off. Don't do it!

REMEMBER Remember why you have your video on in the first place. You want to be able to communicate in full. By having your camera on, you are being respectful of the people you are meeting with because you know it's easier for people to digest your message when it's delivered in the richest way possible. By using video and audio, you make both yourself and your message more memorable.

Deciding on the video culture of your team

The best way to figure out what the video culture of your team is and should be is to look at the norms of your current virtual or hybrid meetings. Does everyone typically log on with their video on or do the majority opt out of turning on their cameras? If most of the people on your team do not turn their cameras on, dig a little deeper into the reasons why. It could be that no one ever set the expectation that they should meet with video on, but there may be additional challenges that you may not expect.

Here are some questions to ask that reveal possible barriers to turning on the camera:

>> Do they possibly have bandwidth issues that don't provide a stable enough environment to allow for both audio and video?

>> Are most meetings held at a challenging time for them personally, say during carpool or dinner time?

>> Could there be privacy concerns or a lack of a perceived "appropriate space" for being on camera?

The answers to each of these questions may require a remedy that you can provide, troubleshoot, or account for as you are determining a video policy for your team. For example, if some of your team members are keeping their cameras off during carpool or dinner time with the kids, you likely will want to hold meetings at times that don't conflict with those timeslots. If someone has bandwidth issues, see if your organization will allow that employee to expense high-speed internet costs. If someone is concerned about not having a professional background or is sharing the space with others, see if you can get them a noise-cancelling headset and make a blurred or virtual background a norm.

Don't be afraid to ask your team their opinions on video use during meetings. Find out why they like to use it or don't like to use it, then share with them the pros and cons that you take away from this book. Often, there is an assumption that if you are going to be on camera, you need to look like you are ready to be interviewed by a news network. While your team should not be showing up in pajamas (unless that happens to be your dress code) they shouldn't feel like they need to be any more dressed up for a video meeting than they would for a meeting in person. Explain to them that keeping the camera on isn't about being "ready for your closeup" but rather a way to improve communication flow in the meeting itself. You want to see their facial expressions, not how skillfully they've styled their hair.

Make the creation of your video policy a team effort. Let everyone weigh in, but realize that you will likely not have universal support for whatever policy you bang out. People's level of comfort on camera varies wildly. Some are completely fine with it and have no problem keeping it on. Others find it terribly invasive. However, if you help the video opposition understand why it is important to use in certain circumstances, you will hopefully find grudging support.

TIP

Here's a checklist that may help guide your decisions about when video is imperative and when it's not for your team. The checklist first appeared in our book, *Suddenly Hybrid: Managing the Modern Meeting* (John Wiley & Sons, Inc., 2022).

Questions to consider when deciding camera on or off

1. Do you not know the people you are meeting with very well?	[ ]Yes [ ]No
2. Does the meeting include important decision-making?	[ ]Yes [ ]No
3. Is the meeting smaller than 10 people?	[ ]Yes [ ]No
4. Are you expected to directly participate by presenting information or providing input?	[ ]Yes [ ]No
5. Are external stakeholders invited to the meeting? If yes:	[ ]Yes [ ]No
a. Is this the first time you are meeting them?	[ ]Yes [ ]No
b. Will the meeting involve negotiation?	[ ]Yes [ ]No
c. Are you trying to make a sale or close a deal?	[ ]Yes [ ]No
6. Is the topic of discussion complicated?	[ ]Yes [ ]No

If you answered yes to two or more of these questions, then you probably should turn the camera on. All of these scenarios play into the idea that you want the richest way of communicating as possible.

WARNING

When a meeting is hybrid, it is absolutely imperative for remote attendees to turn their cameras on if the meeting is one that requires full participation from everyone. Virtual attendees risk disappearing from the meeting when other attendees are present in the physical room. While there may be some flexibility about attending meetings with the camera on when everyone is virtual, a hybrid meeting demands remote participants be on camera to ensure they have as much "presence" in the meeting as possible. Otherwise, their influence and impact on the meeting will be greatly diminished.

Chapter 6

Meeting with Global Participants

S ome time ago, Joe was working with his favorite research collaborator in Germany, Nale Lehmann–Willenbrock, and they were discussing some recent data analyses comparing German and U.S. group meetings. The conversation went something like the following:

> Joe: "So, what do the results indicate?"
>
> Nale: "Looks like Germans spend more time talking about problems than Americans."
>
> Joe: "Interesting. So they dwell on the problem a bit. Could be good for identifying the right solution."
>
> Nale: "Yeah, and Americans tend to jump right to identifying solutions to problems, rather than talking through the problem. At least compared to Germans."
>
> Joe: "Hmm . . . so, Americans are impatient?"
>
> Nale: "Looks that way. But, Germans appear to complain more."
>
> Joe: "Never would've guessed that." (dripping with sarcasm)
>
> Nale: "Yeah, we've sort of guessed this. But, now, if we publish this, we'll never live it down."

That's right. Meeting research confirms what many had already suspected. In general, Americans impatiently jump to identifying a solution to a problem whereas Germans take their time defining the problem a bit more. Oh, and Germans appear, on average, to spend more time than Americans complaining about the problem. Don't blame us. It's in the data.

We don't share this story to provide you ammunition for the blame game but rather to inform you of some cultural undercurrents that may be impacting your meetings (see the nearby sidebar "Beware of cultural stereotypes" for some important considerations).

If you are in a meeting with people from around the world, you need to be aware of culture differences that may be minefields for misunderstanding. Without knowing it, you may inadvertently violate a norm, expectation, or assumption that they have about meeting.

REMEMBER

The world is full of people — people with different personalities, value systems, and priorities. Just as those traits impact their behavior in meetings, the countries and cultures in which they live impact how they act in meetings too.

In this chapter, we discuss the different cultural expectations around meetings. We talk about managing the norms that may differ across cultures while maintaining the benefits of cultural diversity. We also address some of the more pragmatic considerations when working with people around the world, from their corporate or home offices.

WARNING

BEWARE OF CULTURAL STEREOTYPES

Before we jump into all the differences that we've seen in the way people from different cultures meet, let's take a moment to acknowledge a huge caution and caveat.

First, beware of falling into cultural stereotypes. Stereotypes are a useful way for people to help us navigate the workplace and the world around us. But they are often wrong. In fact, they are often used to justify treating people differently and not in a good way. Second, be very cautious when generalities about groups of people are stated, because people are different and rarely do they fit with all the generalities. Scientists often take the average of things being measured. The average temperature for this time of year, the average height, the average amount of time people are late to meetings, and so on. The problem with averages is that people don't typically fit perfectly the average. More people are above and below average than are actually average. More days are above or below the average temperature than are actually at the average.

In a recent set of studies that Joe and Nale did together, they studied meeting lateness. We talk about this a bit in this chapter. We even share some generalities. However, one thing we found was that when we expected a particular culture to differ from another based on previous research on time and behavior, they didn't differ as we expected. People in Italy was not simply "okay" with people showing up late to meetings, even though the literature and science on time would suggest that they'd be a bit more laid back on arriving late to meetings. We actually found a lot more similarities than differences when it comes to how people experience and feel about lateness to meetings across the world.

These studies and our own experiences interacting with others from around the world reminded us that we have to be very careful making general statements about groups of people. We have to be very careful making any kind of assumption about the people we are working with. We have to be aware of and beware of cultural stereotypes. Yes, norms and stereotypes can be useful, but our most important advice is to get to know the people you are meeting with and do your best to make the meeting experience good for you, them, and everyone you meet with, regardless of where they come from.

Understanding Cultural Expectations

REMEMBER

Different cultures have different expectations when it comes to meetings. These differences mean that a one-size-fits-all approach to meetings could lead to disaster. We address some of the norms that differ across a wide range of cultures here, but it is way outside the scope of this book to cover them all.

To help illustrate our point, we'll consider four different countries and their respective cultures as it pertains to meetings in general: the United States, Germany, Japan, and the United Kingdom:

>> **United States:** Typically meetings in the U.S. focus on problem solving, defining roles, and persuading others to help solve the problem. There is often a meeting leader who tries to maintain a positive, friendly rapport, and the meetings are larger compared to many other cultures. The meetings often have a structured approach that follows the agenda, though the agenda is frequently changed during the meeting. Compared to other cultures, their meetings are relatively short, but fast paced.

>> **Germany:** Meetings in Germany are more focused on decision making, using information provided in the meeting, with problem solving and consensus building as secondary aims. They are usually chaired by the highest-ranking person in the room, regardless of who may have called the meeting. The approach is a relatively rigid structure that follows the agenda and any

modifications for the agenda are looked down on. Compared to other cultures, their meetings can be lengthy, detailed, though somewhat governed by the agenda in terms of timing.

>> **Japan:** Typically, meetings in Japan are formal and for presentation purposes, where consensus is built and expected. Before these formal meetings, they often have many informal pre-meetings, one-on-ones, to ensure everyone important is already in agreement with the content of the presentation. For the formal meetings, the hierarchy is very strong and leaders are never (or rarely) challenged openly during the meeting. Small talk occurs only in the beginning of the meeting and the meetings are usually very long. This is in part due to the occasional deliberate split between pre-meetings and the actual meeting. That is, they have lots of conversations about the upcoming meeting, coalition building, and working toward consensus on key points before the actually scheduled meeting even begins.

>> **United Kingdom:** The majority of meetings in the U.K. focus on information sharing about work with some decision making about future next steps. The aim is more on providing information and building relationships rather than hurrying to a decision. The meeting leader or chair is influential in structuring the meeting, though higher-ranking managers typically have final decisions, even when they are not the meeting leader. Small talk often opens the meeting and then the agenda is duly followed, with varying modes for managing discussion. Meetings are relatively long (an hour meeting is considered short), though not as long as those in Japan or similar cultures (where meetings are typical 90 minutes or longer).

REMEMBER

Please remember that these are only four different countries and cultures. Many other differences likely exist and could impact how you run your meetings. However, we can learn from other cultures and it's okay to integrate their meeting styles into how you meet, particular with people from those cultures. Later in this chapter, the section "Maintaining cultural diversity in behavior" presents some ideas on how to do this.

TIP

When you take a look at your roster of meeting attendees, be mindful of the people on that invite list and the cultural differences that may exist. If you are concerned about potential meeting norm conflicts, adjust your approach accordingly, if possible.

Recognizing norms about lateness

Did you know that more than half of all meetings in the United States start late? That's right. It's become almost expected that someone is going to show up late for meetings. For some, starting meetings on time just doesn't happen. In fact, Karin worked with a client that decided to normalize it by saying, "Ten minutes late is the new on time in our organization." Rather than trying to solve the problem, they decided to pretend it wasn't a problem but a reality that simply had to be accepted.

The problem with lateness, though, is that it destroys meeting effectiveness. In most organizations, people have an expectation that meetings will occur in a punctual manner. Now, punctuality is defined differently by different people, their groups, and their organization. Case in point — the example Karin just shared.

Although it's a common counterproductive behavior in the United States, lateness is not uncommon across cultures. In fact, in a study of countries the world over, Joe found that lateness to meetings is pretty much a universal problem and nobody is happy about it.

REMEMBER

Here's the key takeaway. No matter where you are or who you are meeting with, it is rude to show up late for a meeting. If you can arrive on time, do it!

The distinction though, and one worth remembering, is that what is meant by "late" is different across cultures. For example if you look at typical "lateness" in meetings, meetings in Finland, China, and the U.S. started about three minutes late. However in Italy, Germany, and Ukraine, the average late start was around six minutes beyond the advertised start time. But compare those numbers to what you will likely see in Middle Eastern countries, such as Iran and Saudi Arabia: Start times for their meetings averaged around 19 minutes late.

Now that tells us a couple things. First, meetings start late everywhere, meaning they actually kick off later than their scheduled start time. Second, it gives us an idea of what is considered acceptable lateness across the world. In some places, a couple minutes late is fine. In others, you have 15 minutes before people start getting nervous or annoyed.

You might be wondering, "How do you know which lateness norm to lean towards if you are in a meeting with global participants?" Because there is so much variation in norms across cultures, we actually recommend establishing a group norm about lateness. Discuss what you and your team feel is an appropriate norm for lateness, what it means to each person, and make a collaborative decision.

In the United States, we sort of give everyone a five-minute "grace period." If you show up no more than five minutes late, you're fine. However, sometime between five and ten minutes, people who are waiting for the rest of the folks to show up get upset. In fact, in some of Joe's post-meeting surveys, people expressed how they really felt about lateness in no uncertain terms:

>> "They should be written up."

>> "I want to punch them in the face."

>> "Late people should get one warning and then walked to the door."

>> "If I was in charge, I'd fire their @!#$."

These are real comments, on real surveys, from Joe's work. People get angry. They get mad. They want people to pay for being late.

TIP

Establish your group-specific norm for any groups that meet regularly.

Building a group norm is great for your regularly scheduled group meetings. But, for meetings with new people from different cultures, we suggest a slightly different approach discussed in the next section. One of sensitivity and inclusion, as you don't have the opportunity to establish a meeting norm.

Maintaining cultural diversity in behavior

Now, you might be tempted to say that given the cultural differences outlined earlier in this chapter, it is best to just set the meeting ground rules to fit with the majority of participants and leave it at that. In some cases, that may be what has to happen. But, we want to provide a meaningful caution.

WARNING

If you stamp out diversity in behavior in relation to your meetings, you harm potential innovation and creativity in problem solving.

Essentially, differences in cultural expectations around how people meet are a good thing, much like diversity in background, experiences, nationality, and ethnicity also are a good thing. Organizations the world over are desperately trying to figure out how to ensure that diversity, equity, and inclusion are maintained.

Part of that motivation is a moral imperative (it's just the right thing to do). We should, as good human beings, value all our similarities and differences. How we are alike makes us part of the human family. How we are different makes us interesting, unique, and fun.

However, part of the motivation to ensure diversity is maintained has a direct business case. Diversity is associated with better performance on complex tasks, particularly those that require innovation and creativity. The meeting is a location where there are minimal costs to valuing and encouraging diversity of behavior. Meanwhile, there are actual solid benefits for doing so.

Let's give you an example. Earlier we talked about how Germans tend to spend more time on problems and Americans spend more time on solutions. Well, the process for identifying a creative solution takes both. You have to define the problem, elaborate upon it to understand it nuances, then consider the varied potential solutions, elaborate upon them, and then collaboratively decide on which solution to apply. In other words, you need the strengths of both the German problem focus and the American solution focus to get the desirable innovation and creativity. We are better together!

WARNING

Some cultural norms in meetings are not as positive, though. For example, in certain countries, talking over one another during a meeting is common practice. In a face-to-face meeting, this isn't a huge problem (even though it may take some getting used to by those who come from cultures where interrupting someone is considered the height of rudeness). The real issues crop up when the meeting is held in a virtual or hybrid format. For those attending virtually, they are often limited by one audio stream and people talking over each other can result in them hearing only snippets of sentences and not the full thought.

REMEMBER

When considering how to incorporate and value diversity in meeting norms, think about what makes sense within the context of the meeting format as well as the meeting processes. Allowing for a free-for-all of verbal participation can mean a mess and a subpar experience for remote attendees in a hybrid or virtual meeting.

Allowing for cultural tolerance of silence

While working with a global client, Karin was delivering virtual training for their employees in APAC (Asia-Pacific). The webinar was not intended to be hyper-interactive. Mostly she was just relaying best practices for enhancing your virtual presence. However, she did provide plenty of opportunity throughout for attendees to ask questions. In fact, at the beginning of the session, she told the group that she would stop periodically to field any questions that they might have.

Any time she would stop to take questions though, she noticed a trend. The Australians in attendance were quick to raise their hands (emoji or physical ones) to pose their questions. In fact, so many of them raised their hands at once, that she had a hard time determining the order in which to answer them. However, those who were from Asian countries like Japan and China asked very few questions at all.

What Karin saw play out in real life is something you may see in your meetings — cultural differences in tolerances of conversational silence. This hits hard in meetings across cultures where silence has different connotations. In some cultures, silence may be a sign of respect. In other cultures, it's a cue to keep going in a conversation. In meetings where the expectations and tolerance of silence are varied, it can result in nonproductive conversations that are lopsided where a few people talk the whole time while others, who are waiting for silence as a cue to potentially add their thoughts, never get a chance to say a word.

REMEMBER

Some cultures have a higher tolerance and even expectation for conversational silence during a meeting. Knowing these differences may be the key to a successful or painful meeting experience. Not knowing them may lead to uneven participation and a lost opportunity to receive valuable input from everyone in the room.

Here are a few norms related to silence that are important to consider in your meetings that include folks from various cultures:

>> Many Asian cultures are comfortable with a minute or two of silence when consider alternatives.

>> North Americans begin to get uncomfortable after about one or two seconds of silence during a conversation.

>> After a question, people in Asian cultures consider it polite to pause as though giving thought to the question.

>> After a question, Western countries, particularly the U.S., view that silence as a void to be filled and consider a pause to indicate disagreement or even anger.

>> Silence confuses and confounds Americans who think their team is disengaged, whereas Asians would consider such silence as a sign of respect and consideration.

TIP

From a practical standpoint, you want to keep these cultural silence norms in mind when trying to pull out participation. Create a turn-taking policy that involves calling on people rather than allowing anyone to speak up when a bit of airtime presents itself. (Otherwise, you may end up with a scenario like Karin did where the Australians . . . or the Americans . . . or the Canadians end up dominating the conversation.) Let people put their thoughts initially in chat too. Someone who doesn't feel comfortable immediately speaking up might find it easier to participate in a nonverbal way. You can then invite that person who commented in chat to elaborate on their thoughts verbally.

You also want to be aware of other norms related to silence that matter for different types of meetings and situations. For example, in strong hierarchical cultures, such as the Chinese culture, the most senior person should speak first and silence may precede their contribution out of respect. Recognize who that person is in the room and make sure you don't violate that cultural norm by addressing someone of lower status first within the organization. It may be off-putting to their team if you do.

Be aware of the power of silence too, especially when it involves negotiations. For those who tolerate silence better than others, it can be an effective tool. For example, those in China who culturally have a high tolerance for silence may sit silently for a moment considering an offer. Meanwhile, their American negotiating partner is interpreting that silence as disgust at the offer and might chime in with a better offer prematurely.

REMEMBER

How you interpret silence may be very different from how your fellow meeting attendees interpret silence. Become familiar with the silence norms of the cultures represented in your meetings and use those norms to your advantage.

Taking the Setting into Account

When meeting with people around the world, the setting matters even more than ever. Yes, it matters in your corporate office or when meeting virtually with people you may have been co-located with at some point. But, the issue of the setting gets bigger when you are meeting with colleagues in different geographic locations, including other countries, where both the time and the culture introduce nontrivial differences.

For example, meeting time matters when a given culture has a longer lunch. If you inadvertently try to schedule a meeting during a time that is considered taboo or generally inconvenient, then you may be labeled a "meeting pariah."

Another consideration is where people are meeting from. In some places, large homes allow for nice quiet locations away from the busy household environment. Other places, homes and living locations are not nearly so large, and so meeting from the kitchen table in a remote-work-required situation, may introduce interruptions from others who are sharing the same space. How do you deal with that?

TIP

Be mindful of the environment that you are in and the environments that others are in to help yourself and others have the most positive meeting experience possible.

By now we've all seen the kid cameo or the cat cameo. It's less about being embarrassed and more about how to minimize the disruption to the meeting itself. In some cases, this may require the normalization of family pets getting some screen time in a virtual meeting. Or, it may require flexibility with the mandatory "cameras on" ground rule that you and your team adopted after reading our book (see Chapter 9 for more on this).

Adaptation when necessary and uniformity when required needs to be your motto to embrace the diversity of the many people you meet with, while making sure you can actually meet well.

Avoiding the time zone tragedy

One of the biggest issues with variable settings are time zones. In the United States, the East Coast is three hours ahead of the West Coast. A 9 a.m. stand-up meeting for the corporate headquarters in New York would require the San Francisco affiliates to join the meeting at 6 a.m. That likely infringes upon personal time and can create bad feelings between the coasts.

Now, let's layer in the possibility of collaborating with people in France, or India, or China, or Australia. The issue of time zones becomes a real challenge (and a math problem) to manage.

Beware the time zone tragedy, where your lack of sensitivity of the location of your team members may create impossible meeting times.

The time zone tragedy occurs when a leader schedules their meetings at times that are personally convenient for them, without regard to those in other locations. It's a tragedy because at minimum, you make it difficult for people to participate in the meeting (waking up early or staying on after hours). At worst, you make it impossible for people to participate. Joe's been asked on multiple occasions to meet at 2 a.m. and had to remind the organizer that he would not be awake at that time.

In some cases, Karin has seen some far-flung team members voluntarily reset their work day to accommodate the majority. A teammate for one client works in India while the rest of their colleagues are based in the U.S. Rather than trying to stick to typical business hours in India, they make themselves available for at least a portion of the day that would coincide with regular business hours in the U.S. Their work day typically begins late in the day, India-time. While there are certain circumstances like this that exist, it is unfair to expect that mindset to be the norm.

So, what do you do?

When scheduling a meeting, note the time zone representation, and propose a time, if at all possible, that is within business hours.

Typically just noting where people are and looking at yours and their calendar can solve the tragedy. However, what happens when there isn't a time within 9 a.m. and 5 p.m., or whatever your normal business hours are, that works for everyone because of time zones? Well, then you have to humanize the decision and actually ask the person whose schedule will be impacted most. Go to the person who you are thinking of scheduling either before their normal work day or after their day should end, and see if it's even possible.

REMEMBER

Before even suggesting such an imposition, though, don't forget to check and see if you even need that person at the meeting.

If you've checked and you need them, then you need to talk to them about the feasibility of meeting at a time before or after hours. And be respectful. These simple courtesies can really go a long way to establishing a positive rapport with your colleagues even as you practice good meeting hygiene.

Normalizing differences in environment

Online meeting platforms mean people can meet from anywhere with good internet, but that's also created a wide variety of settings from which people are meeting when attending virtually.

Sure, some people might have gone all out with their remote office setups. They bought all of the hardware (webcam, external microphone, studio-worthy lighting). Their set (also known as their office space) looks like a picture from a trendy lifestyle magazine. In our experience, this is the exception not the norm, and the differences can be even more pronounced when meeting with global participants hailing from countries where space is at a premium.

Joe noticed this early on in the COVID-19 pandemic. One of his good colleagues was meeting from her living room and her pets were climbing all over her. She kept saying sorry and moving the cat or dog out of the camera view. After several meetings and many, many "sorry, hang on a second" moments, Joe finally said to her, "You know, I really don't mind the pets. Just let them do their thing while we do ours." The relief was written all over his colleagues face. It didn't seem to register with her pets.

What Joe did was normalize the difference, and in this case, a distraction. From then on, the meetings were much more productive and when a pet just would not cooperate, it provided some additional entertainment.

REMEMBER

People meet everywhere. They can now meet from anywhere. Most distractions become non-distractions when they are normalized and acknowledged. This is true of pets, kids, trains, cars, TV programs, books on a shelf, and so on. Naming the difference takes the power out of the difference. The worst thing you can do is pretend like there is nothing out of the ordinary going on. Don't pretend like it's not happening. We all know it's happening. Acknowledge it. Deal with it if necessary, and then get back down to business as quickly as possible. The longer you linger in the awkwardness, the worse it'll be for you as well as your fellow meeting participants.

Let's give you another example.

Joe met with a bunch of students, talking about how to be successful in graduate school, and what it was like to be an organizational psychologist. The meeting was hybrid, so Joe was in his office at home with his bookshelf behind him, and the students were in a conference room two time zones away. They asked lots of questions. He gave lots of answers. It all seemed to go quite well. It wasn't until later when he spoke with his colleague who invited him to guest mentor these students that his shelves were identified as a distraction. Now this happened a few years ago, when a particular book series featuring vampires was all the rage. It just so happened, those books were on prime real-estate behind him, and the students talked for a good while after the meeting about whether or not he read them and was a fan or not.

In this case, the distraction didn't get normalized until later once the items that pulled focus were brought to his attention. During the next meeting, Joe made the books a point of conversation, and then never mentioned them again. The distraction became normalized, so it no longer distracted from the meeting.

TIP

It's best to identify differences early and quickly so they can be normalized into non-distractions.

Allowing for differences in video use

When the world became fully virtual during the pandemic, video use in meetings rose exponentially. However, people around the world have different expectations and norms about video use today.

TECHNICAL STUFF

In certain countries or even areas within countries, there are limitations in bandwidth for connections across long distances. Joe experienced it himself when he tried to interview a potential student from India who had such bad connectivity that he was fortunate to even be able to meet with audio alone. Spotty or weak internet isn't always a choice; sometimes it's the only option to connect. So if you find yourself being annoyed that a team member never turns their camera on, instead of stewing about it, ask about their bandwidth. Maybe you can collaborate on a solution to address a signal that is lacking.

Circumstances may require the video being off when you'd really prefer that it remain on. This is not the end of the world, but it does require some changes in behavior.

If you are in a meeting that is complex or with new people, and video is not cooperating or not allowed, your voice has to do a lot more work. What you lack in nonverbal cues, you need to make up for in your verbal delivery. You have to exaggerate your emotions, feelings, and thoughts with your voice. Be more excited about good ideas and more reserved about things you disagree with when all you have is your voice to communicate the message.

However, you need to recognize that there are some situations in which video use is not encouraged or allowed due to cultural norms. Some cultures would find having a camera on in their home a major personal invasion of their private space. And even in cultures where it appears normative to use cameras for virtual or hybrid meetings, some will still have strong feelings about their use. We talk about this in more detail elsewhere — check out Chapter 5.

Use the video as much as you can, but be flexible with your meeting participants. It is more important to show respect than risk offense.

You might be thinking, these all seem like virtual or hybrid-related setting differences that emerge from meeting with people around the country and around the world. And you'd be right. However, there are others that emerge when meeting with people face to face around the world. For example, conference room setups are not the same. Technology available for use is not the same everywhere. Seating arrangements are not the same everywhere.

Our best advice is to be prepared to experience differences. And, plan accordingly. Sometimes these differences prove to be distractions that need normalizing. Sometimes these difference are not distractions, but just how things are done in this different environment. Get to know the environment you are in, own your knowledge limitations, and be kind as you learn to navigate the cultural differences that make for a richer experience for us all.

2

Setting Up for Success — What to do Before a Meeting

Whether your meeting is a rousing success or an utter failure can largely depend upon what you do before you even before you've got the meeting underway.

In this part, you'll find out the key questions to help you decide whether that meeting you want to call should even happen in the first place. You'll also learn why it's important to design your meeting to match its goals as well as how to set expectations for yourself and others during the actual live session.

Chapter **7**

Determining if You Even Need a Meeting

We're guessing that many of you have experienced times when you left a meeting thinking, "I've just lost an hour of my life that I'll *never* get back." In fact, Joe just had one of those experiences yesterday. He was invited (voluntold) to attend a meeting where curriculum changes were to be discussed for an academic program that he supports. As the meeting leader called the meeting to order, they announced that one of the faculty would be sharing their insights into the proposed changes. This person then proceeded to discuss the merits of the proposed changes for the next 50 minutes. The meeting leader then said something like, "Well, it looks like we're about out of time. Any last second thoughts?" No one piped in because everyone was ready to leave (in other words, checked out 30 minutes ago).

This is a prime example of a meeting that never should have been a meeting in the first place. There was no interaction. There was no collaboration. It was just a nearly hour-long monologue with one person sucking up all the air time while the rest of the attendees were forced to listen attentively (or at least appear to). This calendar clog could have been easily unplugged. Couldn't this meeting have been an email? The answer is yes, and for the sake of everyone's overstuffed schedules, it should have been.

Meetings do not have to be a waste of time.

REMEMBER

In this chapter we discuss the idea that not all meetings should be meetings. You and your calendar are probably breathing a sigh of relief, but how do you know what should be a meeting and what should not? We dig into the questions that every meeting leader or organizer needs to ask themselves before they schedule a meeting. If you take the time to answer these questions honestly and thoughtfully, you will immediately see a difference in how your electronic calendar looks. We also explore what kinds of gatherings shouldn't be meetings at all but rather something else. Colleagues having drinks? Not a meeting but certainly a worthwhile endeavor that can build team cohesion.

Knowing What Should be a Meeting

REMEMBER

Not everything should be a meeting. Not everything that is labeled a meeting is a meeting. But whether they fit the definition of a meeting or not, you may find these scheduled gatherings dominate your days. Partly it's due to the fact that meetings are so easy to schedule. You just send a calendar invite with a few clicks and somehow you feel like you have moved business forward (often a costly misconception; time spent in a bad meeting means time spent not doing something more productive). Partly it's due to a lack of recognition of what truly requires a meeting in the first place.

Let's give you a few examples. Let's say Karin would like to present the results of a recent survey she conducted on video call fatigue to her team. She calls a meeting to do just that. That presentation is not a meeting, unless she also allows time for dialogue, discussion, and active interaction with the audience or other meeting participants. What about those weekly standups that block out an hour each Friday for the team to meet? If there is no specific reason for folks to gather around the conference room table, that's not a meeting either. At least not immediately. And here's why . . .

REMEMBER

According to the science of meetings, a group meeting is a gathering of three or more people to discuss something together. So before you hit send on any invitation link, consider the two key elements of any meeting. All meetings should have:

>> A defined purpose

>> The need for collaboration

If these two things are not present before and then take place during a meeting, then it's not a meeting; it's a gathering of people.

Now, you might say, "But, we always have a staff meeting on Monday morning at 9 a.m. and we start by identifying what we're going to talk about." That's backwards. You should be walking into the meeting knowing what you're going to talk about, what agenda items you are expected to report out on, and what decisions need to be made as a group. Agenda item number one should not be "Determine why we are meeting in the first place."

Let's dig a little deeper.

Meeting with purpose

The first question a meeting leader must ask themselves before scheduling a meeting is, "Does the meeting have a purpose?" If yes, proceed. If no, stop! Define the purpose, and then move on. If you can't come up with a defined purpose, don't schedule the meeting at all. Purposeless meetings are terrible meetings, and that's a scientific fact.

But, what do we mean by purpose? Well, usually that means that you've identified the overarching goal of the meeting, what you ultimately want to accomplish in the meeting, as well as a few key agenda items. That makes for a clearly defined purpose. However, sometimes the purpose is a bit more vague. For example, the purpose could be "follow up on recent activities." Assuming there are some recent activities to follow up on, then you can comfortably say, "Yes, my meeting has a purpose."

Have you ever been to a purposeless meeting? Of course you have. We all have, but it's even more annoying when you are forced to schedule one as a meeting scientist. Joe recently set up a meeting with leaders from two universities "to discuss a partnership." He cringed a bit as a meeting scientist at the lack of agenda and clear purpose, but given that these specific instructions came from his boss, he proceeded as requested. When it came time to meet, the first 15 minutes of the meeting between high-level officials at these universities were spent answering the question, "So, what are we talking about?" People showed up, but they weren't prepared because the purpose was not clear. More importantly, a few minutes after the purpose was co-defined by the group, it became shamefully clear that the right people and the key information were not in the room. And the meeting adjourned.

Guess what Joe told his boss after the meeting? Something like, "We need a clearly defined purpose and an agenda next time." Thankfully, his boss agreed, and Joe found himself with a new task on his to-do list, to define the purpose and prepare the agenda for the next meeting. No good deed goes unpunished!

Meeting for collaboration

The second thing a meeting leader needs to ask themselves before scheduling a meeting is "Does the purpose require collaboration?" If you need interaction, discussion and collaboration to fulfill that purpose, then you would answer "yes." Go ahead and schedule that meeting.

But, what do we mean by collaboration? Well, usually this means that in order to accomplish the purpose, more than the meeting leader or a designated presenter (or two) will need to talk. In other words, collaboration in meetings occurs when multiple people need to speak up, discuss, and share thoughts in order to move the idea, problem, or discussion item forward. Basically, if the purpose of the meeting can be accomplished without anyone else weighing in — sharing their ideas, thoughts, expertise or opinions, then you probably don't need a meeting.

Think about the meeting example you read about at the beginning of the chapter, the one where Joe and his colleagues sat through a 50-minute soliloquy from another faculty member. Did this gathering require collaboration? Apparently not seeing that there was no opportunity to do so.

TIP

The second question you need to ask yourself before scheduling a meeting is "Does the purpose require collaboration?" If yes, proceed. If no, stop. Don't schedule the meeting at all. You likely can accomplish the purpose by some other communication means that can be created and consumed independently, such as an email. Not all activities need to be a meeting.

Knowing What Shouldn't be a Meeting

Not every gathering of people is a meeting, and that's okay. Take for example one of Karin's webinars. As a communication coach and trainer, she regularly hosts hour-long presentations focused on a particular topic of interest for clients. While she likes to think she's an entertaining presenter providing valuable information, she would not call one of her webinars a meeting, though her clients often do. In this case, the information is only flowing one way; it is not a collaborative experience.

REMEMBER

You don't want to fill up people's calendars with too many things that do not fit the definition of a meeting. A periodic professional development webinar is fine. A full week of webinars is not and will cut into people's time to accomplish other critical tasks.

The label of "meeting" is incorrectly applied to all sorts of common activities done in groups, such as socializing with colleagues. That's not a meeting, or at least it shouldn't be labeled as such. However, it does help to build team cohesion. Still, there are other more problematic examples of mislabeled meetings that you may need to rethink.

Socializing without aims

Socializing without aims is not a meeting. In other words, grabbing a drink at the water cooler with a colleague is not a meeting. It might be nice. In fact, the science of organizations would argue that those "bump into Bob" moments are the social lubrication that organizations need to function effectively. Nothing demonstrated that more than the COVID-19 pandemic, when loneliness, depression, and anxiety emerged, in part, because of reductions in human-to-human social interaction.

However, socializing *with* aims can and probably should be a part of meetings. That non-business small talk, that chit chat that happens before a meeting truly begins actually leads to a more effective subsequent meeting. Why? Because it's easier to chime in when the topic is what you did over the weekend or the results of the big game. That low-stakes opportunity to speak up early on helps individuals who are typically more quiet or reserved feel comfortable to share within the meeting itself. Still, small talk should not be the meeting, but small talk will make the meeting better.

REMEMBER

Take five minutes at the start of your meeting to have a chat about anything that isn't related to work. It will make the meeting better. Notice we said five minutes; not the whole meeting! However, during the COVID-19 pandemic, some meetings were scheduled entirely for the purpose of socializing and talking about non-work stuff. Thus, circumstances may require some necessary variations here, but you get the idea.

Informing without deciding

The bane of our meeting lives — the most common "non-meeting" violation we see — is the *information sharing meeting*. These are the meetings we go to and don't actually get a chance to talk in. Those meetings we go to that could've been an email. Those meetings that would definitely not pass the two-question test mentioned earlier in this chapter (requiring all meetings to have a purpose that requires collaboration). Still, these kinds of meetings happen all too often.

You may be familiar with this one — the weekly stand-up meeting where team members come together to share what they have been working on that week in a round-robin format. Typically, people give their updates, one at a time, and then the meeting immediately adjourns without any discussion. Informing without deciding or discussing is not a meeting. It's just informing. No collaboration is encouraged or required. In short that weekly standup should be cleared off the calendar.

You might argue that those updates are really important for the team to hear. We agree but is there a better way to deliver that information that doesn't eat up designated space on the calendar? There sure is and there are more ways now than ever before.

TIP

If you are simply sharing information, encourage people to use methods that are asynchronous that allow those receiving the message to consume them at a time that fits best into their own schedules. Those round-robin reports could be delivered in text form via email or a channel in a collaboration platform like Teams or Slack. They could even be delivered using richer mediums like self-recorded video and audio. An executive Karin worked with likes to listen to his team's audio updates one after another while exercising — like his own personal podcast.

WARNING

Sharing information in an asynchronous fashion works great provided that no one ends their reporting with, "I need help with this issue. Anyone have some ideas?" Then it's time to call a meeting. Not only is collaboration being invited; it's warranted. The team needs to assemble to share their thoughts and problem solve. They will likely need to make decisions to break up the bottleneck. Now the meeting has a purpose that demands collaboration to get the group moving.

We get information from lots of sources that we wouldn't imagine labeling "a meeting." No one says, "I just had a meeting with the five o'clock news," or "I just had a meeting with the quarterly report," or "I just had a meeting with my email," or "I just had a meeting with *Running Effective Meetings For Dummies.*" Get the point? Lots of things are informing without deciding and are not meetings.

However, many very good meetings include information sharing. In fact, one might even argue that all meetings have information sharing. But, they go further than just a data dump. They also require discussion, idea sharing, and perhaps even decision making. That's the key. Informing without deciding is not a meeting, but informing with dialogue between participants is.

REMEMBER

Informing without deciding is not a meeting. However, most good meetings require information sharing. Add a dash of collaboration (like actually talking about the information) and you have a meeting and likely a good one.

Chapter **8**

Designing the Meeting to Match Your Goals

Afew days ago, Joe received an invite from one of the leaders in his organization to join them and another person for a 30-minute meeting. The invitation just listed the attendees. The purpose was not identified. No agenda was shared. A day or so before the meeting, Joe asked one of the attendees what the meeting was about, and they didn't know either. That's not usually a good sign.

The meeting was a virtual meeting. The three participants arrived and some small talk ensued. A few minutes past start time, they finally identified the purpose of the meeting, to share some bad news for Joe. (Don't worry Joe still has a job!)

What did they do wrong? Take a minute. If you've read any of the other chapters in this book, these few details about the meeting may cue you to a few issues.

First, they didn't identify a purpose for the meeting ahead of the meeting (Chapter 7). Second, they did not share an agenda (Chapter 8). Third, they chose a less rich medium for communicating bad news (Chapter 5). Fourth, they did all this to a meeting scientist (who is now writing about it in this book).

REMEMBER

Design your meeting with your goals in mind. And when doing so, you need to consider all the design features that are relevant to the participants and circumstances. Doing so ensures the goals are achieved in the most effective and collaborative manner. Failing to do so can be at minimum problematic, and at most, a complete disaster for you and your team.

Let's dig into this a bit more.

Choosing Your Format

When it comes to meeting formats, you now have more options than ever before, but not every kind of meeting works well on every format. Choosing the right format for the right meeting is key to your meeting's success. Essentially, there are four different format types: face-to-face, virtual, hybrid, and teleconference.

TIP

Here are some key considerations to keep in mind when choosing how you will meet:

» **Assessing how rich a medium is required.** One of the main considerations for format is the degree to which you need a rich medium to communicate together. What do we mean? *Rich medium* means more cues, more information, more indication of what Bob is really trying to say. A face-to-face meeting is the most rich medium. You have all the audio and visual cues possible. Hybrid is the second most rich because at least some folks have all the cues, and those connected in, assuming they are on video, are doing pretty good with that as well. Virtual is still pretty rich, so long as the video is on. That's why our data shows that these three are pretty close together in terms of overall effectiveness. Using the phone? Richer than text but usually not rich enough for an effective meeting with multiple people.

» **Conducting a challenging conversation.** If the meeting requires complex communication or there is likely to be emotional reactions to the topic of discussion, go rich or go home. That is, if you have to deliver really good or really bad news, try to do it face-to-face. Or, hybrid in a pinch. Also, if the topic is just complicated, with lots of nuances, again go face-to-face. The more rich the medium, the less likely there will be miscommunication, confusion, are a perceived lack of empathy. (Remember Joe's bad news meeting? Empathy nonexistent.)

» **Needing to reach out and touch.** If the meeting requires the physical manipulation of materials, be face-to-face. Now, you'd think this is self-explanatory. But, the fact that we are saying it means it's not. Perhaps you've experienced it? Someone on video yelling at the people in the room to move something or do something. If it's imperative that everyone has the ability to point to, pick up or touch something, you need everyone to be in person. A full sensory experience can only happen face-to-face, not through a screen.

>> **Using teleconferencing sparingly.** Joe would like to remind everyone that he has yet to find any data supporting the use of teleconference, at all. In his previous books with Karin, *Suddenly Virtual* (John Wiley & Sons, Inc., 2021) and *Suddenly Hybrid* (John Wiley & Sons, Inc., 2022), the data shows that teleconference is a less rich form of communicating and therefore worse than all the other formats, without exception. By worse we mean, less satisfying, less effective, lower participation, and more stress/burnout in teleconference. In fact, you can add those data points to the more than 30,000 people who have participated in Joe's other surveys in recent years that consistently show teleconference is bad. We simply cannot recommend that format, in general. For more on the importance of choosing video first, flip back to Chapter 5.

TECHNICAL STUFF

Let's go a little deeper on the teleconference stuff here. The crux of the issue is this: Using the phone truncates your ability to communicate, both as the receiver and the deliverer of communication. When you are on the phone, your conversation partner can't see you waving your arms or rolling your eyes. They don't see you lean in when they speak more softly or see you put them on mute when they monologue about irrelevant content. Absent of these cues, the meeting is going to be worse, particularly if you do not know the person well.

Now for a caveat. You can use telephone for a meeting when you know the people extremely well. For example, Joe knows his research team members very well. He knows what each of them sound like when they are being sarcastic or joking. He knows their mannerisms when they are excited about a project or not excited at all about the next task. He does not need to see them as he communicates because he can picture them in his mind's eye. If you know your your group that way, teleconference will work just fine.

REMEMBER

Choose the richest format possible for your team to meet, particularly when dealing with complex or emotional issues, or when needing to physically manipulate objects together. Do not use teleconference if you can help it.

A few other exceptions are worth noting. Quick chats over the phone can be efficient and effective to clarify a point or fact check, especially if it means you've avoided adding another meeting block of time on everyone's calendar. Some managers also like having "walking meetings" where they hop on a call with a colleague and have a more free-flowing exchange of ideas. They're not as purpose-driven as some meetings that have a specific goal in mind, but they can unleash some creativity which could then lead to a more targeted meeting using a different format.

WARNING

From the years 2020 to 2022, the choice of meeting format was constrained by a global pandemic. Public health concerns led many of us to default to virtual environments or occasionally hybrid, with masks on. We recommend keeping the health and safety of your participants in mind whenever you schedule a meeting of any kind.

Adjusting for internal or external participants

When choosing a format, we recommend you lean towards more rich formats (as outlined in the previous section). This is particularly important when you start to consider the composition of the participants in your meetings. In most meetings, we have two large categories of participants: internal and external.

Internal participants are folks that are inside the organization. They're your team or members of the organization that you likely know. They are within your organization's meeting culture and so they know how meetings typically go around here.

External participants are folks that are outside the organization. They are people who you may be trying to sell products and services to. They may be vendors or potential vendors. Regardless, they are not part of your organization. Therefore, they do not know the organization's meeting culture. They don't know how you meet around here, so you need to make sure the format you choose will match their expectations and needs.

TIP

Who is in your meeting will inform what format you choose. Adjust your format to fit your attendees' expectations.

Weighing the desires of external participants

If you are meeting with external participants, try to find out what their preference is in terms of meeting format (see Chapter 8 for more on meeting formats). If the majority of your meeting attendees are in-house but you have one or two coming in from the outside, you don't need to completely change your meeting format based upon their desires, but if your external participants are the most important people in the meeting, you probably do.

Probe for the preferences of your external participants. Are they sick and tired of virtual meetings and refuse to do anything but a face-to-face meeting? Or do they like how efficient a virtual meeting is and value that above everything else? Maybe their key stakeholders are spread all over the place but there are some who are co-located in the office. For that scenario, they might insist upon a hybrid meeting, so everyone can attend regardless of geography. Listen carefully and choose a format that will make them most at ease, even if it might be at odds with your own preferences.

In sales, selecting a meeting format has become even trickier because what the seller wants may not jive with what the buyer wants. During the pandemic, buyers came to appreciate the flexibility and speed of meeting virtually with vendors. Some even got into the habit of self-serve purchasing without even talking to a person. However, most sales people, who have used the in-person playbook for the majority of their careers, want to get in front of their customers. This can create friction between buyers and sellers.

TIP

Our best advice is to go with the format that the buyer requests. Often times, the sales cycle involves a combination of meeting formats: face-to-face for the initial meeting, virtual for follow up calls and perhaps another face-to-face meeting to actually close the deal, especially one that is high value.

Fitting with format expectations in the organization

If you only have internal participants, it's important for you to be aware of and follow the norms of your organization, provided those norms will allow you to accomplish the goal. What format is expected and is that expectation appropriate for the purpose? There may be times when the way you normally meet isn't suitable for what is being addressed. Let's give you an example.

Say your meeting culture calls for virtual meetings almost all of the time, but the meeting you need to schedule will involve an emotion-heavy conversation. A virtual meeting may not be the best choice for something that demands the highest level of nuance and understanding possible. In this case, you would want to opt out of the meeting norm, increase the richness of the modality, and go for in-person.

Another consideration for internal versus external participants revolves around how well you know the people. You probably know your internal people better than your external participants. Again, look at the roster of participants. If you are meeting with people you don't know, particularly external people, richer formats are typically better.

TIP

If you don't know the people you are meeting with very well, make the meeting format as rich as possible. Try for face-to-face but if that's not possible, choose virtual with cameras on.

Recognizing different geographic locations

As you consider your internal and external participants in any given meeting, think about where they are located. More organizations than ever before have established policies related to remote work, allowing people to work fully virtual or hybrid. For example, they may have decided that employees only need to be in the office on Wednesdays, or that they must be in the office three days a week, or they can remote work 15 days per month, or any number of other policies.

These policies introduce geographic dispersion both internally and externally among your meeting participants. Because of this, you need to match your meeting goals with the format according to the geographic dispersion created. For example, if you have an all-hands meeting, and you have some exciting news, try to schedule it when most people (or even all people) are in the office and co-located.

For external participants, the geographic dispersion may go wider than the greater metropolitan area (though that is becoming more true for people in the same organization than ever before as well). Because of this dispersion, you may have to always choose a format that allows for remote participants. When doing so, always think about the goals of the meeting and lean into more rich formats.

REMEMBER

Face-to-face is richer than hybrid . . . which is richer than virtual . . . which is richer than teleconference. Using this continuum, for meetings that have geographically dispersed participants, hybrid should be your go-to.

Minding time zone differences

Because of remote work policies and roles that require meeting with people across geographic boundaries, time zone issues are likely to emerge. Here again is another reason for surveying who will be in the meeting room. If you know the people well, you probably know where they live, and you know the time difference. If you do not know them well or where they live, you have to ask.

WARNING

Do not assume you know where people are when you schedule a meeting. Verify, verify, verify. In an age of remote work, don't be pulled into the trap of thinking everyone's work hours reflect the time zone of their corporate headquarters. Often, they don't.

Joe's experienced a time zone faux pas on multiple occasions. One example is when he meets regularly with his colleague in Hamburg, Germany. The time difference is eight hours. He's actually become really quite good about remembering the difference. However, there's a little bit of a hitch every year, twice a year. The switch from daylight savings to standard time and back again. Germany and the United States don't do it at the same time. So for a couple weeks every spring and for a couple weeks every fall, they aren't eight hours different. They're seven or nine hours different, depending on the fall-back, spring-forward timing of their respective countries.

TIP

There are countless online tools that do the work for you when translating time zones, so make sure you consult them when scheduling the meeting.

However, that's not enough. We have to also be cognizant of working hours: both ours and the people we are meeting with. West coast workers in the United States are often annoyed by East coast workers who want to meet at 9 a.m. That is, 9 a.m. Eastern Time, which is 6 a.m. Pacific Time. Six a.m. is before some people wake up, and for families, it's before kids are out the door to school. And perhaps the biggest offense of all — it's usually even before the first cup of coffee is in the mug!

When minding time zone differences, also mind workday schedules. If participants in your meeting are traditional office workers with a 9 a.m. to 5 p.m. schedule, don't schedule your 9 a.m. Eastern Time meeting with your Pacific Time colleagues. That creates the potential for work bleeding into personal (and family) time. The same holds true on the other end as well. Starting someone's day too early or extending too late creates resentment.

TECHNICAL STUFF

When meetings overlap with personal time, they run the risk of creating work–family conflict. *Work–family conflict* occurs when work related activities infringe upon or interrupt family or personal life situations. For example, meetings scheduled before 9 a.m. or after 5 p.m. for an office worker are likely to create work–family conflict.

Now you might think, "I don't schedule meetings after or before hours that often. Only when absolutely necessary." Ask yourself, are you okay with burned out employees? Are you willing to risk creating stress among your people? Or worse yet, are you willing to deal with the turnover that work-family conflict causes? We didn't think so.

However, if you're like us, you probably already know this and do your very best not to infringe upon people's personal time. But, many of us occasional make a mistake and schedule someone outside their business hours.

TIP

It's important to establish a ground rule that if a meeting comes onto your calendar after your usual working hours, communicate that to the meeting organizer. Most of the time, it's a mistake because they didn't mind time zone differences. Empowering employees to flag meetings outside of expectations can help to ward off any potential feelings of ill will.

Also remember that "business hours" is a subjective experience for many people. For some, business hours mean 9 to 5. For those with kids, the afternoon hours often need to end earlier, but they add hours in the evening. There are also very different attitudes about working extra hours or overtime. Some people keep track meticulously; others never do. Both types of attitudes impact reactions to meeting scheduling times. Our advice is to try to stick to the organization's standard business hours and get to know your team so you are aware of any exceptions to the organization's norms.

Creating a Comfortable Meeting Space

In order to accomplish the goals of your meetings, you need to make efforts to ensure the meeting space is comfortable and appropriate for the dialogue and interaction anticipated to occur. As one might imagine, the responsibility for the meeting space and what can be done to ensure its comfort varies as you switch modalities.

Historically speaking, when nearly all our meetings were face-to-face, we had to concern ourselves with the physical environment we planned to meet in:

>> **Seating:** When considering seating, you need to ensure there are enough seats for all participants, and a couple extra in case additional people join the meeting unexpectedly. Additionally, the seating needs to be adequately comfortable relative to the expected length of the meeting. Many a manufacturer of office seating could learn a thing or two about comfort.

>> **Lighting:** You have to be able to see each other in a meeting room. This might seem obvious but problems arise if the light is so blinding that you can't see the slides projected on the screen. Make sure your lighting works for you in all the ways you need it to. Dimmer switches are a life-saver. Natural lighting is always a plus.

>> **Table:** There's a reason King Arthur had a round table. No head. Everyone equal. Sometimes that would be absolutely the way to go in your meetings. In other cases, it's better to have "points of power" at the table, which is typically the head/foot on a rectangular table, as well as the middle of each long side (particularly on an oval table).

>> **Positioning:** Where people sit can enable or constrain participation. If you are allowed to assign seating, consider putting people you really want input from in the "points of power." The social dynamics will actually ensure that they will participate more sitting in those seats than they will if they choose their usual, less powerful spot, like the back of the room so they can be ignored, again.

>> **Refreshments:** Especially for a longer meeting (more than an hour), plan to include some sort of refreshment. Even just including water bottles on the table for each participant is a nice gesture. It can also be reciprocated with increased participation among people who are more comfortable.

>> **Basic technology:** Many meetings have a wonderful (or let's face it, perhaps not so wonderful) PowerPoint presentation to click through, but you can't click through it, if it can't be projected for all to see. So, another thing to manage is the basic technology in the room that allows for these presentations to be viewed. Make sure the cords are available for people to plug in if necessary. If logging into a networked computer, make sure there's a way for external participants to use these resources.

POINTS OF POWER (NOT PowerPoint!)

Some of the early research on conference rooms in organizations focused on where the powerful people sit. These locations at the table emerged somewhat naturally in the environment. In fact, anthropological researchers found these to be common behaviors throughout human history, with people routinely identifying where they would sit when meeting with others. More important people would get the better seat, better location, perhaps to be able to see everyone or to be able to direct attention or action around the meeting situation.

For a rectangular or oval table, there's an easily identifiable head and foot of the table. These are often where the meeting leader or the supervisor for the team would sit. Since there are two spots, head and foot, you're likely to see one occupied by the supervisor and if they are not the meeting leader, the other occupied by that person who is leading. The pragmatic reason for doing this, for the meeting leader, is they can see everyone. For facilitating discussion and sharing the communication equally, these two spots are pretty useful.

Additionally, on oval or rectangular tables, there are two additional points of power — the middle of each longer side. Once again, they afford a pretty good view of the people in the room. Based on the research, you'll find that those people with a bit higher rank or who desire to be viewed as such, will sit in these spots if the head and foot are not available.

These examples all suggest a hierarchical structure that is quite salient in the organization. What about in flat organizations? Or perhaps for people who are aware of how these positions communicate power and influence? These organizations and people might deliberately choose to sit in positions that are considered of lesser power in an effort to create a more egalitarian environment. In general, if you want more equal participation, this might be the way to go, if you are the meeting leader.

For the vast majority of folks, scheduling the conference room down the hall takes care of most of these items. However, this becomes more complicated when your work environment doesn't have a conference room and you have to manage this all yourself. Or harder yet, you work outside, or in a factory, or in a hospital, and so on.

The key for creating a suitable meeting space is to do the very best you can to make the meeting space comfortable and supportive of the goals you aim to accomplish.

Enhancing your face-to-face environment

You might wonder why we now have another section about the face-to-face environment given what we shared about the typical meeting space earlier in this chapter. Well, that's because we need to enhance that space.

The stereotypical conference room needs a facelift. No longer is "basic technology" sufficient. We now have to augment the face-to-face environment with features that allow remote participants to participate. In other words, we need to enhance the face-to-face environment so that remote participants feel like they are as much a part of the meeting as those attending face-to-face. Everyone needs to feel seen and heard, regardless of location.

What's that mean? We need to include the computers, cameras, and integrated software into the conference room. There are a number of technology companies eager to enhance your conference room, but be aware that you may not need the fanciest system around. In fact, it comes sometimes backfire when you have so many bells and whistles and that no one knows how to even turn it on. Suffice it say, you need to go beyond a small webcam mounted on the wall to make your conference room video-enabled.

REMEMBER

Being seen and heard is essential for accomplishing your meeting goals and new technology systems allow for video cameras, displays, and audio devices to make that possible.

TECHNICAL STUFF

If you are looking for a list of specific hardware or software to best equip your conference rooms or remote workers' home offices, you won't find it here. We recognize that we are not technology experts and will not discuss all the nuances and technical features available in the market. What we will offer is some advice on what features you should be looking for to make your meeting spaces effective.

Ensuring an effective virtual space

When you think about creating an effective virtual space, you need to consider two locations: the place where your remote attendees are joining from and the place where your remote attendees are beaming to. A breakdown in either of these spots will lead to a breakdown in your meeting or at least a less than optimal experience for one if not all of your participants.

Unfortunately, unless you are the head of the IT department, you may not have much say over what hardware or software is available for your meetings. However, you may be able to offer an informed opinion which will carry more weight, especially if you can demonstrate how your meeting effectiveness is being negatively impacted by what is currently being offered.

Selecting inclusive software

Both virtual and hybrid meetings rely upon software to make them even possible. Without a video collaboration platform, your meetings are relegated to the confines of the conference call bridge or the spider phone smack in the middle of the conference room table. Both of those have pretty much gone the way of the dinosaur, so we are going to assume your organization has some sort of video conferencing solution available to you.

REMEMBER

Whatever software is chosen, it needs to be easy to use. In any organization, you have a wide range of technical proficiency. You may have people who can take apart a hard drive and put it back together again, literally. You may also have people who are just coming around to this idea of texting. You need to account for both of these scenarios and play to the lowest common denominator . . . or perhaps slightly above if you are willing to invest your time into training.

Speaking of training, this is where many organizations fall short. They may spend loads of time shopping for the best possible meeting software solution and finally make the purchase with confidence. They roll it out by installing it on everyone's devices and then send an email with some basic instructions on how to use it. Just handing people the tool doesn't mean they know how to wield it well. You need to empower your people to use it, or they will just manage their way through the basics without venturing beyond. Your head of IT may have fallen in love with some of the super cool new functionalities of the tech tool, but believe us when we say . . . we've encountered a ton of people who consider it a victory to just be able to share their screen.

TIP

Add a meeting to everyone's calendars to navigate technology. Set up a quick session led by someone from the IT department who can walk your people through the software features that matter most. They may not need to know how to spotlight their face in their video box, but they definitely do need to know how to share their slides, how to stop sharing their slides, and how to choose their camera, background, and audio settings.

WHEN VIRTUAL

For any virtual meeting platform, you want to look for features that help keep engagement high. Remember remote attendees are always at risk of mentally checking out or caving in to the distractions around them (see Chapter 5). You want your platform to give you as many tools in your arsenal as possible to combat that.

TIP

Almost every virtual meeting platform has tools that incorporate nonverbal forms of participation. Not only can they be regularly used to keep people engaged, but they also open up participation possibilities for those who may not be able to or feel comfortable with speaking up. Consider the introverts on your team. You may never hear from them unless you call on them specifically. Things like chat, polling, and emoji reactions lower the bar for providing input. Speaking up during a virtual meeting might feel terrifying for some, but writing out a response in chat that can then be read by the meeting leader allows them to fully form their thoughts and then have them entered into the dialogue. Many platforms also now include accessibility features like closed-captioning that enable the hearing-impaired to follow along during a meeting more easily.

With innovation comes updates and that can be difficult to manage. You will find that there are as many software updates as there are days in the year, and that can be annoying if the feature you finally mastered now is in a totally different spot on the interface due to some "upgrade." Be prepared for surprises when you log on and give yourself time to figure out how to adapt to the changes.

The other challenge when it comes to meeting platforms is the evolution of tribes who favor one platform over another. Significant squabbles have erupted within organizations over what platform is best. Without revealing names, we have seen some folks who are firmly in the "Z camp" practically refuse to meet with anyone who insists upon using the platform from the "X camp." It's not pretty. But most IT departments have clamped down on using multiple meeting technology and now enable only one platform (though we have seen plenty of people go rogue and use their favorite through a device that is outside of IT's reach. Shhhh . . . don't tell anyone.).

WARNING

These allegiances to specific platforms becomes even more problematic when working with people outside of the organization. They might be a "Z shop" and you might be a "X shop." They may want you to use their platform to meet but your IT department has blocked it on your device, or vice versa. You may not be able to fully resolve the conflict, but you do need to be aware that it might arise. Make sure you work out any permission problems before you engage with an external stakeholder, or see if you can have limited access to their platform so you can get business done.

TIP

Stick with a platform that is well known and familiar to most. Remember, the software is there to support the meeting; users shouldn't be stressed by trying to figure out how it works. That upstart platform might be really interesting with features that are over the top, but getting people up to speed on it may be more trouble than it's worth. People use what they are comfortable using. It may not be higher quality. It may not even be the best platform for their purposes, but people use what they know.

WHEN HYBRID

The role of software in a hybrid meeting is even more complex because it serves a connective tissue for those who are in person and those who are remote. Typically, the platform itself is the same as the one you would use for a fully virtual meeting (see Chapter 5), but you might be wondering how to incorporate it into your hybrid meeting setup.

TIP

Our best advice is to make sure everyone is logged on regardless of location, but be sure your in-person attendees don't use the audio built into their own devices. You are liable to get nasty feedback. If your physical meeting room is properly equipped, you want your in-person attendees to leverage the camera(s), microphone(s), and speakers built into the conference room to engage with your remote participants.

If people aren't using their own cameras and audio, why would we suggest that even in-person attendees log on to the virtual meeting platform? Because you want everyone to be able to use the nonverbal engagement tools that the platform provides:

>> If you launch a poll, you don't want only the remote attendees to be able to answer. You want everyone to be able to weigh in.

>> If you ask for people to write a response in chat, you don't want to just see the answers from the virtual attendees.

Unlike verbal participation where the in-person attendees have a slight advantage in terms of getting into the conversation, nonverbal participation is one way to level the playing field.

Using the right equipment

So much may be out of your hands when it comes to the equipment available for your meetings, but having the right hardware is essential for creating an effective virtual or hybrid meeting environment. For a meeting to work well, everyone needs to be seen and heard or at least have the chance to be.

TECHNICAL
STUFF

PRESENTING SLIDES IN A HYBRID MEETING

If a slide presentation is part of your meeting, you want to share those slides on the virtual meeting platform itself rather than try to capture the screen using a camera in the room. This allows everyone to see the slides in an equitable manner.

In fact, depending upon where you are sitting in the conference room, those who are remote might have a better view than you do. However, you can control where you sit in the meeting room. Your remote attendees can't change the conference room camera view.

In response to the COVID-19 pandemic, many companies invested heavily in equipping their workers with the right tools, sending out webcams and headsets to make the fully virtual work lives better. But there were many other organizations who left it up to their employees to figure out how to best connect when joining a meeting remotely.

Hybrid meetings added a whole new level of equipment complexity to the mix, and plenty of companies still haven't figured it out . . . or even realized that their current solution isn't working. You are far more likely to walk into a "video-enabled" conference room with one small webcam than one with a fully decked out system. Here, we'll talk about what good looks like (and what bad looks like too) so you can leverage what tools you have at your disposal and perhaps advocate for better ones.

WHEN VIRTUAL

During the COVID-19 pandemic, much of Karin's work involved training sales professionals how to move from a hand-shake mode of selling to a virtual one.

In addition to talking about virtual communication approaches, she also offered advice on how to show up in a professional manner on screen. Some of the advice focused on the equipment while other advice addressed how they should use it.

Many of these coaching sessions went something like this:

> Karin: "Hi Jack. Great to see you. Wow, I can hardly make your face out today. Your image is really pixelated."
>
> Jack: "Oh . . . yeah . . . I see that on the screen. I thought it was just my internet connection."
>
> Karin: "Are you using the webcam that (your company) sent you?"
>
> Jack: "Uh . . . I think it's in my closet."
>
> Karin: "Huh . . . it's not going to do you much good there."
>
> Jack: "I didn't know how to hook it up, so it's still in the box."
>
> Karin: "Well, let's fix that right now. Why don't you grab it and we'll set it up."

Nine times out of ten, using an external webcam for a virtual call will produce significantly better image quality than what is built into your laptop. One of the big differences you will see is the camera's ability to deal with various light levels in your room. External webcams handle low light situations with relative ease and bring everything into sharper focus.

As important as a high-quality webcam is, an even bigger factor in how you come across during a virtual meeting is the quality of your audio. You can have a meeting with someone who has poor video quality. It may be slightly irritating but it's not impossible. But if your audio is bad, you are toast. People are much more tolerant of poor video quality than they are of poor audio quality.

Unfortunately, you may not even know your audio fidelity is bad. After all, on a virtual call, you can't hear yourself, and those on the other end may not let you know, out of fear it might embarrass you. How can you check out how you sound? One of the wonders of virtual meeting platforms is the ability to record yourself. Hop on your platform of choice and record yourself talking. If you have a variety of audio input options, test them all out. You might be surprised by what audio device sounds best.

WARNING

Your room acoustics play a big role in what audio options works best. For many regular business users, the microphones embedded into your laptop might be fine . . . unless you are in a room with a lot of hard surfaces and very little sound absorbing material. If you have hardwood or tile floors, lots of windows with no curtains and high ceilings, you may have a very bouncy sound environment. The laptop microphones may make you sound very echoey. External microphones, like a lavaliere, headset, or standup mic, may be a better choice. If you have kids or pets, noise cancelling headphones can be a lifesaver. They keep the background noise out and help keep you focused on the call itself.

Lighting is an often overlooked by all important element of your webcam setup. Eye contact, even when virtual, is the best way to build trust and believability. If people can't see your eyes, you are putting yourself at a disadvantage. Plus so much of how we communicate a message is through our facial expressions. You want to make sure your nonverbals are coming through loud and clear.

TIP

Focus on front lighting, so your face is well lit. Ideally, it'll be the brightest thing in the frame. You could buy one of the gazillion ring lights available online or one of the higher-end setups created purposefully for virtual calls . . . or you can just sit facing a window. Natural light is the most flattering light of all and is certainly easy to produce. Now granted, you may have times when Mother Nature isn't supplying the light you need (a night-time call or a very gloomy day). For those times, we suggest you have some sort of artificial light source that is illuminating you from the front. Overhead lights will cast shadows around your eyes, impeding your ability to make good eye contact. Look for two desk lamps that you can put on either side of your webcam, so you are evenly lit.

Just having a good webcam isn't enough. You need to know how to position it properly in a place that is comfortable for your viewer. What do we mean by that? You want your camera to be positioned at eye level, so it will appear to your conversation partner or partners like you are looking them straight in the eye. Too often, you will see people use their webcams built into their laptops. They keep them on their desks and appear to be peering down at their audience. It's an easy fix. Simply elevate your laptop on a stack of books or a box that raises it up to the point where you can draw a level line from your eyeballs to your camera lens. You can also make it easy on yourself by purchasing a laptop stand that keeps your webcam and your device in a fixed spot.

If you are using an external webcam, maybe you have it perched on the top of your monitor. That's also not a great option because you likely will appear to be looking up at your conversation partner . . . like a little kid asking a parent for permission. Here's what we suggest: Put that external webcam on a desktop tripod and position it at eye level in a spot that makes sense. Say you have two monitors and you often look at both. Place the webcam between the two monitors so you can easily glance from the camera to either of the monitors.

WARNING

Make sure your camera is pointing directly behind you and isn't angled up. Not only do you risk having a less than attractive shot up your nostril but it also will feel uncomfortable to your audience. One giveaway that your camera is pointing up is if you see the ceiling in your shot. If that's the case, angle your camera down so there is no ceiling in view. The adjustment will also likely allow more of you to be seen on screen. You want to maximize your presence in the frame which means situating yourself so you are seen at least from mid-chest up. Be careful to create some headspace too. Don't cut off the top of your head. It'll make you appear crammed which in turn will appear awkward and distracting on screen.

WHEN HYBRID

There are two sides of the equipment equation that you need to worry about when in a hybrid meeting: the virtual attendee side and the in-room attendee side.

If your virtual attendees use the equipment the way we discussed in the previous section, you know at least one side of the equation will be in good shape. The in-room attendee side is a little harder to control but can make or break the meeting itself. Karin experienced this first-hand in one week . . . check out the nearby sidebar for the full story.

When it comes to choosing the right equipment for a hybrid meeting, you have to consider the needs of the remote attendees first. How can they not only be connected to the action but *feel* connected to what is occurring in the room. That means having cameras in the conference room beyond just a static shot that may only show some of the people present. That means having a way for them to access the information (the slides example in Karin's nearby sidebar) as easily as their in-room counterparts. That means ensuring it can be a two-way conversation with speakers and microphones that allows everyone to be seen and heard.

LEARNING TOUGH LESSONS ON HYBRID CLASSROOMS

In one week, Karin taught two hybrid classes at two separate institutions of higher education. For the first class, Karin was guest lecturing on how to plan a hybrid event at an international business school. There were seven different countries represented with students attending both in person and virtually. Karin herself was leading the class virtually, but she had the help of the professors to moderate (and perhaps corral) the in-person attendee contributions. The room was equipped admirably with three giant monitors, all showing different things. On the first monitor were here slides. On the second monitor were the images of the virtual attendees in their boxes as well the chat. On the third monitor was just Karin herself, looming large.

The classroom itself was equipped with three separate cameras — one that had a wide shot of the entire class, one that had a different angle of the classroom and one that could capture the face of the in-person professor.

Karin proceeded through her class, working in interactive exercises and stopping for Q&A. When students in-person had questions, the professor called on them. The microphones had good enough range for Karin to hear them and she answered them accordingly. When virtual students had questions, Karin called on them because she could see their hands were raised on the platform that she was also on.

Overall, Karin felt like this hybrid class was a big success.

A few days later, Karin taught another hybrid class but this time she lead it from the classroom itself. However, she didn't even know the class was going to be hybrid . . . and in many ways, it didn't make a difference. Why? This university's version of a hybrid class-room consisted of an extra laptop. The professor opened a meeting link and pointed the built-in webcam at Karin as she stood in front of the room and taught the class.

She was using visually appealing and interesting slides that conveyed key points, and the class involved a very interactive exercise that the virtual attendees could neither see nor take part in. At the end of the class, Karin spoke to the virtual attendees briefly who asked if she could send along her slides. Turns out they couldn't see them because they were not shared on the platform. Rather, they were being beamed to the in-room projector directly through an HDMI cord.

While the in-person students were thrilled with the experience, the virtual attendees probably felt like they were no more than an afterthought. She felt terrible.

Scheduling the Meeting

We've talked about time zone differences and geographical challenges when selecting a format, earlier in this chapter. We even brought up the issue of scheduling outside business hours, and the unintended consequences of that. With these and your goals in mind, it's time to schedule the meeting. You could blindly throw out a few days and times that work for you, but here's where technology can ease the process.

TIP

Where possible, allow the electronic calendar to aid you in identifying the appropriate time. If you are setting up a meeting with people inside your organization, many of these tools will show you all your potential participants' schedules, but before you just snag a slot that looks open for all, you need to take a step back and be more mindful.

When looking at your participants' availability, there are a few things to look for:

» **Do any participants have back-to-back meetings leading to your meeting?** If yes, consider starting five minutes later, giving them a chance to grab a drink, find the restroom, and mentally transition to your meeting.

» **Are any invitees in different time zones and does this impact your preferred time?** Though we already discussed this, now that you're in the scheduling system, be sure to use its features to your advantage to avoid before or after hours meetings.

» **Do any of your participants have a meeting right after your intended scheduled time?** If yes, consider, once again, ending a few minutes before their next meeting. Joe started doing this and literally received emails and texts thanking him for introducing a little humanity into the day.

Once you've identified your time and sized your meeting time appropriately, there are many other things to consider before hitting the final button to schedule the meeting. Let's take a look at them.

Inviting the right people

FOMO is a four letter word. Yes, it stands for fear of missing out. Yes, it is real. However, no, it is not a good reason to invite everyone to your meetings or to allow others to invite themselves to your meeting.

REMEMBER

Your goals and your purpose should drive your invite list. It is okay to exclude people from a meeting who don't need to be there. Most will thank you for it, particularly if you send them a brief email update after the meeting with any relevant information. If your meeting is virtual or hybrid and company policies allow you to record your meetings, you can also send along the recorded version of it, so they can watch it at a time that fits into their workflow.

Further, expanding the meeting invite under the umbrella of inclusion is also not a good practice. Yes, we want our workplaces to be more inclusive. We want all our employees, our managers, and our leaders to feel safe and secure to be who they are, as diverse or as non-diverse as that may be. However, recently, we are hearing people using inclusion as an excuse to invite more people to their meetings. You are not doing anyone any favors by adding another meeting to their already-busy workday. Go back to the original goals and aims of your meeting and include only those who must be there to accomplish those goals and aims.

TIP

Everyone who is invited should have something important to add to the discussion. If you use this idea, then it's easy to start to identify people who can be removed from a meeting invite. Some will be confused at first and FOMO might rear its ugly head. Comfort them. Reassure them they are not missing out. Include them by informing them. But ultimately, don't invite them.

Accounting for attendees' schedules

It's important to recognize that your calendar is not the only schedule to consider when identifying a time to meet. You must consider each and every attendees' schedule and do all that you can to avoid the pitfalls of time zones, after-hours meetings, back-to-back meetings, and a lack of recovery time.

Since we've already discussed the first three, let's focus on the last one, recovery time. *Recovery time* is that period after a meeting where you reflect on what just happened and then prep for what comes next. In other words, recovery time is mental transition time, an opportunity for us to task switch in our heads.

It's hard to transition from something you are deeply focused on to something else. For example, Joe has a very tough time transitioning from watching basketball to answering his kids' questions about when dinner will be ready. He is very focused on the game. He can't even hear anything else.

Yes, now that you are hopefully laughing at this relatable scenario. This is not unique to Joe or to people who like sports. We all get fixated on a work task or caught up in a meeting, and it's hard to transition. Recovery time between meetings is about giving the brain a few minutes to move out of that task or meeting and move onto the next thing.

If you still aren't convinced about the need for adequate recovery time, consider these data points. According to Joe's research, people need 17 minutes to recover from a bad meeting. From a good meeting, they only need five minutes.

REMEMBER

It doesn't take a meeting scientist to tell you what to do . . . but Joe will tell you anyway. Make your meetings good, so your attendees don't need more than three times the recovery time required for a bad meeting. Considering the fact that many people still suffer from back-to-back meetings, they may get no recovery time at all, regardless of how good or bad the meeting was. If you want to get immediate gratification, try just cut your meeting times back by five minutes. Your meetings are more likely to land in the "good meeting" category and your change should allow everyone the recovery time they need.

Picking a suitable meeting length

We saved this to the end of the chapter because everything that has come up to this point is relevant to determining the appropriate meeting length. In fact, here's a list of some of the things you need to consider in question form to help facilitate your decision-making:

>> **What is the purpose of the meeting?** Some purposes naturally require more time than others.

>> **How many items are on the agenda?** Just the sheer number of different topics will impact length.

>> **How much time does each agenda item need?** Obviously an announcement needs much less time than a discussion. That should be consider when deciding on time.

>> **Does everyone know everyone in the meeting?** Introductions take time. However, they are essential when you have internal and external folks on the call who may not know one another.

>> **What's the time of the day for the meeting?** People tend to have more stamina for longer meetings in the morning than in the afternoon. Thus, keep your longer meetings in the morning and make your afternoon meetings shorter (or canceled).

>> **How much time is needed for pre-meeting talk?** This is discussed in detail in Chapter 10, but essentially for some formats, you'll need five minutes at the beginning for a bit of small talk.

>> **How much time is needed at the end of the meeting for recovery time?** Based on the calendars you see, if folks have back-to-back meetings, consider how to give them five minutes to recover and transition.

Rather than provide a fully comprehensive list of all the questions and considerations when determining the appropriate length, we provide this generally strongly worded guideline: Ensure the meeting length is long enough to achieve your goals, but not so long as to be burdensome or result in wasted time.

Too often at the end of an agenda we have the dreaded "open forum" statement. That's the part of the agenda where anyone can bring up anything to the team. We generally don't recommend having such an opportunity in your tightly scheduled meetings. Joe absolutely despises the "open forum" option on agenda. And here's why . . .

Supposed you go to a meeting that's scheduled for 50 minutes (your meeting leader is providing recovery time at the end by making it shorter than an hour), and at 35 minutes all the items on the agenda have been thoroughly discussed. The meeting leader then opens up the floor to any remaining items from anyone in the meeting. What happens next is the remaining time, all of it and sometimes more, gets filled with items that did not make the agenda (some purposefully). People fill the time. So, even if the agenda is accomplished, we linger until we are at time, often on useless items that do not get resolved.

When the purpose or goal of the meeting is accomplished, end the meeting!

When in person

When you start considering meeting format, the appropriate length does need to consider situational factors. For in person meetings, particularly in a comfortable, well-lit, refreshment laden conference room, meetings can be longer and it's okay. This does not mean that your meeting should be longer, just that it can be.

Therefore, our advice is that if a meeting is going to need to be longer, consider having it in person in a comfortable meeting space. However, right sizing the meeting length to the meeting purpose and agenda should be your primary consideration.

When virtual

Virtual meetings are a bit more complicated from a meeting length perspective. That's because you do not have control over the meeting space, the way you do in an in person meeting. As such, in general, virtual meetings should be shorter than in person meetings.

However, there are further considerations:

>> **Virtual meetings do suffer from the potential of video conference fatigue.** The science is clear, seeing oneself on video does drain people

psychologically. No, this does not mean turn off the camera. But, it does mean that you should try to make these meetings shorter.

>> **Because you do not have control over the meeting space, it is not safe to assume that everyone is comfortable**. Distractions in the remote environment can derail the meeting. For example, most children's favorite television show is relatively short, 20 to 30 minutes. If that's someone's go to as a distraction for their kids while they have a virtual meeting, they'll be calculating the number of episodes their going to allow them to watch. Let's help them by keeping it to one or two.

When hybrid

Since hybrid has both features, in person and virtual, you need to err on the side of the virtual meeting recommendation. Keep them as short as possible to accomplish the goals and purposes of the meeting.

In fact, that's the truth about all meetings. They should be as short as they can be and still accomplish their goals. Stretching out the meeting in any way for any reason shows a lack of respect for people's time and hinders their opportunities for deep work throughout the day.

REMEMBER

Sizing your meeting length is a skill that requires practice. If you start doing this, you will have times when you schedule too much or too little time. For groups that you meet with regularly, you'll get better at it quicker because you know the personalities, the quirks, and the tendencies of your team. For groups that you meet with only once or with less regularity, there will always be factors outside your control that could blow up the meeting and interfere with your best laid plans. Do not get discouraged. Even just getting your day-to-day team meetings sized properly is a great place to start.

Chapter **9**

Setting Meeting Expectations

D id you ever look at your calendar for the day and see a mystery meeting — a meeting that is eating up space on your schedule but has no assigned purpose? You try to guess what it might be about by checking out the list of invitees. Hmmm . . . Carol is going to be there. So is Bob. What do these two have in common that might require us all to be in the same room to chat?

This might seem like a ridiculous scenario, but it plays out over and over and over again. A meeting is scheduled without any context included in the invite. You simply know the location or have the meeting link to click. You may know who will also be in the room if all of the attendees have been listed. However, you have no clue as to why you are all getting together.

Technology has made it really easy to schedule meetings with a few mouse clicks, but it has almost made it too easy. Before you decide to call a meeting, you owe it to the potential participants to really think through why you need the meeting in the first place, what you hope to accomplish, and who truly needs to be there to make that happen — and then let them know the answers you came up with to those questions so they are left wondering why they're meeting with Carol and Bob at a designated time.

In this chapter, we share with you the steps you should take before clicking send on that meeting invite — what you need to consider and the actions you need to take. We also discuss ways you can make the meeting itself more productive by assigning pre-work which allows you to start the meeting at a higher level of understanding of the agenda items being covered. Any great meeting has a lot of participation throughout.

We wrap up this chapter by talking about how to set participation expectations, so your attendees will come prepared to share their ideas, thoughts, questions, and opinions on the topic on the table.

REMEMBER

If you don't set expectations in advance, expect to get very little out of the meeting.

Drafting an Agenda

Calendaring software (that allows you to view your own and other people's calendar and availability) has been a gamechanger for scheduling meetings, allowing you to skip the back and forth of finding times that work for all parties. You can send off your meeting invite to participants who can respond by clicking accept, decline or maybe without you even exchanging an unautomated email.

But the software that makes it easy to schedule a meeting can also make it easy to cancel a meeting. Last-minute cancellations can gum up the flow of your workday and leave you scrambling to find a new time to get everyone together.

TIP

One way to avoid this lack of meeting follow-through is to get your participants invested in attending. Let them know this meeting is well worth their time. How do you do that? By telling them what you're going to be discussing and why they need to be there. In other words, you need to give them a reason to say "yes." Not only will it better ensure they are prepared for the meeting, but it also will increase the chances that they actually show up.

Clarifying the meeting goal or purpose

Imagine you are going on a road trip, but you have no destination in mind. Sure you could drive around aimlessly until you eventually run out of gas, but where would that get you? Maybe you might discover something along the way that actually piques your interest, but it's more likely that you'll end up wasting a full tank of gas and not accomplishing much.

REMEMBER

Holding a meeting without a goal in mind is like setting off on a trip without an endpoint. Unless your goal is a meander in the countryside, you want to plug your destination into your GPS which like magic, tells you exactly how you need to get there, turn by turn. What's the meeting equivalent of inputting your endpoint into your GPS? Identifying your meeting purpose and goal.

Determine what you actually want to get out of the meeting. Is the purpose of the gathering to brainstorm or generate new ideas? Are you needing to make a decision on something and it requires all of the lead stakeholders to be in the room to inform that decision? Are you trying to map out your long-term strategy and need to outline the steps you need to take along the way?

Any meeting needs to have a defined purpose, a purpose that requires collaboration. Don't just call people together without a goal in mind. It's a waste of everyone's time.

REMEMBER

Whatever the purpose is of your meeting, knowing what you are trying to accomplish allows you to then create a plan to achieve it during the time allotted. That plan hinges upon one of the most important and underutilized tools in the meeting leader's toolbox — the agenda.

WARNING

We have to admit something. This is not a comprehensive list. And every "self-help" book on meetings may have their own list. We by no means want you to adopt this as your list of meeting types. You will definitely have meetings that do not fit this list. That's because the meeting is the most flexible collaborative environment known to humankind. The purposes we include here are just examples with some pointers to assist you. If we tried to list all the many purposes and elaborate upon them, we would probably need a few more volumes.

In Chapter 4, we present a quick list of some meeting purposes. Let's elaborate on the more common ones you will likely encounter.

Staff meetings

In many organizations, you may find a weekly staff meeting is on repeat on a certain day of the week and at a certain time. It can also take on many names like a weekly standup. The purpose of these meetings can shift based upon what is top of mind for the team or what has happened since the previous meeting. Often there's reporting out that occurs in these meetings. And, as a weekly meeting, the agenda can get a little stale (meaning redundant and boring). Don't hesitate to shake things up on that agenda from time to time.

Product and services development discussions

These kinds of meetings take many different shapes depending upon where the product or service is in its development. Early on, the meetings may be more brainstorming oriented while later on, they may be more structured with planned updates from each stakeholder team or group.

Promotion or advancement decisions

When there is a vacancy to be filled or a new position created, often there is a discussion of who might be the right candidate to take on the job. You may be asked to be a part of or even lead a meeting like this where promotional or advancement decisions need to be made. The process may actually require a series of interviews (meetings) and decisions (more meetings).

Long-term strategy

A meeting called to develop a long-term strategy is often multi-faceted and longer than usual. After all, the purpose of the meeting is to plot out the path for the organization over the long haul. There is a lot to consider and a need for many voices to be heard. Expect this kind of meeting to be a bit more formal because when talking about "the big picture," there is a tendency for the discussion to be all over the place unless you properly plan for a productive discussion with defined outcomes.

HR decisions

WARNING

As a manager of people, you will likely encounter situations where you need to meet to discuss whether to hire someone, write-up someone, reward someone, or fire someone. All of these can be delicate situations, and some are fraught with legal implications (for example, hiring and firing). Proceed with caution and recognize the gravitas a meeting like this requires. That should motivate you to embrace the practices discussed throughout this book.

Quarterly Business Reviews

Just like performance reviews, the structure of what is often called a QBR (Quarterly Business Review) depends upon the organization's culture, template and norms. In some companies, there is little wiggle room outside of a prescribed way of conducting these kinds of meetings. In others, it's up to you to determine what needs to be covered, who needs to weigh in, and what action steps need to be determined and assigned.

Quick project updates

For ongoing projects, you may find it not only helpful but necessary to get all the stakeholders in one room on a regular basis in order to move the project forward. The purpose of these meetings is to make sure progress isn't being held back by a lack of communication between the various constituencies working on it. Those quick updates can free up any logjams or create them if you don't plan the meeting carefully.

Targeted brainstorming sessions

The "wisdom of crowds" refers to leveraging the collective experience and ideas from many people. Brainstorming sessions can allow you to do just that. If there is a particular problem that needs to be solved and the answer isn't readily apparent, conducting a targeted brainstorming session with the right people in the room who have unique perspectives can often illuminate an answer. Structuring your brainstorming session is essential to getting the most out of everyone's input.

Debriefs

Many organizations engage in various extensive activities that require multiple people or teams to collaborate. Upon completion of these tasks, the people or groups come together to discuss how things went. That's a debrief. It's used in healthcare for surgery teams, in the fire service for firefighters, and in business for after, for example, a product launch. The goal is to learn from what just happened, the good and the bad, and do better in the future.

Site-wide meetings

Also known as an "all hands" meeting, these meetings are often paired with retreats or other company-wide activities. The purpose is often to announce major changes or information that everyone at the site or in the company need to know. These can be very useful to ensure information gets to everyone simultaneously, but Joe likes to remind folks that a real meeting has collaboration. So, consider creative ways to make your site-wide meeting interactive (for example, break into small groups to discuss the changes or opportunities announced).

Shift change meetings

Many businesses work in the 24-7 cycle with two or three shifts working throughout a given day. Every time there is a shift change, there is the potential need to have a quick hand-off meeting. In healthcare this is when a nursing crew passes off to the next crew, ensuring that important patient information is shared with the next group. In factory work, this is when one crew passes the torch to the next on the production line, and updates on product counts and deliverables are discussed, albeit briefly. Again, the point is sharing information just-in-time. This is one of the few, truly information sharing forms of meetings that we agree probably need to continue to occur!

Rightsizing the list of agenda items

REMEMBER

Every meeting should have an agenda or purpose. Most meetings don't, and we would suggest that's why the majority of meetings are "meh" or worse.

To carry the GPS metaphor forward, a meeting's goal is the destination you input into your navigation software. Think of the agenda as the turn-by-turn directions that you receive as a result.

Most navigation applications will give you several ways you can get from Point A to Point B. Some of them might be the most direct, others may avoid tolls. Still more might offer a more scenic route. The one you choose is based on the purpose. If you are hoping to get everyone in the same room to simply get to know each other and build some team cohesion, you may opt for the "scenic route" agenda. If your meeting's purpose is to get something done, you will likely want to select the "direct route" agenda — the one that shows you how to accomplish your goal as efficiently as possible within the timeframe you allotted.

WARNING

It is really tempting to try to jampack your agenda with as much as possible, and this is where you may slip up. After all, especially if your team is dispersed, it may be a rare occurrence to have everyone in the same room, and you want to make the most of it. But beware of agenda-creep. Every agenda item should be related to and building towards the goal of your meeting. Don't let it spill over into other topics of discussion outside the scope of the meeting's purpose. The more purpose-driven you are in crafting your agenda, the more productive, efficient and effective your meeting will be.

TIP

How do you know how many agenda items can be covered in the period of time you designated for the meeting? Rely upon your past experience. Look at each topic of discussion you would like to cover and realistically consider how long people might want to talk about it. A status update on an ongoing initiative might take five minutes but a brainstorming session about how best to launch a new product might take the entire hour you've set aside (or more).

If possible, err on the side of allowing for more time than you think you will need to provide yourself a little bit of a buffer. Estimates of discussion time are just that — estimates. You want to make sure you don't cut yourself or the meeting short without actually meeting your goal.

If your meeting is going to extend beyond an hour, you need to account for one more item in your agenda — breaks. There are limits to attention and endurance for attendees in any meeting format. If you have any virtual attendees, you need to have even more breaks than if you are conducting a fully in-person meeting. Digital exhaustion is real, and time spent in a meeting as a remote attendee can be more draining than time spent as an in-person participant. See Chapter 5 for more about video call fatigue.

Breaks are an important component of longer meetings because it allows people to get up, stretch, grab something to drink or eat or simply have a brain reboot. You may formally insert those times into your agenda, but you also should be on the lookout for signs that you need a break *now*. As a meeting leader, you may be able to sense when the energy in the room starts to flag. Maybe people start to participate less or fidget more in their seats. Be aware of these red flags and be quick to call for a break even if it's not at the scheduled time. Pushing through an agenda when participants are struggling to stay focused has diminishing returns.

Sharing your agenda beforehand for attendees to review

Once you create your agenda, don't keep it to yourself! You want to share your agenda with all of the attendees. Why? Because you want to give them time to review what is going to be covered.

You may be thinking, "I always share the agenda for the meeting. I pass it out right at the beginning of the meeting." While we applaud you actually having an agenda in the first place, your timing is a bit off. You need to send out the agenda in advance so your participants can come prepared. Handing it out at the beginning of the session forces your attendees to process the information in real-time. You also may encounter pushback from participants who were hoping to talk about a topic that isn't on the agenda at all, or worse yet, list an agenda item that they care a lot about but feel ill-prepared to discuss without doing some research ahead of time.

REMEMBER

How far ahead of time you send out the agenda depends upon the degree to which you need feedback on the agenda before the meeting, as well as the pace of change within the organization. Sometimes important items come up just before a meeting, that could not have been anticipated when the meeting was scheduled. However, if the content being covered will require people to prepare reports or presentations, you need to send it out with enough notice to give those who are assigned those duties time to create them. In most cases, you just want people to review the agenda and spend a second to see if the meeting is relevant to them and where they might need to be prepared to share their thoughts. Whatever lead time you choose, remember it's all about showing respect for your participants. You want to give them an opportunity to contribute in the most meaningful way possible, and it's hard for them to do that if they aren't given proper notice of what will be discussed.

Soliciting feedback and adjusting your agenda

TIP

If you want people to buy into something, give them ownership of it. That's why we advocate not just socializing the meeting agenda to those on the invite list but also asking for their feedback on it. Often times, they will have suggested tweaks that will make the agenda even better.

You may think you nailed the design of your agenda, but you are looking at it from just your perspective. There may be very important points that should be discussed that you haven't even thought about. That's where the input from your team can make all the difference. Your team can make your agenda even more rich and targeted because of their own experiences. They may be closer to the problem or topic or issue being addressed in the meeting, and they may recognize a gap in the agenda. That's why you want to encourage their input and then be sure to make adjustments to it based upon it. Soliciting feedback and then not responding to it will make you appear tone deaf and put a damper on any future efforts you make for them to weigh in.

TIP

Consider soliciting agenda feedback a fact-finding mission too. Their suggestions could help you unearth some problems or issues that you were unaware of but should definitely be put on the table for discussion. You want the meeting itself to be collaborative, so it follows that you would want the meeting agenda to be a joint process as well.

Once you have updated the agenda, make sure you send out the revised version once you have it set. That way, everyone will go into the meeting, feeling like they will have an opportunity to be seen and heard on the topics that matter most to them.

Leaning into Pre-Work

As a manager, you can bet that a good portion of your day will be spent in meetings, and plenty of those meetings will leave you shaking your head, wondering how you can get that time back that was just wasted. This isn't a new phenomenon. Over the past several decades, managers have been battling a steadily increasing meeting burden that takes away from time they could be spending doing other things — such as business analysis, mentoring or strategic planning for their team.

In 2006, the widely cited estimate of the number of meetings per day in the United States was 11 million. In 2013, that number was re-estimated in to 55 million. In 2022, that number was again re-estimated to be more than 150 million.

Essentially, the meeting overload got worse during the COVID-19 pandemic. We had more meetings than ever before, and when we were fully virtual, commuting time was replaced with meeting time. There's been some recalibration due to this "meeting-ization" of our work lives. Companies have instituted things like No Meeting Mondays or limits on the length of meetings, turning the hour-long meeting into 50 minutes. But, these efforts don't tackle the real issue: Bad meetings cause more meetings. However, there's one strategy that can help make the time spent in any meeting much more impactful. Assign pre-work.

Assigning work before the meeting

Coming into anything cold can be hard — whether it's a social function, a work event, or an even a sports contest. Think about what an athlete does before any competition. They warm up — stretching their muscles, focusing on technique, getting their mindset straight. They do this so they can enhance their performance when they take the field, hit the court, or step up to the plate.

Pre-work is a way to warmup for a meeting — a best practice that will allow all attendees to come prepared to participate to the best of their ability and not come in cold. If you assign the right pre-work relative to the meeting purpose you can kick off the meeting at a higher level of collective understanding of what needs to be discussed. There's no need to get everyone "up to speed" because they've already done that on their own.

What kind of pre-work should you assign? Well, it depends upon the topic at hand. Let's say it's an update on first quarter financials. You could spend oodles of time initially sharing the spreadsheets with the team and pouring over the data together in the meeting room. Or, you could send out those reports in advance and allow each team member to digest them on their own time. Each person could do their own individual analysis and come up with a list of questions that they could bring to the meeting itself. The latter scenario allows you to start the meeting with collaborative and meaningful dialogue and skip over the tedious process of consuming the data when it's first presented.

REMEMBER

Not only can pre-work make a meeting shorter, it can also make it more meaningful. The initial information transfer is done on an individual basis before you even get to the meeting. Instead, you can start with discussing how to respond to it.

Determining the right amount of pre-work

You might be thinking, "How can I expect people to do a lot of pre-work when their days are filled with back-to-back meetings?" You've got a point there, but pre-work is actually the antidote to meeting overload. If you make a practice of assigning pre-work, your meetings will automatically be shorter because you won't be spending as much time in the meeting room simply sharing basic information. If you consistently encourage asynchronous pre-work (work done on your own, on your own time) you will be giving time back to your team. Check out the nearby sidebar for more information on synchronous and asynchronous work.

How much pre-work you assign is determined by a variety of factors. How much lead time is available for your team to accomplish it? How complex is the issue being discussed? How much other work is currently on their plates?

One factor that you may not have considered is how much pre-work is appropriate based upon the format you will be meeting in. Are you meeting in person, virtually or hybrid?

TECHNICAL STUFF

SYNCHRONOUS AND ASYNCHRONOUS WORK

Let's explain the difference between synchronous and asynchronous work. *Synchronous work* is any kind of work done with someone else at the same time and often in the same place, either physical or virtual. When you are conducting a live meeting, you are doing a form of synchronous work because everyone is expected to be doing the same thing at the same time — meeting together.

Asynchronous work is any kind of work that can be done on your own and at any time of your choosing. Now granted you will likely have a deadline for the asynchronous task to be completed, but you are not required to be working on it at a specific time. When you are asked to prepare a presentation for an upcoming town hall meeting, you are doing asynchronous work while putting together the presentation in advance of a synchronous event, the town hall meeting.

Pre-work, by and large, is mostly done asynchronously, and with the rise of flexible work models, pre-work that you can do on your own schedule reflects the preference that many employees have expressed to work when they want and how they want.

When in person

A face-to-face meeting is the richest meeting format available and also the most forgiving. You don't have to worry as much about messages being lost in translation because in-person communication can be delivered with ultimate nuance, both verbally and nonverbally.

People also have greater staying power in a face-to-face meeting because they have more mobility. They can get up to refill their water glass or politely excuse themselves for a few minutes to take a bio break.

For both of these reasons, pre-work prior to a face-to-face meeting isn't as essential as it is when you are using other meeting formats. Participants in an in-person meeting have more stamina than those who are attending a virtual or hybrid meeting, so saving time by skipping over the information-transfer portion isn't as valuable. You also can more easily read nonverbal cues in a fully in-person meeting. For example, you can look for a squinty expression or a blank stare to detect if someone is confused by what they are hearing. You can then immediately ask for clarification or probe for the reason behind the very telling body language signal.

TIP

While pre-work isn't as critical in a face-to-face meeting as in other meeting formats, we would still suggest you use it as much as you can simply to reduce the number of hours people spend in meetings. Pre-work significantly reduces the duration of meetings and makes the conversation more productive when everyone has a good grasp of what is being discussed before they walk in the door.

When virtual

Virtual meetings are best when they are purpose-driven and with the right people in the room. If you are using this format, we're going to assume your meeting has both. Given the typical "get stuff done" goal of a virtual meeting, assigning pre-work can help you accomplish your goal as efficiently as possible.

Let's say you are trying to figure out next steps for product launch. You are midstream with the project right now with various groups working on different aspects of it. Your upcoming meeting aims to come up with a list of next steps. You could just invite all of the stakeholders to come to your virtual meeting, ask them to give updates on what they've done and then determine what needs to happen next, or . . . you can ask each group to prepare a summary report of their progress, send it out a day or so prior to the meeting itself, and spend the time in the actual meeting coming up with next steps. The latter version allows you to push a lot of the synchronous work (live meeting time) to asynchronous work (individual tasks done independently).

Virtual meetings can be draining and there are limits on people's attention spans when they are in them. When a meeting involves a lot of around-the-horn reporting, those who are not actively speaking can be distracted and possibly check out. When a meeting is primarily discussion-based, there's little room for distraction because attendees are asked to participate actively, not be spectators.

TIP

We suggest you lean in heavily on pre-work prior to virtual meetings when possible. It allows you to get more done in a shorter period while helping everyone stay better focused.

When hybrid

If you are holding your meeting in a hybrid format, we would encourage you to assign pre-work as much as possible. A hybrid meeting, by definition, involves a combination of in-person and remote attendees. When in this environment, you need to prioritize the limitations of endurance and attention spans of the remote participants.

REMEMBER

Virtual attendance at a meeting saps more energy than if you are attending a meeting in person. Anything you can do to shorten the time spent in the live meeting will be appreciated by your remote attendees — and probably your in-person attendees too.

As with a virtual meeting, pre-work allows you to devote your hybrid meeting time to discussion rather than simple information-sharing. You may need to elaborate on certain points that people may not have understood on their own, but in general, participants will be able to jump into the conversation with a communal frame of reference.

You may also derive another benefit from assigning pre-work prior to a hybrid meeting. You can avoid technology inequities that might arise due to the nature of how the meeting needs to be conducted and the innate hybrid meeting disparities. Let's give you an example.

Say someone is sharing a spreadsheet. The remote attendees are viewing the rows of data on their external monitors. The in-person attendees are seeing the spreadsheet projected on the monitor on the conference room wall. In this case, the remote attendees have an advantage because they can more easily see the numbers being referenced. After all, their screens are only a few feet from their faces. How easily the in-room attendees can take in the data depends upon where each person is seated. Those sitting close to the monitor can make out the data pretty well, but those situated at the far end of the room need to squint to make it out.

How much better would it have been if that spreadsheet would've been sent out in advance? Each attendee would've had the same opportunity to explore the data on their own and instead of trying to figure it out on the fly, they could've absorbed it individually at their own pace. The pre-work would have primed them to ask questions like "What does this mean?" rather than "What does this say?"

In the examples you just read, we focused on pre-work that is a bit more time-intensive, like reviewing or preparing reports. However, pre-work doesn't have to be that involved for you to get a big benefit from it. Asking your team to review the agenda beforehand is a form of pre-work that should only take a few minutes, but it puts them in the right frame of mind to have a more fruitful discussion. Simply reviewing the list of topics orients their brain to the intent of the meeting and serves as a warmup the main event.

Laying out Participation Ground Rules

"Geez, I couldn't get a word in edge-wise."

It's a common lament heard after meetings where certain — let's call them strong — personalities, love to hear the sound of their own voices. Usually, at least one person in a meeting falls into that category, and they often manage to suck up all of the air time allotted, for them and often for almost everyone else.

You could blame the meeting leader for not corralling that bad meeting behavior which we would call *monologuing*, and you wouldn't be wrong. A good meeting leader would be quick to cut off the long-winded response and pass the baton to someone else in the room. However, not all meeting leaders are skilled at doing this . . . and not all meeting monologuers are capable of being redirected without some serious strong-arming from a facilitator. One way to ward off one or two people monopolizing the conversation is to establish some participation ground rules before the meeting.

Why is this such a critical step?

One of the most important indicators of whether a meeting is a success or failure is how many people participate. Because it is such a significant factor, you want to do everything in your power as a meeting leader to ensure that everyone feels like they have been seen and heard. The good news is you don't have to just go into overdrive to pull out participation once the meeting starts. You can do a lot prior to the actual session to set yourself up for a lively and engaging discussion.

Establishing participation expectations

A meeting, by definition, calls for collaboration to meet a defined goal. That collaboration should not involve just a handful of people but rather everyone who appears on that invite list. You may think attendees will be aware that their participation is not only requested but required, but that's not always the case. With the increase in the number of meetings on everyone's docket, a lot of us have gotten into the practice of "sort of" attending a meeting.

You know what we're talking about. You technically are present and accounted for. You have physically shown up, either on screen or in person, but your mind is elsewhere. Maybe you are thinking about a project deadline you have tomorrow that is unrelated to this meeting. Maybe you are attending a meeting virtually and have another tab open to allow you to skim your email. Multitasking, whether hidden or overt, is an epidemic. (See Chapter 5 for more about multitasking.)

Don't assume your meeting participants will be ready to engage just because you have included them on the attendee list. Instead, be explicit in laying out participation expectations right in the meeting invite. Along with the purpose of the meeting or even a full agenda if appropriate, clearly state that you want everyone to be a part of the action. Let them know you expect everyone to show up, ready to engage.

WARNING

Meetings should not be a spectator sport. If someone on the invite list just needs to be a "fly on the wall," swat that fly off the attendee list. The more people you have in a meeting, the more unwieldy it becomes.

TIP

Shoot for that sweet spot of five to seven people when a meeting's purpose is to be dialogue-based and lead to a decision. This holds true for every meeting format.

Participation expectations, and the ground rules related to them, vary based upon whether your meeting is face-to-face, virtual, or hybrid. Let's talk about ways to prime the pump for participation based on format.

When in person

Think back to your high school or college days. Did you have any classes that allowed you to pick where you sat? If so, did you gravitate to the front of the room or did you try to hide in the back row?

In-person meetings aren't all that different. Some of your team members may be eager to engage and situate themselves as close to you as possible. Still others might try to hide at the end of the conference room table preferably behind a colleague who blocks them from your line of sight.

Just because everyone is in the same room doesn't mean there will be universal enthusiasm to participate as much as possible. It's up to you to make sure no one can hide in the corner . . . or behind Jim.

TIP

One way to increase in-person participation is to actually assign certain agenda items to individuals in the room. Let Kay lead the conversation about the upcoming sales call. Let Tom talk about the latest update on the video collaboration platform that the team uses regularly. Giving people ownership of parts of the agenda typically will keep them engaged for the entire meeting, not just the sliver they are directly responsible for.

The key is making sure all attendees are aware that they are expected to be actively engaged:

>> Let them know in the meeting invite.

>> Let them know at the start of the meeting itself.

>> Let them know as they are crossing the threshold into the meeting room itself.

Allow us to explain.

Karin was a keynote speaker at one of her client's sales meetings. After her speech, she attended a breakout session being conducted by one of the sales trainers. As she walked into the room, she heard a distinct crinkle of paper underfoot. She had inadvertently stepped on a clever way to set participation expectations. The sales trainer had duct-taped a piece of flipchart paper on the floor. On it, he had drawn a picture of a laptop computer with a big "X" over it. Under the image, he had written "Multitasking Free Zone." Every person who walked into that room couldn't help but hear the crinkle and look down. The message was clear. The meeting they were entering demanded their focus and full attention. Message received.

WARNING

Letting people keep their computers open during a face-to-face meeting sometimes invites danger. Even if they had not planned on multitasking, those pop-up notifications on their screens are almost impossible to ignore (even if the pings, dings, and whooshes have been silenced). If you want people to give you their full attention, make your in-person meeting a laptop closed environment. You might be confused by this advice, given that in Chapter 8, we suggest in-room attendees keep their laptops open when in a hybrid meeting. But here's the difference, in an in-person meeting, all of the action is occurring in the same room shared by all participants. In a hybrid meeting, you have action occurring in the physical meeting room as well as the virtual one (for example, a lively chat stream or emoji reactions). If you are in a fully-face-to-face meeting, you aren't using a virtual meeting platform, so you only need to worry about what is going on in the meeting room itself. Keep the laptop closed. There may be some exceptions to the rule. Maybe someone has their laptop open to take notes or you've asked everyone to collaborate on a coauthoring document. In those situations, having the laptop open makes sense. Barring those exceptions, keeping laptops open only opens the door to distraction.

The same holds true for mobile phones, but it's perhaps not as tantalizing of a distraction. Sure, a notification might appear for a short time on the screen but most people's settings allow those notifications to either disappear or the screen to turn off after a relatively short period of time. Plus, people can easily see if someone is messing around on their phone. If someone is waiting for an important call, communicate that it's okay to have their phone out, but they shouldn't be on it while in the meeting. If an urgent call comes in, they can excuse themselves and take it outside the meeting room.

When virtual

If you plan to hold your meeting on a virtual platform, it's even more important to communicate participation expectations. Why? Because people want to adopt the default position of passive observer. It's how we've been conditioned to interact with screens. We watch tv. We watch a movie. But a virtual meeting requires attendees to move from that passive observer role to that of an active participant, and that can be tough for a lot of folks.

One surefire way to bring up the level of engagement is to encourage everyone to turn their webcams on. It helps you, the meeting leader, as well as the attendees. For more on the importance of meeting culture that supports video use, check out Chapter 6.

REMEMBER

As a meeting leader, it is only natural for you to focus your attention on those who have the most "presence" in the virtual room. If you ask a question, you are much more likely to call upon someone you can both see and hear. It's the virtual equivalent of calling upon the people who are sitting in the front row during an in-person event. If someone chooses the front row seat, they are demonstrating that they want to be engaged and are ready for it.

Calling on someone who has not turned on their video can feel scary. What if you ask "Bob in the Black Box" a question, and you get no response. It's certainly embarrassing for Bob, but it's also embarrassing for you. You may be worried that it's a bad reflection on how you are running your meetings — you have so little control over the proceedings that your attendees don't even feel like they have to stick around.

Asking everyone to turn their cameras on makes it easier for you to spread the participation opportunities around. You can avoid the natural bias to rely too heavily upon the input of those who choose to use video. If everyone has their cameras on, it better ensures more even participation by the entire team.

By making it a camera-on meeting, you are also helping your participants to be accountable to themselves. If you are using your computer for a virtual meeting, it is so easy to open another tab and start checking your email or finish off that report or online shop! The camera lens sees everything and the actions of even the sneakiest of multitaskers are still readily apparent. Yes, everyone can see Emily fixated on her phone. Yes, everyone can see that John is fully engrossed in something other than what is happening in the meeting itself. Still, you are likely to get push back from at least some of your team members who are either suffering from video call fatigue or just don't like being on camera.

TIP

One way to encourage people to turn on their webcams is to make it clear why you want to see their faces. There is a misconception by many an employee that they can only turn the camera on when they are "camera ready." Make sure you set the expectation that you are not looking for them to appear as if they are ready to anchor the six o'clock news. You just want to be able to read their facial expressions and body language to make the communication process richer and better. Having a bad hair day is not a good reason for keeping video off.

Another way to increase participation in a virtual meeting is to use the engagement tools built into most virtual meeting platforms. Things like polling, chat, and break out rooms can take your meeting from something people passively sit through to something people actively enjoy.

TECHNICAL
STUFF

There are also plenty of technology tools that you can layer on to the platform itself. For example, the use of virtual whiteboards exploded during the pandemic and their adoption has held beyond it. However, if you plan to use tools that might be unfamiliar to your attendees, make sure you empower your team to use them well. In advance of the meeting, send out a text or video tutorial on how to get started with <insert whatever tech tool you are introducing> so everyone can feel comfortable using it right away. For more on this, flip to Chapter 12.

Participation is harder to pull out in a virtual meeting due to the inclination most people have to just "show up" and not "do" anything during them other than occupy space. That's why you want to clearly communicate to your attendees that your meeting will be interactive by design and execution. It's the only way to avoid people mentally checking out of your meeting.

When hybrid

Participation expectations during a hybrid meeting can often break down along the fault lines created by the medium through which people are attending. You might find the people who are gathering in the physical conference room have no problem staying engaged and offer their two-cents-worth . . . or even a full dollar's worth of input. You also might find that your remote attendees are on mute — literally and figuratively.

Some of the suggestions we made for setting participation expectations in in-person and virtual meetings also hold true here. For example, assigning agenda items to individuals can increase investment and engagement in the meeting, but that means handing out discussion responsibilities to both the in-person as well as remote attendees. If you plan to use new tech tools in the meeting, make sure everyone is put on notice and given ways to get up to speed on how to use them. Above all, as with a virtual or face-to-face meeting, everyone needs to understand that the meeting is supposed to be collaborative — a sharing of opinions, perspectives and thoughts from all who are present, not just a select few.

TIP

We would encourage you to consider making "camera on" mandatory for those who are joining remotely during a hybrid meeting that is designed to be discussion-based. For more details on this tip, check out Chapter 5.

Proximity bias is not a character flaw; it's human nature. People pay better attention to those who are literally close by. Think about how it feels when you are at a sporting event. You are very aware of the people sitting in the rows around you, but you probably aren't even thinking about those beyond your immediate location.

In a hybrid meeting, proximity bias can impact how you run a meeting. If you are leading the meeting from within the conference room, you might be great at keeping the people sharing that space with you fully engaged, but you may not be so hot at paying equal attention to your remote team members. Hopefully, you are aware of this potential pitfall and you are making extra efforts to bring the remote attendees into the action as much as possible. However, this task becomes much more challenging if remote attendees don't have their cameras on.

REMEMBER

Everyone in the meeting needs a tangible reminder of who is present:

>> For in-room attendees, it's a given because they are seen on the conference room camera.

>> For virtual attendees, it's up to them to establish themselves visually in the meeting itself.

Requiring remote attendees to use video helps you, the meeting leader, to spread out participation across all attendees, regardless of location. Remote attendees who have their cameras on are more likely to be recognized and called upon to contribute than those who opt out of using video. It also helps the in-room attendees to remember there are others in the meeting, not just those gathered around the table.

Calling on individuals in the meeting

Another way to add clarity to participation expectations is to explain how you plan to manage the conversational flow. Your plan may change dramatically based on the format you are using for your meeting. You can't exactly pass a physical baton if you are meeting virtually. By the same token, you can't raise your emoji hand if you are sitting around a conference room table. If you want people to participate, you need to let them know how to do it.

When in person

Every organization, every team, even every manager has their own norms for participation in a meeting. Some managers love to throw a topic on the table and let a free-for-all exchange of ideas and opinions fill the room. At the other end of the spectrum, you may be part of an organization that passes out *Roberts Rules of Order* to every management trainee to make sure they are well versed in parliamentary procedure. One method isn't better than the other; they're just different. What is important though is to establish how you plan to run your meeting. Without that insight, half of your participants could come into the session, ready to spitball their ideas, interrupting at will, while the other half enter the session, wondering how the chair can recognize them.

How you manage participation depends upon the purpose of the meeting and the personalities in the room. If your meeting is a brainstorming session, you want to encourage creativity and innovation, both of which might be stymied by a more formalized participation process. We'll talk more about how to run an effective brainstorming session in Chapter 11.

If you absolutely have to make a decision on something and your time is limited, you may want to tighten the reins on how people weigh in. You may choose to call on people one at a time to make sure everyone's voice is heard before you ultimately decide what needs to be done. Try to match how you want to manage the conversation flow based upon what you are trying to accomplish in the meeting. Does a less formal approach make more sense or does a more structured style hold more promise for what you need to get done?

But what if you have an exceptionally verbose team member who is likely to take over the talk track? That brainstorming session may turn into a one-man-show. What if you have brilliant but introverted members of your team who rarely speak up unless they are officially invited to do so?

TIP

Determining how you want people to participate is product of the purpose of and people in your meeting. If you truly want to create an equitable environment, you need to account for both of these factors when choosing what participation ground rules you want to establish.

That may mean adjusting your typical participation ground rules to account for a changing team dynamic. Some team members have worked together so long that they may practically finish each other's sentences . . . and often do. Your meetings are typically like a lively conversation around the family dinner table. But what happens if you introduce a new person to the mix who doesn't feel comfortable just interrupting someone that they don't know very well?

When you are considering how you want to manage the participation flow, think first about the people who are least likely to speak up. How can you make it easy for them to engage in a meaningful way? You can:

>> Ask people to raise their hands if they have something to say rather than simply butting in.

>> Call people by name to proactively give them the floor. This may be an adjustment for those who have been used to a different meeting participation process, but it's a necessary one, at least for the time being.

>> Let your team know that this switch to a more formal participation flow is to help your new team member get acclimated to the team.

Once the new person has gained their footing, you may be able to migrate back to the previous less formal participation practice.

When virtual

When you are meeting virtually, the conversation flow can often feel stunted and stilted unless you take active control of it as the meeting leader. Why is this the case? Because the technology often limits how many streams of audio can be heard at one time. Consequently, if two people talk at the same time, you will likely hear only snippets of each person's sentences. The natural rhythm of in-person conversation is often disrupted by the technology that even allows people to meet virtually in the first place.

For this reason, brainstorming sessions like we described where people interrupt each other and jump in at the slightest whiff of airspace do not work well. Instead of hearing a variety of ideas, you are more likely to hear simply the loudest or the most long-winded one. That's why we strongly suggest you actively manage the conversation by calling on people by name.

You'll find that one of the biggest barriers to a smooth flow of communication during a virtual meeting is no one really knows who has the floor. Those who are extroverted might speak up on their own, but others might wait it out, not wanting to step on anyone's toes. By calling on people by name, you are not only inviting them to speak but giving them permission to do so. Some members of your team may not need that extra nudge, but others will. To avoid you only hearing from your extroverted team members, you need to moderate the discussion to include everyone. By establishing that you plan to call on people by name, you can more easily do that.

There will be some people who will happily raise their hands (their physical ones or emoji ones) and they will wait their turn to be brought into the dialogue. However, you will also encounter plenty of people who would rather keep their hands securely in their laps or off their screens.

In order to bring everyone into the conversation, we advocate doing what we call "cold calling with good intention." This refers to calling on an individual by name who hasn't readily made known that they would like to speak. If this makes you uncomfortable, it's understandable. No one likes to put someone on the spot — well, maybe some people do, but that's not you, right? Here's where the "good intention" comes in. Your goal in calling on that person is not to give them a personal pop quiz in front of their colleagues. No, your goal is to ensure they have an opportunity to provide their thoughts and perspectives which you believe would be valuable for the group.

Cold calling with good intention is all about the approach and the motivation behind it. Let's give you an example.

The purpose of your virtual meeting is to explore new markets for your much improved widget. In fact, you've been focusing on a specific industry that your organization hasn't gained traction in yet. You know that one of your team members, Rich, worked in this industry before coming to your team. During the course of discussion, you expected Rich to be an active participant in the conversation, but he's a bit of an introvert and hasn't spoken up. After waiting for Rich to speak up himself, you decide to take matters into your own hands and say something like this, "Rich, I know you spent a lot of time in the X industry. I'd love to hear your take on it." Yes, you are cold-calling on Rich, but what you are asking him to do isn't a heavy lift. You are asking for his opinion based upon his own experience.

Now let's give you an alternative that we would not recommend. What if you had said, "Rich, I know you spent a lot of time in the X industry. Can you tell us how to best enter this market?" Yes, you are cold-calling but the "good intention" part is fuzzy. You might truly want to know the answer to that question, but it's not fair to ask Rich to provide it on the spot.

When virtual, cold calling with good intention becomes a valuable tool given the inherent challenge of reading the room. You can't hear the intakes of air that precede someone speaking up. You may miss a nonverbal cue that you normally would pick up on if you were in person, a cue that indicates they have something to add.

TIP

Let your meeting attendees know that you may use this technique to make sure you don't miss out on including everyone in the conversation who wants to be included. That way they're prepared for it. If you establish this ground rule for every meeting, your attendees will come to expect it and it won't be a big deal. It'll just be the way you run meetings.

WARNING

There's one thing that you need to keep in mind if you plan on cold-calling during a meeting: *psychological safety* (the degree to which a person feels safe to share their ideas and thoughts without fear of retaliation or negative reactions by those around them). Even if you are calling on them with good intention, it can still feel terrifying for some. (Think about how it felt to be called on to answer a question when you were in school, and you had no clue what the right answer was. Maybe that wasn't cold-calling with *good intention* though?) In order to take away some anxiety around this practice, establish that it is perfectly okay to say "pass" if you don't have anything to add. You are simply giving them an opportunity to be heard. If they don't feel like they have anything to add that can further the conversation, there's no expectation that they make something up on the fly.

When hybrid

Like a virtual meeting, a hybrid meeting suffers from the same limitations of audio technology, but the effects aren't felt universally. If you are in the meeting room, you may find it really easy to speak up when the mood strikes and insert yourself into the dialogue. You can easily read the nonverbals of your fellow face-to-face colleagues and see when they're wrapping up their thoughts, allowing you to follow. But the remote attendees may be pulling their hair out, trying to get the attention of the in-room folks, to let them know they have something to say. If they're lucky, someone in the physical meeting room might spy the remote attendee wildly waving their arms. Aha . . . Chris would like to speak. But often, participation can be an uneven mess if left to its own devices.

TIP

For a hybrid meeting, setting up a more formal style of participation is often necessary to prevent a two-tiered experience where in-person attendees gobble up the talk time and the remote attendees are barely heard. Calling on people, giving them the floor, helps you to keep control of the conversation flow that otherwise would likely end up being chaotic and counter-productive . . . and possibly marginalizing for the remote attendees.

3

Facilitating an Effective Meeting — What to do During a Meeting

The time has come to kick that meeting off. On your mark, get set, go!

Wait . . . not so fast. There's a lot that you need to know to make sure your meeting accomplishes its goals.

In this part, you discover the right way to start a meeting and identify key behaviors that ensure participation by everyone in attendance. Many meetings include presentations, so we cover the essential skills needed to deliver them in an impactful way. We also arm you with information on what bad meeting behaviors might crop up, and most importantly, how to stop them.

Chapter **10**

Starting a Meeting

Y ou may think the way you start a meeting is pretty obvious. You say a few words of welcome, take a quick glance at the agenda, and then dive in to agenda item number one.

Sure, you could do that, but you are missing out on a huge opportunity to optimize your meeting's success.

Presumably, you've put a good amount of thought and effort into designing your meeting to fit a certain purpose. You've selected the right people to have in the room. You've probably even put a lot of thought into what kind of room you are using — a physical one, a virtual one, or a combination of both (if not, check out Chapter 8). Why wouldn't you want to put as much effort into kicking it off right as you did with everything leading up to it?

You may be thinking, "But there's not that much to think about when it comes to starting a meeting." There's where you're wrong. Consider the examples of what not to do when starting a meeting, as described in the nearby sidebars.

WARNING

Don't let all of your pre-meeting work go to waste. Determine the best way to kick off your meeting so that bad execution doesn't ruin your meeting design.

HOW NOT TO START A MEETING EXAMPLE #1

Like most days, your calendar is full of back-to-back meetings, but on this day, you've been an attendee up until this one with your team. You are drained from a full day on video calls. You haven't even had a chance to eat lunch, so you're hangry. You click on your meeting link. Take a quick look at the gallery view and see no one has their camera on. You let it go because you just can't summon the effort to cajole your team to use their video too. You turn off your camera and after a quick hello, start delivering the latest update on the product launch.

In this chapter, you discover how to set you and your team up for a productive session by taking action just before meeting gets underway — whether it's troubleshooting your technology foibles or allowing more time for chit-chat than you normally would because the situation calls for it. We also describe how to kick it off right — right on time — and offer additional tips for sticking to the structure you designed. And we wrap up by discussing what participation policies you need to explicitly state depending upon the kind of meeting format you are using.

HOW NOT TO START A MEETING EXAMPLE #2

You are excited to hold your first hybrid meeting with your team. The IT department has told you that all of the conference rooms have been equipped with the latest audio and video equipment needed to conduct your team meeting, half of which will be in the room with you and half of which will be joining remotely. You've had a crazy day, so you get to the conference room with just a few minutes to spare, only to find that the IT department's idea of being "equipped" means an extra laptop that can be used to open the meeting link and no in-room camera or microphone other than the one built in to that device. It's too late to figure out other options now. You greet the gang assembled around the conference room, open the virtual meeting on the extra laptop, awkwardly wave at the embedded webcam, and get started. You are told by one of your remote attendees after the meeting that they could only hear every other word said in the conference room.

Setting the Tone Just Before the Meeting

As any business traveler would tell you, one of the most stressful parts of any trip is trying to make a flight connection, especially if it's in an airport that is unfamiliar to you. Even if your itinerary seems reasonable, allowing plenty of time to get from one gate to another, flights are regularly delayed and gates are often changed, even at the last minute.

Karin recalls a rather harrowing experience in Newark International Airport. She was flying in from LAX and knew her layover was tight — only 45 minutes before her next flight would board, a quick hop from Newark to Raleigh-Durham. She wasn't even all that concerned when the pilot of her plane at LAX came over the loudspeaker: "Sorry folks, we're going to be a bit delayed. They need to check out a mechanical issue before we push back from the gate." No worries, airlines always build in time padding for such occasions. Plus, she had her boarding pass for the second flight, which listed the gate for her Newark flight that was in the same terminal. Even though that 45-minute buffer had reduced down to about 20 minutes by the time they took off, Karin still felt confident.

When she walked off the plane in Newark, though, she showed an airline employee the gate number she was seeking. Apparently, it was at the far end of the terminal and down a few flights of stairs. She took off, walking briskly but not running . . . yet. When she arrived at the gate designated on the mobile boarding pass, the sign indicated they were boarding . . . for a flight to Boston. Wait, Karin was going to Raleigh-Durham. She consulted the arrivals and departures board. Sure enough, they had changed the gate — to a gate that was directly across from where she had disembarked . . . a gate that was now at the exact opposite side of the terminal from where she was. The word "Boarding" flashed on the digital screen.

At this point, she ran, trying to keep her roller bag from taking flight while trying to dodge other travelers who were moving at a normal pace, not the panicked speed Karin was moving at. When she arrived at the gate, she was the only person there aside from one airline employee who told her she needed to gate-check her bag and get on. At that point, Karin would've left her bag in Newark as long as she could make her flight home. When she finally flopped into her seat, the sweat was rolling down her forehead as she offered a quick apology to the poor guy who had to sit beside her while she tried to stop hyperventilating.

What does this story have to do with starting a meeting?

REMEMBER

You don't want to be that leader who comes flying into a meeting, throws down their stuff, and stresses everyone else out by their apparent lack of composure. You want to be in control of yourself and your meeting, and it's hard to do that when you are arriving at the last minute, appearing totally unprepared for what is about to occur.

Arriving before the meeting start time

Sliding into the room and skidding to a stop (whether literally or digitally) is no way to begin a meeting. In fact, we would suggest that you do more of a mosey into the meeting itself, and that mosey should go into motion well before the official meeting start time.

Arriving early is better for you because it allows you time to prepare for what is about to happen. You may have created the agenda and have a good sense of what you are going to cover, but it's always helpful to take one last look at the items on your docket to give yourself that 15,000-foot view. To put it in GPS navigation terms, you don't need to go over the turn-by-turn directions, but you probably want to look at the overview of the entire route. That way, the starting point and ending point are fresh in your mind and will help you stay on the right path.

You also don't want time to deal with any unexpected situations. What if there is a scheduling snafu and the conference room you are expecting to hold your meeting in was somehow double-booked? You either have to boot the current residents out of your space or find another location for your meeting. You don't want to be figuring this out in the presence of your entire team.

You may have experienced the virtual version of this. Some calendaring software automatically adds a virtual meeting link that aligns with their software stack. However, your team uses a different meeting platform outside of that stack. You send off the calendar invite with the appropriate meeting link in the notes. However, unbeknownst to you, the calendar app added one by default. The result? Dueling meeting links. When it's time to meet, half of your people might be on one meeting platform with you, while the other half are waiting on the other platform, wondering where everyone else is.

TIP

Scheduling issues, whether physical or virtual, happen, and as the meeting leader, you want to head them off as quickly as possible. By arriving early, you can sort out the scheduling mess and hopefully resolve it before anyone else shows up.

Arriving early is better for your team too because you'll be mentally equipped to more effectively run the meeting. Not only does it provide time padding for sorting out schedule bumps or any other meeting space issues, but it also gives you time to settle in and assume the proper mentality to lead your team.

REMEMBER

How you show up is heavily influenced by when you show up, and in turn, it will influence the tone of the meeting for your team. Your attendees will appreciate seeing a meeting leader who is calm, cool, and collected. They won't be absorbing any of the frantic and negative energy that a frazzled arrival can create. Rather, the energy in the meeting room will be positive and any potential issues will already be smoothed out.

Knowing how early to arrive

Determining how early you should arrive before your meeting depends upon a variety of factors including your own level of comfort and your relationship with the attendees, as well as the format in which you are meeting.

Early is in the eye of the beholder, you might say. Let's go back to the airport analogy. Some people wouldn't even dream of arriving at the airport later than a full two hours before their flight. Others (and yes, Karin, we are looking at you) have no problem whisking into the terminal about an hour in advance of takeoff . . . provided that they aren't checking bags.

TIP

How much lead time you give yourself also depends upon who will be in the room with you. If you are meeting with your team, it may feel like a lower stakes situation that requires perhaps ten minutes of ramp up time to make sure everything is set and ready to go. If you are hosting a meeting with senior leadership or very important clients, you want to give yourself plenty of time to settle your nerves and stomach and ensure your meeting room and your mind are ready to go.

If you are meeting face-to-face in a conference room that you regularly use, you won't need much time to orient yourself to your surroundings. Ten minutes ahead of time might be plenty. However, if you are using a conference room that is new to you, you may want to tack on an extra 20 minutes to acclimate yourself to the accommodations. Are the blinds lowered to keep out the sun glaring through the windows? Does the whiteboard have markers that actually write and aren't dried out? Do you have enough chairs in the room for everyone who plans to be in attendance? These minor considerations can have an outsized impact on your meeting if you don't address them beforehand. Instead, they end up eating precious time during the actual session as you, for example, have to hustle to find extra seating.

TIP

If you are meeting in virtual setting, we recommend opening up a meeting link at least ten minutes before the official meeting start time. It gives you time to reacquaint yourself with the platform and plot out how you might use it to best effect. It also lets you troubleshoot any tech challenges, which we will discuss a little bit later in this chapter.

If you are leading a hybrid meeting, how early you arrive is dictated by whether you are leading from a virtual position or an in-person one. If you are leading it remotely, then you want to make sure someone else can help with the setup within the physical conference room while you navigate the virtual meeting room setup. If you are leading the hybrid meeting in person, allot enough time to prepare the conference room setup as well as the virtual meeting room setup to ensure that all attendees can interact as seamlessly as possible.

Elevating your personal production value

If you are leading a meeting virtually, you want to give yourself time to check what we call your *personal production value* — how you show up on your video box based upon your webcam and audio setup.

REMEMBER

Paying attention to your lighting, background, camera position, and audio quality aren't signs of vanity. They're signs of respect for those who are joining you on the call. You want them to be able to communicate with you as easily as possible. In other words, attending to your on-camera presence is not about you; it's about them, your team.

When leading a meeting virtually, how you appear on screen will also dictate how your team will. If you join your virtual meeting in your pajamas with your face in shadow and a persistent hum in your audio, you will likely find it difficult to inspire your team to greatness. You are also sending a dangerous message to your team; you don't care how you show up for your meeting, so they shouldn't care how they show up either.

As a meeting leader, you want to make sure you are setting a good example by showing up in a polished and professional manner, and that means taking the time to check how you appear in your little video window.

TIP

Run through this checklist before the rest of your attendees join:

>> **Is your camera at eye level?** You want your audience to feel like you are looking directly at them, not looking down at them or looking up at them, when you look into the camera lens.

>> **Are you situated squarely in the frame?** You don't want to cut off any body parts like your chin or forehead. Try to take up at least three-quarters of the box with your body so you have maybe three fingers worth of space between the top of your head and the top of your screen.

>> **Is your face well lit?** Focus on lighting up your face so people can read your facial expressions.

>> **Is your background free of distractions?** Try to keep your background neutral with perhaps one conversation starter if appropriate.

>> **Is your audio coming through loud and clear?** Most platforms have a way to test your microphone and speakers prior to the meeting getting underway.

WARNING

YOUR VIRTUAL DRESS CODE

A quick word about what to wear when on virtual calls: Before you protest that pajamas are perfectly acceptable attire in your organization, allow us to add a caveat. While what you wear depends largely on your organization's culture, do know that the significant move to remote work has done a number on office dress codes, largely due to the fact that people are working from home more than ever. That more relaxed environment has sometimes translated into a relaxation of the level of professionalism that manifests on screen. Often, people have interpreted "business casual" with too much emphasis on the "casual" and too little emphasis on "business." Your team will be looking to you to set the standard and they will take their cues from you. Our advice is to let your team know that they should match audience expectations. Suggest that they ask themselves what they'd wear if the meeting were in person. The way you show up for a meeting with your team will likely be different from the way you show up for a meeting with external stakeholders. You might be fine with a nice shirt for your team meetings, but if you are meeting with senior leadership, you likely want to step up your wardrobe game as a sign of respect.

Making sure meeting technology is functional

You might think that meeting technology is only applicable to virtual and hybrid formats, but now, all of our meetings are infused with digital capabilities that make our meetings better . . . or worse if they don't work.

While you may already have your IT department on speed dial, as a meeting leader, you want to empower yourself to do some basic tech checks and troubleshooting if necessary. Let's give you a few examples.

When in person

One of the main laments we hear about technology in the meeting room is the lack of standardization. You might know exactly what button to push to close the blinds, lower the screen, and power on the projector in one room, but that's no guarantee that you know how to do all of those things in another room, even if it's in the same building.

Often, you'll find a single-page document that claims to be a step-by-step guide to how this room works, but this may end up being more of a hindrance than a help. They may be written by people who have much more technical proficiency than you do or have even installed everything in the room themselves. Their step-by-step instructions are equivalent to the multi-page manual to put together self-assembly furniture. At least one of the steps reads: Throw temper tantrum out of frustration.

TIP

With any luck, the room that you have booked for your face-to-face meeting is meeting-leader friendly, meaning it is intuitively set up to allow you to do things such as project slides or lower the mechanical blinds if necessary. Even if you aren't planning to share slides during the session, you still want to make sure you know how someone can do so in that particular room. Maybe it's connecting using HDMI. Maybe it means logging into a website that allows you to present through Wi-Fi. Maybe it's using Airplay to project your device to the monitor in the room. Whatever system is set up, you want to know how it works so you can show them with confidence how to connect.

When virtual

For as much as some people bemoan video collaboration platforms, they have opened up a world of work that would not have been possible just a few years ago. Virtual meetings have embedded themselves into the meeting lexicon and unleashed an appetite and expectation for flexible work arrangements. But technology can be fickle, and that's why it is imperative that you log on early to your meeting platform of choice to make sure it is working the way you want it to.

What can possibly go wrong? If you are asking this question, you probably haven't done many virtual meetings yet, because technology glitches are relatively common. Sometimes a setting will default to something that you don't want due to a software update that happened automatically. Changes to the functionality may have been made at the enterprise level that you hadn't realized had been made, and now you are wondering why your virtual background isn't available any more . . . or your polling questions disappeared . . . or your breakout rooms need to be created all over again.

You don't want to find out that changes are afoot in the system as you enter the meeting room with all of your attendees. You won't have enough time to identify potential problems and react to fix them. Instead, give yourself a grace period by logging in early enough to take a look around your virtual space without being watched by all of your team members.

REMEMBER

If your meeting includes any people from outside the organization, you want to build in even more time just in case the security measures put in place to keep shady characters out somehow keep your key external stakeholders out as well. Often permissions need to be granted by the IT department well before for the outsider to be able to take part in the meeting on certain platforms . . . something one of Karin's clients learned the hard way (check out the sidebar, "On the outside looking in").

ON THE OUTSIDE LOOKING IN

In 2020, Karin was hired by a large biotech company to do a webinar for 5,000 sales and sales operations people on virtual communication. The platform they had selected to hold the meeting on was known to be a bit, let's call it "buggy." Knowing this, Karin suggested they do a tech check about a week before the session and the client agreed, sending a meeting link for Karin to use to get onto the company's meeting platform.

On the day of the tech check, Karin hit the link and received an error message. She hit the link again. Same response. She hit the link one more time with the same result and then reached out by phone to her main contact who in turn got their IT lead on the line. After an hour of attempting and failing to get her past the firewall, the client and Karin agreed to try again the next day. The IT lead insisted he would change the permissions for the site that would allow her to get in.

Tech check number two: The same thing occurred. Karin couldn't get into the meeting, and her client was flummoxed and promised to fix the problem.

Tech check number three: No luck.

Tech check number four: Eureka! Whatever tweaks the client made on the backend allowed Karin to get onto the platform, albeit without all of the functionality of someone within the organization. For example, she couldn't see the chat thread, but for her, just being able to be in the room was a win.

Fast forward to the day of the event, Karin decided to log on about a half hour ahead of time, just in case. Good thing she did because once again, she was denied entry but this time, the stakes were higher. She had 5,000 people who were waiting to see her deliver her presentation. After nearly 30 minutes of attempting to get Karin in to the session, the client threw in the towel. They announced to those gathered that due to technical difficulties, the Virtual Presence Training would need to be rescheduled.

TIP

Some of the technical challenges that you might encounter with virtual meetings can be solved through tech support 101 — close the meeting and/or log off and log back in again. The platforms sometimes just need a quick reboot to work the way they are supposed to. However, there are others that are out of your control that you can't possibly fix on your own. If you arrive early, it gives you enough time to distinguish between the two.

When hybrid

Remember the tech checks to do for face-to-face meetings? Remember the ones to do for virtual meetings? For hybrid, you need to accomplish all of those, plus some new ones that are necessary due to the additional technology required to connect those who are attending remotely and in person.

In a hybrid meeting, you need to:

» Make sure your meeting room is fully operational with a camera that can capture the body language of those who are gathered in person and perhaps even auto-focus to zoom in on the person who is speaking around the conference room table.

» Do an audio test with another attendee who can hop on early as a remote attendee to make sure the sound quality is sufficient for the virtual attendees to follow the in-room conversation.

» Check the monitor (or ideally monitors) in the conference room. Can you project the meeting room window onto the monitor so in-room attendees can see the faces of the remote participants as well as the chat window?

The other side of the technology coin is out of your hands and under the control of the remote attendees. You can't ensure their webcams are beaming a clear image or that their microphones provide high audio fidelity. However, as soon as someone joins as a virtual attendee, check both as quickly as possible to avoid any tech trouble that can waylay the meeting itself. If you spot an issue prior to the start of the session, let them know what the problem is ("Marge, there's a loud hum in your audio!") and ask them to log off and log back in. If the problem remains, you can ask them to either troubleshoot it on their own or have them attend in a way that won't be disruptive for the rest. For example, Marge can attend on mute. It's not ideal, but at least it won't derail the whole meeting.

TIP

This scenario enhances the case for assigning a technology lead for your hybrid meetings. The technology or tech lead should be someone who is attending virtually who can help manage any individual tech challenges that crop up for remote attendees. A tech lead would be a valuable resource for those occasions we just mentioned. Let's say Marge is actually supposed to be playing a big role in the meeting. In fact, she's going to be leading the discussion around a report she sent out in advance. Having her attend on mute isn't a viable solution. Instead of just cancelling the session and rescheduling once her audio has been fixed, you can put Marge and your assigned tech lead into a breakout room to sort out the issue while the rest of the meeting continues. The discussion about Marge's report can wait until her audio is up to snuff. If the tech lead can't help, then you can decide to table the discussion for a later time.

Engaging in pre-meeting talk

Remember how we said flying into a room, dropping your stuff, stealing a quick glance at the agenda, and diving into the meeting was bad? That's because doing so is very jarring for the meeting leader, you. You need time to cognitively transition to the purpose of the meeting. You need time to ease into the meeting. That's okay and it's actually a good thing to take a second and do just that.

Well, just as running into the room can be jarring for the meeting leader, it's also uncomfortable for the meeting attendees. They may be in the middle of a conversation, and though you are starting on time, that conversation is interrupted. They too need a few minutes to transition, potentially, to the agenda at hand (particularly if the agendas were in your hand when you ran into the room).

TIP

Take a few minutes before the meeting to create the space needed to cognitively transition to the purpose of the meeting. With a little bit of planning and effort, pre-meeting talk will start to be simply part of your meeting routine, and you'll notice a change in your meetings and in your team. Trust and cohesion will emerge naturally as a sense of care and concern will foster collegiality and even friendship among team members.

But, what do we mean by creating the space for cognitive transition? Hand out the agenda and tell everyone to read it quietly? If you don't have a physical agenda, are we suggesting you just sit there and stare at each other for three to four minutes so our brains can catch up?

Neither. If you've done things right, the agenda or main purpose for the meeting is already available to the attendees (for more on getting this in place, see Chapter 9). Instead, we recommend engaging in pre-meeting talk. What's that you say? Well, *pre-meeting talk* is the conversations that occur as you gather for your meeting. Historically speaking, it's those brief catch-up conversations we had when we walked from our office to the conference room. We'd often run into folks heading the same direction and ask them how their day is going. Or, what's new in their lives? Or, how are their kids or family? In other words, we'd chat a bit before the meeting.

REMEMBER

Applying the principle of pre-meeting talk has implications for other things you need to do to make the meeting effective. If you absorb five minutes of meeting time with pre-meeting talk, that's time taken from the agenda. So, you'll need to keep that in mind when designing your meeting, and make sure you schedule the meeting for the right length of time to accommodate it.

Some of Joe's earliest research on workplace meetings focused on pre-meeting talk. His efforts involved building on the work of other researchers who described four different types of pre-meeting talk as follows:

>> **Small talk:** This form of pre-meeting talk is all about stuff outside of work, like the weather, sporting events, family life, the latest episode of that reality TV show you really shouldn't spend time watching but do because you can't help yourself. It's the casual conversation content.

>> **Work talk:** As a form of pre-meeting talk, this includes conversations about ongoing projects, work tasks, new projects, job duties, and other work-related topics not currently relevant to the meeting at hand.

>> **Meeting preparatory talk:** This form of pre-meeting talk is about the upcoming meeting. What it's about. What we think about the agenda items. It can sometimes include coalition-building around a decision point with colleagues ahead of the meeting. This type of talk often happens when a meeting does not have a clear agenda or purpose.

>> **Shop talk:** Now, you might be thinking, "Wait a minute, how is shop talk different from work talk?" Well, shop talk is more about colleagues, office politics, who are the top performers (or terrible performers) in the company, the personality of the boss, and other interpersonal topics. So, it's not about the work itself, but about the environment in which work takes place and the people in it.

Using these working definitions of pre-meeting talk, Joe and his colleagues wanted to see which type of talk made for better meetings. The focus here was on which type of talk related most strongly to the overall effectiveness of the meeting. Any guesses? Time to reveal all!

If you guessed small talk, you would be right. And here's why we think that is: Although the other forms of talk are important and help accomplish the work of the day, only small talk inserts a bit of social interaction into the work environment. Humans need social interaction, and usually that interaction creates more positive feelings between people.

It's also a lower-stakes form of communication. If someone asks you what you think of the weather, you can have any opinion and it's okay. If someone asks you what you think about the project you're working on together, your opinion could impact your relationship with that person or your boss, depending upon whether or not they agree with you. Clearly, the weather is safe and the project may not be, at least in terms of topics.

However, what Joe and his colleagues concluded was a bit more technical. They believed that it had something to do with the personalities of the members of the team or meeting group:

>> Extroverts don't need any help getting their ideas shared. They are energized by meeting with others, so they'll enthusiastically engage.

>> Introverts not so much. Many are nervous communicators. They don't like to just interject their opinions, and when they do, they are often well thought out, if not articulated as eloquently as others.

Joe had a student a few years ago who was extremely introverted. Even when they were called upon in class and were expected to answer, they would look down and only mumble their responses. However, one-on-one and discussing a topic of mutual interest, they would go on and on and on. The difference? The environment and the comfort of the situation. For introverts, pre-meeting talk that is low stakes in nature can provide a pathway to participation.

REMEMBER

Pre-meeting talk has the potential to help put introverts at ease, simulating a smaller more intimate conversation, thereby unlocking their voices a bit and helping them contribute more openly with the group.

So, getting pre-meeting talk going is actually a very good thing! But, how you do it differs by meeting format.

When in person

We alluded to how to do this for in person meetings already: Arrive early to the meeting room.

Well, that's in part to make sure the setup is adequate for the meetings' goals and purpose. Is the projector warmed up and can the presenter(s) connect okay?

However, a greater motivation to arriving early is so that pre-meeting talk can be fostered. By being there early, you get to greet people as they arrive. You can ask how they are doing. You can lament the cold or hot weather you are having. You can engage in small talk with them.

TIP

By showing up ten minutes early, you have five minutes to make sure the room is ready to go, and five minutes to greet attendees as they arrive and engage in pre-meeting talk.

For those who struggle with jumping in on small talk, it's actually okay to do a little pre-meeting talk preparation. Look at the attendee list and think about them just briefly. Maybe for some attendees you know them and their family, so you can ask how the kids are doing. Maybe for others, you don't know them as well, so the weather is the entry point. Maybe for others, you've got a history of trying to get small-talk going and they've been less than interested, but you know what projects they are on. Ask them how they're doing with one of their projects.

Although pre-meeting small talk is the best form of pre-meeting talk for improving overall meeting effectiveness, the other forms of pre-meeting talk are useful in moving the work and organizational culture forward in a positive light. Embrace the opportunity to talk with your colleagues and friends.

When virtual

Gathering for the virtual meeting is a matter of three or four clicks on your computer or other device. Because of that, pre-meeting talk is a bit harder to emerge naturally. The current trend is people click the button to join the meeting when it's scheduled to start. And, if they have back-to-back meetings, they might even be a minute or two late because the previous meeting ran long (or perhaps nature called). Therefore, you have to take a different approach to pre-meeting talk in a virtual environment.

In March of 2020, when many people became "Suddenly Virtual" due to the COVID-19 pandemic, Joe and Karen were inundated with calls from clients looking for help. They wanted to know what to do to make sure these new virtual meetings worked well. Joe recalls one client saying, "Something is just off about these meetings. I can't seem to get into a flow with my team like we did in person." Guess what Joe asked? "Are you engaging in pre-meeting talk?" This was a longer-term client, so the person was well aware of this practice. His response was that he wasn't really sure how to do that in this new environment. People show up at the meeting start time. Our advice — do it anyway! That's right, pre-meeting talk is important enough to do it, even when it will cut into meeting time.

A common complaint about virtual meetings is how they can feel sterile. When in person, you benefit from social lubrication that occurs as you walk down the hall, enter the conference room and settle into your seat. You joke around, you chit-chat, you banter back and forth. In a virtual meeting, you enter the virtual room and bam — you're on. There's no warm up embedded into the meeting unless it's planned. But that social lubrication is key to fostering the relationships and building the cohesion that is an essential part of working well as a team. Carving out time for pre-meeting talk will make the actual meeting better and tighten the ties between your team members.

When you open a virtual meeting early, it allows you to do what you would normally do during an in-person meeting. You can greet everyone individually when they arrive. As we mentioned many times over, people want to feel like they are seen and heard in a meeting. By acknowledging their arrival in the room and waiting for them to respond in kind, you accomplish that right away.

Addressing people individually also sets the tone that you intend for everyone to participate in the meeting. There's no hiding behind the black box with a name. If you say hello to someone, they will feel compelled to respond. They are on official notice that they are not there to just be spectators.

Don't just stop at the quick greeting either. We recommend starting every virtual meeting with the question, "How is everyone today?" And then wait for answers. Don't rush past this. If it's a one-on-one, wait for your partner to respond. If it's a group meeting, wait for a few attendees to respond. Let people vent a bit. But, don't let it go too long.

For a 30-minute meeting, let pre-meeting talk take 3 to 5 minutes of the meeting time. For a 60-minute meeting, let pre-meeting talk take 5 to 7 minutes of the meeting time. Look for a way to transition to the task at hand without appearing like you are cutting people off. Wait for an opportunity to wrap it up graciously and then turn your attention to the agenda.

When hybrid

How do you handle pre-meeting talk in a hybrid meeting? As with most hybrid meeting best practices, it's a combination of techniques used for in-person and virtual meetings. How you are leading the meeting, in-person or virtually, does have an impact.

For example, if you are physically in the room and have arrived early as we advise, you can foster that pre-meeting talk with your face-to-face attendees as they gather in the room. You also want to be on the lookout for the arrival of your virtual attendees. (In fact, in some cases, it's up to you to even let them in to the meeting itself if you've set up a waiting room.) When your remote participants show up on screen, greet them one by one, and get the conversation going there as well. You may need to manage the flow a bit more to make sure the in-room attendees don't talk over the virtual ones too much, but this actually is one time where you can afford to be looser in how you manage the conversation.

If you are leading a hybrid meeting remotely, you will likely need an in-person helper to get the system up and running. That person can also serve as the go-between you and your in-room attendees. Perhaps you can address them as they enter the conference room, but your in-room helper might be in a better position to moderate that exchange. As with any hybrid meeting, you want to make sure you give equal attention to those remote and in-person, so be sure to engage your virtual team members as you would in a fully virtual meeting too. However, with a hybrid meeting, you may not need to carve out time allotted to the actual meeting proceedings if you were able to sufficiently engage with all attendees prior to the start.

Getting Off to a Good Start

If you have followed our advice (wise move!) and arrived early to your meeting, you might find it challenging to transition to actually getting the meeting in motion. Maybe you've been really enjoying the conversation about your coworker's crazy weekend antics and you don't want to seem rude to cut them off. However, as the meeting leader, it's your job to move from the informal chit-chat to the first item on the agenda, but it requires some finesse and focus. If you interrupt a sincere moment of levity with your team by robotically calling the meeting to order, you are liable to rub everyone the wrong way. Instead look for an opportunity to link the casual conversation to the reason why you are gathered and then guide the team through the agenda.

Starting the meeting on time

TIP

Start on time! Meetings that do so are always better than those that do not start on time. No amount of lateness is good.

As a meeting leader, you are constantly sending signals to your team, often without you even realizing it. Sometimes those signals may inadvertently be sending the wrong message even if you have the best of intentions.

It's become common practice for meeting leaders to wait to start a meeting until everyone has arrived, even if that means ten people are ready to roll but one person has yet to show up. You might think you are being gracious in giving that one person a few extra minutes to appear, but trust us, you are really ticking off the other ten who were punctual. They found a way to be on time. Why should they have their time wasted, waiting on their colleague who was somehow waylaid?

REMEMBER

Meetings 101 says "Start your meetings on time." This time-honored best practice cannot be overstated or underscored. In fact, no other meeting leader behavior has a greater consistent impact on the potential for meetings to engage employees than being courteous with people's time, specifically starting and ending on time.

Joe's dissertation, many moons ago, focused on the things managers can do to engage their employees via their meetings. He looked at participation, meeting relevance, and time courtesy. Of these things, meeting time courtesy had the strongest consistent relationship with engagement. That is, if you want to inspire and engage employees through your meetings, respect their time. Start on time, end on time, and manage the meeting effectively from a time perspective.

TECHNICAL STUFF

After learning how important time courtesy was, Joe and his team engaged in a series of studies about meeting lateness. The focus was, in part, on what people even consider late and how late is problematic and so forth. In an experimental study with working adults, they found that meetings that start one to five minutes late are just about as good as meetings that start on time. However, somewhere between five minutes and ten minutes, people start to get angry. And we mean really angry. According to Joe's data, the waiting people want the late person fired. They want them sanctioned. And even one person wanted to punch them in the face. No, we do not condone violence or over-reaction to late attendees. But, on an anonymous survey, it's clear this really irks some people.

But what about the person who missed out on the first few minutes because they were late? That's on them — and it's not your job to catch them up either. They may be annoyed that they are a bit lost at first, but that may be enough to encourage them to break their lateness habit. They need to respect your time and the time of their colleagues. By not accommodating their lack of punctuality, you are sending a strong signal to everyone else that their time matters and their on-time appearance is appreciated.

Clarifying meeting purpose or goal

You may have sent out the purpose of the meeting in your meeting invitation, and if you followed best practices, you certainly did (see Chapter 9). But it is well worth your time and effort to reiterate it at the top of the meeting itself. Your team may also be suffering from meeting overload and may barely know what time it is when they show up for your particular gathering. Help them out by stating why you are meeting and the ultimate goal for the proceedings.

By refreshing their memories of the purpose for the meeting, you establish guardrails for the dialogue that's about to take place. You all have a collective job to do, and you need to work together to get it done. That means that if someone starts to veer the conversation off the road, you can more easily steer it back by reminding them again of the reason why you are here. We'll talk a lot more about how to keep the meeting on track in Chapter 11.

Assigning an attendee to record notes (meeting minutes)

You've heard the question, "If a tree falls in the forest and nobody is around, does it make a sound?" When it comes to meetings, you have to ask, "If a meeting happens and no one records what occurred, does that meeting move business forward?"

Creating a written record of what happens in your meeting is critical to its ultimate effectiveness. It's too easy for people to forget what was said, what action items were assigned and what decisions were made without someone actually documenting it. That's why we are big fans of assigning a meeting attendee to take notes or even record the meeting minutes.

TIP

How detailed those minutes are vary widely from organization to organization. In fact, in some companies, there is a policy that you are not to record minutes but rather just action items. Figure out what fits your purposes and then ask someone to record the pertinent information which can then be disseminated afterward.

WARNING

If you are leading the meeting, don't try to be the meeting minder as well. You have enough to worry about just driving the discussion and keeping everyone on point. Don't add note-taker to your list of duties. You can easily delegate that role and should. It also allows you to actively engage another meeting participant by giving them a pivotal job.

Reiterating participation ground rules

WARNING

Lively and active participation is a huge determinant of how effective your meeting will ultimately be. That's why you want to encourage people to speak up, provide input and offer their thoughts throughout the meeting itself. However, unfettered airing of opinions without proper facilitation can be counterproductive. People who like to hear the sounds of their own voices may never stop talking, and those who would rather sit in silence will find it easy to do so — even though they may have a really valuable point of view that could better inform the decision-making process.

Before your meeting gets underway in earnest, determine how you want people to participate and then communicate your plan at the beginning of the meeting.

Explaining how to get in conversation queue

As discussed in Chapter 6, there are significant cultural differences related to conversational silence. In certain Eastern cultures, there is not just a tolerance of silence but an expectation of silence of more than eight seconds. In most Western cultures, people get uncomfortable with a pause in the verbal action within two seconds and will quickly try to fill it.

This is just one example of why it is important to establish how meeting participants can get into the conversation queue. If the invite list was carefully curated, all attendees are there to provide valuable input. You want to make it crystal clear how they can do so, but that varies based on your meeting format.

WHEN IN PERSON

It is relatively easy to read the room when you are in person for a meeting. If you are an adept facilitator, you will know to look for nonverbal signs that someone has something to say. Maybe they are leaning forward in their seat or they are purposely making strong eye contact with you to signal that they would like a chance to speak next. If all of the participants are respectful of each other and aren't chronic interrupters, you may be able to get away with not having an overly formal way of engaging in conversation. They may have established their own rhythm of listening and speaking up only after someone finishes their thought.

This is ideal but often not practical due to the variety of personalities that populate most teams. You will have some extroverts who are quick to offer their insights and some introverts who are not. As a meeting leader, you have to figure out how to let everyone have some airtime.

The most common and traditional way of getting into the conversation queue when in person is to have people raise their hands. Most of us had plenty of practice doing so in school. Raising your hand may seem a little juvenile but it does keep people from cutting each other off.

If you would like a more creative solution, consider using a talking stick. Joe has seen some of his clients implement it, and it added some uniformity and uniqueness to the proceedings.

Whatever system you come up with, make sure your people adhere to it. There's nothing more annoying than seeing a rule be established and then completely ignored without repercussion. If someone tries to interrupt someone else, gently remind them of how they can enter the conversation and make them wait their turn.

WHEN VIRTUAL

A virtual meeting will be a mess if you don't have some guidelines for participation that are outlined at the beginning of the session. Often, you'll see meeting leaders start with "a little housekeeping," which usually includes expectations for attendee interactions.

Due to the limitations of the technology, you simply can't have people speaking over each other. You will end up with half sentences and no real flow to the conversation. Instead, let people know you'd like to hear from everyone and give them the ways they can make it known that they have something to say. Maybe you tell people to raise their physical hands or their emoji hands if they have a comment or question. You can make it your responsibility to be on the lookout for the digital or real raised hands and call on them one at a time. A better option might be to call upon someone else in the meeting to be a moderator for you — someone who can make you aware that a hand has been raised, which can be easy to miss if you focus on listening and leading the dialogue.

While we encourage you to give people voice opportunities (a chance for attendees to speak up) we also suggest you use the nonverbal tools of the platform to broaden participation. Let attendees know that they can also put their comments or questions in chat in addition to raising their hands. Then it's up to you to make sure what is in text form becomes part of the verbal discourse. This is another place where it helps to spread the responsibility throughout the team. Ask one of the attendees to be your chat monitor. Their job is to keep an eye on what is appearing on the text thread and letting you know if there are any comments or questions that should be incorporated into the discussion.

TIP

The ability to use nonverbal forms of participation is actually a significant benefit of meeting virtually. It presents another avenue for input that can feel less intimidating for some who are leery of speaking up on a group setting.

WHEN HYBRID

Hybrid meetings are more complex when it comes to how people can get into the conversation queue. Given all the different ways attendees are joining the meeting, you need to explain the rules of engagement for those who are in-person and for those who are remote — while ensuring that one group doesn't have easier access to the floor than the other group.

As discussed in Chapter 9, following a turn-taking policy is really crucial in a hybrid meeting because of the inherent risks of participation inequality. It's easy to imagine those in the physical meeting room steamrollering in the meeting and having a rollicking good time while the remote attendees feel like they are on the outside looking in at a really fun gathering that they aren't a part of.

Let your participants know from the start that you want everyone to have equal opportunity to let their voices be heard. Make it clear to the in-room attendees that they can't just wait for their colleague beside them to stop talking and jump right in. They need to let you, the leader, guide the conversation purposely by calling on people by name. By the same token, let the remote attendees know it is their responsibility to be active participants too. They need to raise their hands, the real ones or digital ones, to let you know they have something to say. As with a purely virtual meeting, you also want to let everyone know that chat is a viable way to insert themselves in the conversation queue.

Activating participation

The interesting thing about participation is that it doesn't just happen on its own. In the years Joe's been teaching large lecture classes, there's often a diffusion of responsibility that occurs in larger groups. That is, everyone assumes that everyone else will participate, so why should they, as an individual, participate at all. Because of this, Joe often has to *activate participation*. Instead of just hoping that the students will respond and when the awkward silence becomes uncomfortable, just answer the question, Joe takes a different approach. He waits longer.

Essentially, people in Western cultures don't like silence. Because of that, they feel the need to fill the silence, even when it's not necessary. That urge to fill the silence is real. But, Joe just ignores it. He waits for the silence to get uncomfortable and then he waits another 30 seconds or even longer. Eventually, it becomes so uncomfortable for folks that they chime in.

In other words, Joe uses his knowledge of human nature to activate participation in the classroom. Silence is a powerful tool to motivate folks. After a couple times of waiting, the students get the idea and never again does Joe have to wait for responses. They freely flow from the students. You can do the same and should do the same with your meetings.

However, it doesn't have to be silence. You can activate participation in other ways. As we discuss in Chapter 9, you can call on people by name or remind them that the chat works. You can even put names next to agenda items, so people know that they will kick off that part of the conversation.

Don't leave participation to chance. Decide how you plan to activate participation among your attendees, and do it. The meeting will be manyfold better because of it. But, once again, what you do might differ by meeting format.

WHEN IN PERSON

In person, silence works pretty well as a facilitator of participation. However, people in a work group might take it the wrong way. It's great with a teacher-student relationship, but not so much for peers.

With that in mind, we recommend two potential approaches;

>> You could just establish the ground rule that you will call on people. Let everyone know that you are going to do that and follow through accordingly.

>> You can, either alternatively or in addition to, use the agenda as a mechanism to activate participation. Put a name next to each agenda item and ask that person to kick off the conversation. That takes the pressure off of you to facilitate every item and it gets another person engaged.

We've found that once a person is activated, they stay active in terms of participation. In less science-y terms, once you get people to speak up, they will typically speak up for the duration of the meeting.

TIP

One technique that Karin often uses when conducting training in person is to move closer to someone who appears to be a bit mentally checked out. If she sees someone on their phone during a workshop, she adjusts her position in the room, so she is standing right in front of them. The mere closeness of her presence causes them to re-engage, perhaps even sheepishly look up from their phone.

WHEN VIRTUAL

Interestingly, what we recommend you do in person actually works well virtually too. This confirms, once again, what we've already said. Most best practices for face-to-face meetings apply to virtual and hybrid meetings with perhaps a little nuance thrown in.

In a virtual meeting, try calling on people by name, provided you set the expectation that you will do so and have established that it's perfectly okay to say "pass." You also can assign agenda items to different people, so they know in advance that they'll be leading the discussion on that particular topic.

But, in virtual meetings, you have one more tool in your toolchest. Most virtual platforms have chat. Lean into it. Embrace it as a legitimate form of participation. And activate it.

By activate it, we mean that you, as a meeting leader, should let people know the chat function can be and should be used. Try saying something like, "Please feel to throw questions and comments in chat and I'll make sure to keep an eye on what's coming in." But if you set this expectation, they will expect you to check it. Don't disappoint them. One sure way to turn off participation in chat is to make it simply a parking lot for comments that are never brought into the verbal conversation.

Sometimes participation on chat requires an extra nudge. One way you can do that is to kick off your meeting with a low stakes question that you ask them to answer on chat. A popular one during the pandemic when so many people were working from home was "describe your footwear." The answers ranged from "Fuzzy bunny slippers" to "Shoes? Who wears shoes anymore?"

TIP

Granted, trying to keep track of what is being said out loud and what is being written in chat can be a lot for a meeting leader to manage. In cases where the meeting is larger than a few people, you may find it helpful to assign a chat monitor who can make you aware when someone has a comment or question to add to the dialogue. It allows you to facilitate the discussion but not ignore the nonverbal input. You can give the chat monitor free license to interrupt you if the meeting is more informal or there's a burning question that needs to be asked in the moment, or you can clarify that you plan to stop periodically to address whatever comments or questions have come in through chat. Your chat monitor can then guide you through what needs to be elevated to the group discussion. If your chat is active, you may have a hard time finding that one pertinent insight in the text thread because it is embedded in basic team banter. Your chat monitor can help weed out what really needs to be addressed . . . and allow you to ignore the smiley face emojis or gifs that may have been added for entertainment purposes.

WHEN HYBRID

In hybrid meetings you have it all. The good and the bad. And that includes the means by which people participate. You have hands being physically and electronically raised. You have digital chats and you have side chats. You have people eager to participate and those who turn off their camera and disappear (literally).

Our advice here is to do "all of the above" to activate participation:

>> Call on people by name

>> Put people on the agenda

>> Lean into chat

>> Assign a chat monitor

Doing all of these things ensures that participation is activated and not just assumed or passively encouraged.

REMEMBER

If you are leading a hybrid meeting from a virtual position, you will need to elicit the services of your in-room helper (as described earlier in this chapter). They will play an important role in activating participation from the in-person cohort because you won't be able to read the room as easily as you would if you were sharing the same space. Let your in-room helper be your eyes and ears. Depending upon your conference room camera setup, you may miss seeing someone's hand being raised. Encourage your de facto in-room moderator to speak up by saying something like, "Allison has her hand raised." You can then give Allison the floor.

Chapter **11**

Managing the Conversation Flow

There he goes again! You put your head in your hands and know you have five to ten minutes before you'll need to wake up and say anything more. You really like this guy. He does good work. In fact, he's been with the company for longer than just about everyone on the team put together. He has institutional knowledge that goes back forever and is often extremely helpful in that manner. You would consider him an important colleague and a friend. However, he is . . . a monologuer.

If you're thinking, "What's that?" allow us to explain. A *monologuer* is a person who likes to go off on a topic during meetings. Perhaps they have a favorite topic that they like to talk about. Perhaps, like the person just described, they know the history of every activity or project the organization has performed and likes to tell stories about them. Perhaps they just take a while to articulate their point, which many could make in a few statements. The point is, they like to talk. Maybe they feel like it's their duty to share what they are sure are critical insights or perhaps they just like the sound of their own voices. Whatever the reason, they can derail a meeting simply by doing just that . . . talking . . . a lot.

You've been in meetings like this. A monologuer goes off and before you know it, you're running out of time. There's no way you'll complete what's on the agenda now. Their pattern of behavior might make you afraid to even schedule a meeting with this person on the invite list because you feel like it's a hopeless cause. If you include them in the meeting, you know you'll never get done what needs to get done.

REMEMBER

Fear not! You are in control of this meeting, and it's in your power to keep it on track. In fact, you may already be demonstrating these conversation control techniques now. The key is using them more frequently and to greater effect, so your meeting doesn't even have a chance to go too far off the rails.

In this chapter, we share ideas, recommendations, and science-based instructions on how to manage the conversation flow of your meetings. We provide you with powerful phrases you can use word-for-word to block problematic communicators on your team. We also introduce some strategies to help you move the dialogue along and then give you guidelines for how to bring the meeting to a moment of decision-making.

Ready to learn? Let's go!

Keeping the Meeting on Track

Although we described how a meeting can be pulled off track, we want to spend much more time discussing how to keep the meeting on track. After all, you've worked hard up to this point to define the purpose and goal of your meeting. You may have an agenda chock full of important topics for discussion. You need to keep things on track so that all the aims of the meeting are actually accomplished.

TIP

Remember your meeting goal is your guidepost. Always be pushing towards your purpose and move the conversation towards that end. This isn't to say that conversations about topics peripheral to the main purpose of the meeting are bad or wrong. However, when they become excessive, they change the meeting dynamic sufficiently enough to derail the meeting altogether. (For more on meeting goals, see Chapter 8.)

One of the biggest culprits for this can come in the form of a story. Recently, Joe was in a meeting with some colleagues discussing next steps in a project. A final report was about to be created and the goal of the meeting was to review the data, see what was most important, and outline the final report. However, a few minutes into the meeting, the group was talking about executive summaries, and a colleague said, "Oh, that reminds me of a story" and then they launched into a ten-minute recitation of an experience they had with a badly assembled executive summary.

Notice that this was not wholly off topic. However, for a 30-minute meeting, this took one-third of the total time. The story was instructive and humorous, but it put the main goal of the meeting at serious risk of failing. The team needed instructions on all the report components, not just executive summaries.

So, what should Joe have done instead of let the ten-minute story happen? Politely interject by pulling the rest of the group into the agenda. The key here is *politely*, and it's often all about timing. It's much harder to cut someone off once they've started weaving their tale. You have to head them off at the pass. Before the story gets going, you compliment them for their use of illustrative stories and remind them of the limited time. Usually that's all it takes to either shut the story down entirely, or more likely, get the five minute version instead of the ten-minute one.

Sticking to the agenda

Let's suppose you prepared an agenda for your meeting. And, let's suppose you followed these agenda usage steps as outlined more fully in Chapter 9:

>> Build the agenda related to the overall purpose.

>> Share the agenda with potential attendees ahead of the meeting.

>> Incorporate feedback and curate the attendee list. (For example, let Bob out of the meeting because nothing on the agenda needs his input.)

>> Share the final agenda with ample time for meeting preparation.

Assuming you did all these things, why on earth would you not stick to your agenda? That's right, one of the more frustrating things that Joe's observed in his research is the abandonment of a well-thought-out agenda. It happens on a fairly regular basis but it's even more painful when meeting leaders have invested the time and energy into doing all of the steps just mentioned . . . and then they practically ignore the agenda once the meeting gets underway.

You'll find there are many reasons why the agenda gets abandoned. Sometimes meetings have an unclear meeting leader. In a recent strategy session, Joe prepared a comprehensive agenda, shared it ahead of time, got feedback, updated the final agenda and was prepared to stick to it. (In other words, Joe tries to practice what he preaches, as does Karin.) However, even our best and well-informed intentions fall victim to circumstances that are beyond our control.

Case in point — Joe's strategy session. As the meeting began, another leader, one with more authority, decided to declare what they wanted to focus on, an item that was in no way, shape, or form on the agenda. Joe knew he needed to defer to the more senior leader, and could only stand by to watch a big chunk of his meeting time be eaten up by something that was not even supposed to be discussed. Even more disappointing? The majority of the time was taken up by a monologue by someone the leader engaged and let loose. Joe returned to the curated agenda as quickly as he could, but he lost 15 minutes of precious meeting time in the process.

REMEMBER

You put the effort into building the agenda or identifying the purpose — so stick to it! Don't let boneheaded attendee's butt in with their personal agendas. Even when they are the leader.

You might be thinking, but we don't want Joe to get in trouble by interrupting his indirect boss! We appreciate your concern and the sentiment. So, what should've happened?

The best way to ensure that you stick to the agenda is to establish the expectation that the meeting must follow it. You have several opportunities to make that clear:

>> When you first send out the agenda and ask for feedback.

>> When you send out the amended agenda.

>> Right at the beginning of the meeting itself.

TIP

Use these magic words, "We plan to cover only the things on the agenda." If someone dares to depart from the agenda, remind them of the stated plan. Make it plain. Make it clear. Make it normal to stick to the agenda. To do so, you'll have to use pre-meeting communication (see Chapter 9) to set that expectation and then you have to demonstrate what you mean by sticking to the agenda. Do that a few times, and you'll get a reputation for staying on task in your meetings. And that's a good thing!

Monitoring time spent on each topic

One of the more common tips in books on running meetings is to set time stamps on the agenda. A *time stamp* means that for each item on the agenda, you predetermine how much time the group will spend on the topic. This is generally a good practice to do, and we recommend it for many more formal meetings, particularly when many of the items are less discussion-oriented and more informational with Q&A.

However, for most meetings, where discussion is expected, and collaboration is required, setting specific time stamps and putting them on the agenda can inadvertently shut down conversation prematurely.

Here's where we mean.

When people are deep into a discussion, there is both discussing and thinking going on. The best deep discussions include a bit of silence where everyone is considering the issues at hand. This can be uncomfortable for extroverted folks who prefer to fill in the pause with more discussion. What typically occurs is the extroverted attendees will continue to discuss while the more introverted folks will think. Then, what tends to happen is that really good ideas can come out of the deep thinking that is occurring, but they will only surface if you create an opening for comments.

WARNING

This is where time stamps on the agenda can create an artificial barrier to good ideas. Imagine this scenario: Your team has been deeply engaged on discussing a path forward for a new product. The conversation has been dynamic and constant with very little dead air. One less verbose team member has been silently taking it all in and then . . . eureka! . . . has an idea that truly could be a game changer, but when they look at the agenda and consult their watch, they realize they are already over the time allotted. Instead of sharing their idea, they self-select out of commenting out of deference for the time stamps. Consider this a cautionary tale.

TIP

While it is valuable for you, the leader, to have time stamps on your agenda, you may want to keep them to yourself, especially if the meeting purpose is oriented towards creativity and innovation. You don't want to artificially stifle that by shutting down idea momentum with a time barrier that isn't imperative.

This is not to say that you shouldn't ever put time stamps on the official agenda. Some meetings would benefit from that. But, even if the time stamps aren't shared to the group, you, the meeting leader should always either have written time stamps or at least some idea of how long you think each agenda item should take. Knowing this serves two purposes:

>> First, it hopefully allows you to schedule the right length for your meeting in the first place.

>> Second, it helps you to drive the conversation at a speed that will allow you to get to your destination within the planned time.

Monitor the time spent on a topic and if you feel it's going longer than needed, it probably is. Make the transition to the next topic.

Using Communication Strategies to Drive Productive Dialogue

In the previous section of this chapter, we talked about intervening and driving the discussion forward. Stopping the monologuer. Pulling people back to the topic, when the story-teller wants to tell a story. We've suggested doing so politely and in a goal-oriented way. And, although that's nice, we didn't really tell you how — what words to use or even just what kind of phrases to deploy to make it those transitions, and in a way that leaves no offense.

WARNING

As you may know, this is harder than it looks. Too often we make what ought to be a benign statement. We pull people back to the topic. Then, later, we find out we've deeply offended someone because we cut them off or we made them feel as though their ideas were not important. That wasn't the intent at all, but it happens. Check out Joe's experience in the nearby sidebar.

Understanding procedural communication

Everyone in a meeting wants to be seen and heard but it won't happen without employing communication strategies that allow that to happen. One tool to add to your toolbox is what is called procedural communication.

MONOLOGUING WITH GOOD INTENTION

A number of years ago, Joe was in graduate school class with his peers. He liked to engage in the dialogue and the topic that week was particularly interesting to him: group collaboration. As the class went on, he asked lots of questions, made many comments, and took lots of notes. It was one of the best class session he'd had to date.

What he didn't realize, and was informed of later, is that it came at the expense of his peers. Unaware of his behavior, he cut people off, he spoke over people, and he generally upset everyone in the room, except maybe the instructor.

This experience never left Joe and actually inspired him to follow a career path. A few years after that classroom experience, he had the opportunity to study meetings to understand what kinds of communication are effective and what are not. In other words, he decided to study the thing that, at least on that occasion (and probably others), he was terrible at: facilitating an effective, collaborative, and inclusive meeting.

What is procedural communication? Great question. It was the question that drove Joe to work with his favorite scientific partner, Dr. Nale Lehmmann-Willenbrock. Her work on interaction dynamics in meetings is unparalleled, and, one of their first studies focused on procedural communication, what it is and what it does in meetings.

Procedural communication is defined as verbal behaviors that structure group discussion to facilitate goal accomplishment. In other words, it's the things we say in meetings to keep things on track, to move the discussion forward, to eliminate bad behaviors, and to get us to our goal in a timely manner.

Here are a few examples of procedural communication:

» Clarifying statements ("What did you mean when you said that?")

» Asking a procedural question ("What are we talking about next?")

» Prioritizing statements ("I think we should do this first and that last.")

» Time management statements ("We need to move on to our next item on the agenda.")

We use these kinds of statement all the time in meetings. They are more common among meeting leaders, but attendees can use them as well to great effect.

TECHNICAL STUFF

In 2013, Joe and Nale published a study focused on the consequences of procedural communication in team meetings. This study showed that after procedural statements, people tended to engage in more proactive communication. For example, they would start talking about how they support the idea being discussed, or they might help identify who will do what and when. In other words, they take the hint and try to make things move forward as they should.

The study also showed that procedural statements greatly inhibit dysfunctional meeting behaviors. For example, few people lost their train of thought, or criticized others, or started complaining. Maybe you have a complainer on your team and they often derail the team. It's often not because they complain, but rather their complaints are legitimized by team members and so they go on, and on about it. Procedural statements can stop that from happening.

Engage in procedural statements to keep things moving right along towards your goals and to reduce the bad behaviors that make meetings tough to endure. Here's a list of a few different procedural statements for you to consider using. We bet you've used some or all of these before:

>> "Thank you! Our next topic is. . ."

>> "What I think Joe is trying to say is. . ."

>> "The next thing on the agenda is. . ."

>> "Great thoughts! I think we should do this first and that second."

>> "I think we've gone a bit astray. What about. . ."

>> To keep us within time, we need to transition to our next discussion item."

>> "We need to wrap up so we have time to recover and get to our next task."

>> "That's an important thing to address but it deserves a longer discussion than what we can do here. Let's set up a different time to talk about it."

Making the right statements

Now that we've given you some specific phrases that you can use (see the previous section), you might be eager to give them a test run, but you need to make sure you are choosing the right ones for the right time.

When engaging in procedural communication, you need to match your statement with what you're trying to do because the same statement doesn't work for every situation. If you're running out of time, you might say something like, "We're getting close on time, so let's tackle this last discussion item." It wouldn't make sense to say, "Great thought, Karin. Joe, do you have any input on this?" While that procedural statement might help you to politely turn off a monologuer, you are inviting even more discussion when you are already in danger of running over time.

Let the situation determine the kind of procedural communication you use. Don't use a time management statement when what you really need to do is clarify the meaning of something that was just said. Match your statement with the situation and then deliver it in a way that will be well received.

Let's illustrate the point. Suppose you are in a meeting discussing a very complex solution to a production issue at a printing factory. The engineers are using some typical jargon to describe it, but the line manager who manages the people, not the machines, is clearly lost. You can see it on their face and they are about to transition to some classic multitasking. ("Oh look, my phone is in my pocket, I should look at that rather than listen to the engineers go on and on and on and on.")

Time to intervene. But what do you do? Simple, you ask a clarifying question. You may not need the clarification yourself. You may already be familiar with the jargon, but you read the room. You see that clarification is needed, and you help it happen.

Regardless of the meeting format, if you suspect confusion, clarify. Or ask whomever was talking to clarify. This is just one example of different types of procedural communication. Use these statements wisely and towards the goals of your meeting.

Transitioning between topics

Agenda items don't happen in a vacuum. They either are preceded or followed up by another topic. However, navigating from one item to the next can be tricky and is often where teams get stuck.

You've probably experienced it yourself in team meetings that you've been a part of. Maybe there's been enthusiastic discussion of a topic from every angle imaginable. Perhaps there's even a list of action items as a result, but now everyone is starting to talk in circles and they aren't sure how to proceed. In fact, some members of the team have even looked at the meeting leader in hopes that that will prompt them to move things along to the next agenda item. No such luck. The dialogue continues to peter out but there's no move to move along. Awkward!

As a meeting leader, don't wait for it to get awkward. Listen. Engage. And when a decision is made, either by you if you're the decision maker, or by whomever that is, that's your big cue to transition.

Another obvious sign that it's time to transition? Repetition in the conversation. Let's say the dialogue is generating a ton of different ideas, solutions, challenges to solutions, and elaboration of the problem. By all means, keep that conversation going. However, as soon as things start to get repetitive, figure out a way to gracefully close the discussion down and open up a new one focusing on what comes next. Sometimes that might be decision time. Sometimes it's the next item on the agenda. Either way, the key here is to be prepared to enable the transition. It won't happen without your help.

So, how do you do it? Well, if a decision has been made, the transition is easy to do. Just say something like, "Great! Everyone okay with that direction? [Nods, yeps, etc.] Good! The next topic on the agenda is. . ."

You can adjust the language and make it your own. One thing that you may want to include is a summarizing statement to make sure everyone heard and understood the decision. But, regardless, something like that statement would do the trick.

But, what if no decision is made and repetitive talk continues, or more likely, complaining or other dysfunctional behavior starts occurring? That's when a different approach needs to be taken.

WARNING

Transitioning between topics before people feel like the topic has been exhausted can step on toes. Be judicious in how you approach this. Listen closely to be sure the topic has run its course. Be prepared to adjust and give more time if someone has something more to say. In fact, if you actually voice your plan to extend the discussion time, that is actually a good thing because your procedural communication still moved things forward, just not to the next topic.

With that warning in mind, consider saying something like, "I feel like we're getting a bit repetitive in our conversation here. Do we have a decision?"

If no decision is needed or the group is far from one, something like this may be more appropriate, "It sounds like we have more to say on this, but we are running a bit over on time for this discussion. Let's table this until the next meeting and transition to our next topic."

The only problem with that approach is when the next topic of discussion is dependent upon a decision on the previous one. That's when you have to use a different kind of procedural communication, a proactive statement which would be designed to push the group towards a decision. How that unfolds is determined by who has decision-making authority and the group dynamics. We address that more in the final section of this chapter.

TIP

Not all agenda items are independent. Sometimes, they are inter-related and dependent upon each other. Look for those dependencies in your agenda and recognize any potential breakdowns that can occur if one agenda item isn't addressed and resolved. When you encounter those items during those meeting, gear your procedural communication towards driving decisions and goal accomplishment.

Driving Discussion

Too often, you'll hear *meeting practitioners* (management consultants who advise people on how to run meetings effectively) suggest letting the discussion happen. Not getting in the way of the ideas as they flow. Making sure you are a facilitator who lets people participate rather than keep people from participating. Of all the advice just offered, only that last statement is correct.

If you just "let the conversation flow," you will end up having a lot of unrelated content or no content at all in your discussions. Let us illustrate.

As a meeting scientist, Joe can't help himself from trying out some of his ideas with unsuspecting colleagues (shhh . . . don't tell them). On one of these occasions, he followed best practices. He prepared an agenda, shared it ahead of time, and then started the meeting off as normal. However, when the group got to the discussion items section, instead of driving discussion, Joe just "let it happen." He introduced the topic and said, "What do you all think?" Here's how it played out:

>> The extroverted colleagues chimed in immediately, some even talking over the others.

>> The introverted colleagues were attentive to their extroverted friends, but remained quiet.

>> Of the seven people on the team, three people talked. Four people said nothing.

>> No one asked the silent people to chime in.

>> Ultimately, no decision was made because Joe didn't engage in procedural communication to ensure that. Instead, Joe just jumped to the next topic.

Now, one colleague knew something was up and said, "Joe, you feeling okay?" At that point, he came clean and let them in on his little experiment. His hands-off approach provided a valuable lesson about driving discussion and the importance of active facilitation. The discussion of this particular item was supposed to lead to a decision, but no decision was ever made because no one guided the process towards that goal. And if a decision was made, it would have been based on input from less than half of the people present. They all had valuable insights to share. That's why they were invited in the first place, but without proactive facilitation, more than half of them opted out of speaking up.

TIP

Don't let the discussion drive itself. It'll likely either run out of gas or run into a ditch without your guidance. Remain in the drivers' seat of the discussion and empower participation among all meeting attendees. Don't "let it happen." Make it happen.

A quick caveat here: there's nothing wrong with starting with a statement such as "What do you think?" when kicking off a discussion. But, you have to do the next three things as well:

>> Call on folks who did not talk by name.

>> Clarify any statements that were not clear by asking clarifying questions.

>> Add your own input to the conversation as an active participation, not just as a moderator.

If you don't do those three things, you run a risk of making a decision that's based on lopsided input. Those who have strong feelings about the topic or who are extroverted or who are in-person (rather than remote) will have a disproportionate impact on the decisions that are made. Everyone needs and should have a voice. Give them the opportunity to express it. (See Chapter 12.)

Some people will be upset if you call them by name. Set a ground rule in your meetings that you'll be asking everyone to participate. Calling people by name becomes absolutely essential in virtual and hybrid meetings. People will get used to it, once you establish it as a norm (see Chapter 9 for more on this).

Listen actively

You may already know the outward manifestation of what is known as *active listening* (where you make an intentional effort to hear, digest, and comprehend what is being said). Here are a few hallmarks of active listening:

>> Look people in the eye.

>> Nod when you agree.

>> Use audible confirmations that you are listening such as "yeah" and "mhm."

However, sometimes these active listening signals can be misinterpreted, especially if you only do these behaviors or do them too much. Someone who says "mhm" all the time may just be passively half-listening at best, but those quick audibles allow them to feign interest.

Active listening signals can also be minimized when a meeting involves remote attendees. Good meeting etiquette calls for you to mute yourself if you are not constantly engaging in conversation. However, you may also be muting those audible confirmations that encourage people to continue speaking. That's why those head nods, visual manifestations of active listening, are even more important when you are a remote attendee. They fill in the audio gap created by the mute button.

TIP

Another way to demonstrate you are actively listening is by taking notes. In a face-to-face meeting, this action can easily be seen and everyone knows that you are following along. In a virtual meeting, it's a little harder to detect. In fact, if you are looking down at your notepad and away from the camera, note-taking can be misconstrued as you not paying attention. Let your conversation partner or partners know you are capturing their thoughts and ideas on paper which is why you aren't looking at the screen. In fact, if you give them the heads up that you are taking notes, they might even slow down, enabling you to get the true essence of their comments.

Paraphrasing comments and repeating questions

Another way to demonstrate active listening is paraphrasing comments and repeating questions. These are two separate kinds of procedural communication that are often paired, and that's a good thing.

When you *paraphrase* someone else's comments, you are confirming that you understand them. It gives the person a chance to chime in to clarify and to gauge how well they've transferred their message as well. In fact, you might even consider starting such a paraphrase with "Let me make sure I understand you. What you are saying is. . . ." That cues them to know that you are trying to get on the same page with them, and they will likely try to help you do just that.

Paraphrasing comments has also become a common practice in virtual and hybrid meetings. Sometimes this is a good thing and sometimes it's not. It's a good thing when you are paraphrasing as an indication that you were listening and want to understand. It's a bad thing when paraphrasing is used to catch-up someone who was clearly multi-tasking.

We've all heard it before.

> Karin: "Hey Joe, what do you think?"
>
> (Big pause as Joe looks up, presumably mid-text, from his lap where his phone was assuredly residing.)
>
> Joe: "Oh, sorry, you were breaking up. Can you repeat what the question was?"
>
> Karin is kind enough to bring Joe up to speed, and for at least a minute, Joe is kind enough to stop multi-tasking and focus on the meeting he's "just sort of" attending.

REMEMBER

Whether it's seeking common understanding or pulling someone back into focus, paraphrasing is a handy tool, even though the latter use is annoying for the meeting leader who is merely asking for attendees to actually pay attention. Strongly discourage multi-tasking among your meeting attendees. It slows down the meeting and makes it harder to achieve the aims of the meeting in the first place.

Another useful technique related to paraphrasing is the repeating of questions. Again, this can be good and bad. It's good to repeat a question when you are fully engaged, have been listening, and are just making sure you understand what they are asking. It's bad when you have not been fully engaged and are unaware of the premise of the question. The question repeat is just a way for them to catch you up.

Whatever the reason for the paraphrase or question repeat, these forms of procedural communication do have value. They help to bring everyone back into the conversation. In other words, they driving the discussion forward.

Probing for deeper dialogue

If you want to generate a creative solution, you need to spend a lot of time defining the problem, but too often, we rush to a find a solution without figuring out the nature of the problem in the first place. Sometimes we like to apply a solution to that problem before we even know what the consequences are of that given solution. As a meeting leader, your job is to identify a situation that warrants a closer look and then push your people to dig a little deeper.

REMEMBER

Creative problem solving takes an investment of time. If you put in the time, you can spark solutions that are of innovative and of high quality. If you rush the process, you will reap what you sow — a suboptimal solution that may or may not work well.

While we've focused a lot on moving the conversation along, you don't want to do so at the expense of the best outcome or missed insights. In certain circumstances, like the one we just mentioned, probing for deeper discussion is not only warranted but advised.

Sometimes you need to take a diagnostic approach to a meeting — like a medical doctor does when trying to find the root cause of a patient's illness. The physician might be able to easily identify the symptoms and even pinpoint the affliction, but discovering what caused the illness usually requires more digging. In the case of a serious illness, doctors want to know not just the what but the why. Figuring that out can mean more tests, probing (literally) and deeper dialogue with the patient. That sustained inquiry, though, is what allows them to find the answer to the question that can best inform their course of action — why is this person sick?

TIP

In meetings, thankfully, there is minimal *physical* probing required but *verbal* probing is advisable for uncovering root causes of issues that demand a resolution. With that in mind, we strongly suggest the following method of probing:

» Begin by describing the problem that led to the discussion.

» Ask questions to get additional information.

» Clarify the meaning of people's comments so everyone understands what is being said.

» Don't settle for the first solution. Ask for alternatives, even if you land on the first solution in the end.

» If the problem is complex, keep asking questions until you get to the root cause(s).

All of these steps and suggestions are designed to help you come to the right decision. They also take time. That's right, the meeting might take a bit longer, but that's okay if that extra time helps you uncover the real problem that needs to be addressed and leads to a better solution. If that's the case, plan accordingly. Don't assume that a problem can and should be solved in a 30-minute meeting. It's okay if you have to discuss things a few times to get to the right answer.

TIP

Probe deeper by ensuring everyone has an opportunity to share their ideas, their opinions, their potential solutions to problems, and so on. Doing so enables the potential for creativity in your team. Failing to do so can be catastrophic.

Managing a Brainstorming Session

One of the primary purposes of meetings is to brainstorm ideas or solutions. There are entire books and a whole ton of research on the topic of brainstorming, including how to do it along with tricks and tips for including everyone in the task. We're not going to address all of the options that you have at your disposal. Instead, we focus on helping you understand the main purpose of brainstorming and how your approach to a brainstorming changes based on the modality of the meeting.

Let's start with why you want to conduct a brainstorming session. The main purpose of *brainstorming* is to gather ideas around a specific task, initiative, or project. The topic can be weighty . . . or not so much. You could conduct a brainstorming session on potential solutions to a problem that's been plaguing your organization. You could conduct a session on what colors to use for painting an office. The sky's the limit when it comes to the topic of the brainstorm. But the purpose is always the same: Give me your ideas, as many as you can muster, as quickly as you can, so we can pick the right one.

TIP

When doing a brainstorming session, make sure you describe your goal to your team and ensure they feel secure in sharing any and all ideas. Too often people self-censure really good ideas. They do so because maybe they are off the wall, out of the box, or some other cliché that describes ideas that seem a bit weird or potentially weird. Weird is good! Weird can sometimes generate the most effective and creative solution. Be weird!

REMEMBER

Research confirms if you want a large number of ideas, it's better to give everyone a few minutes to brainstorm on their own before then sharing all their ideas together. It's more effective to unlock the potential of everyone's ideas first and then bring them together for elaboration and evaluation.

When in person

It's fairly easy to communicate your openness to weird ideas that have potential for success when meeting in person. You can just tell them. You can look them in the eye and tell them: "No idea is weird. Bring them on!"

In-person meetings also fit the mold of old-school brainstorming. You can buy a million sticky notes and let people write down every solution that comes to mind. You can then sort them based upon common themes and physically manipulate the idea notes into a certain hierarchy that flexes as the discussion progresses. Brainstorming sessions like this often get high marks because they involve active engagement by everyone who has access to the post-it note pad and a marker. Sometimes, old-fashioned, non-technical approaches are the way to go.

TIP

If you are able to be in person, it's really okay and actually quite effective to take the old-school approach. However, make sure you assign a scribe (or several) to record what is plastered all over the wall and then convert it into electronic form for sharing and developing the ideas further.

When virtual

Virtual brainstorming sessions are made possible through technology tools that seek to mirror the in-person version as much as possible. Barring a discussion of specific tech options out there, suffice it to say, there are plenty at your disposal whether they're virtual whiteboards built into the platform or software canvases with digital sticky notes and such that can effectively integrate with whatever platform you use.

Sometimes, it's as simple as having everyone open online document applications that allow multiple people to add content at the same time. Coauthoring in real-time can emulate the in-person experience even though it might feel less organic or free flowing.

If you want to know the latest and greatest tools out there, trying doing an online search using the keywords "virtual collaboration software."

Many of these software tools allow for both the generation of ideas and the voting on ideas. That's sort of what you do when you start grouping ideas together with the sticky notes in person. In the virtual world, you vote ideas up or down. Those that receive the most votes may get further attention.

A word of caution! Just because something gets a lot of votes, doesn't mean it's a great solution. For example, in a simulated brainstorming session about how to improve package delivery time for a large retailer, one of the ideas suggested is giving all the delivery people jet packs. It got the most votes out of all the ideas. However, the technology is not readily available to the masses, and it's certainly impractical. But, it sure does sound fun. And if you ask a bunch of delivery people for ideas on how to make delivering packages more effective, you'll get things like this.

Here's the bottom line: Even though you can generate a ton of ideas using software tools in a virtual setting, it is still important to evaluate the ideas on both their feasibility and creativity. (In fact, this applies to all modalities.)

When hybrid

Big surprise for you here: Hybrid lands somewhere in-between. Technically, you could use the old-school way for the in-person folks, but you run the risk of marginalizing the remote attendees who can't participate as fully in that kind of location-dependent exercise. You could try to bring them into the activity by transcribing the ideas on the sticky notes onto an online interface for the remote folks, but that sounds like a ton of extra work.

Our best advice is to lean towards the option that is most inclusive and that means software tools that are equally accessible to the remote and in-person attendees. That's the only way to create an equitable environment where everyone can take part in the brainstorming generation.

You also need to be aware of a potential pitfall that can occur in a hybrid brainstorming session — a two tiered set of results. That is, you get independent responses from all the remote folks and interdependent responses from all the in-person folks. How does that happen? Well, the in-person people talk to each other and generate similar ideas, often using just one person who serves as a scribe and writes down all of the ideas for the group. Meanwhile the remote people generate their own separate ideas and submit them individually. While there may be value in incorporating both options (collaborative idea generation and independent idea generation) there is a potential problem that could crop up. If you do it during a hybrid meeting, you can get a coalition of in-person people voting for their own ideas, dismissing the ideas submitted by their remote colleagues and creating a messed up and biased set of results.

So a word to the wise meeting leader: Make sure you try to keep the idea generation process as equitable as possible by using inclusive brainstorming software for all parties.

Leading Discussion Until Moment of Decision

When you lead a discussion, there comes a moment when a decision needs to be made. If you've led a lot of meetings, you probably can feel when that moment arrives. Sometimes it's obvious. People stop talking and look at you for the decision.

Sometimes it's less obvious. You're running out of time in the meeting, and people need a decision to move forward. Either way, it's time to decide and it's up to you to make it happen.

TIP

Lead the discussion all the way to the moment of decision and then stop. Don't go beyond that point or you risk undercutting the process.

If you lead past the moment of decision, it makes you appear indecisive. If a decision has been made, stick with it and determine next steps. If you appear to waffle or circle back after the decision has been made, you are opening up the door to those who may question whether the solution was the right one, undermining the buy-in that should've emerged during the discussion. Plus, if you have new people on the team, they might even get the impression that you are not interested in leading and can't be trusted to take a steady hand in guiding them forward.

WARNING

While going beyond the point of decision making can undercut your authority, you also threaten to undercut the process by making a decision prematurely. You can come across as authoritarian. Perhaps that's what you want. However, a century of research looking at the dynamics of teams would suggest you're in for a tough experience leading the team. When people get a chance to discuss the idea and you lead them gently to a desired conclusion and decision, you now have their support. And support in an interdependent team environment is essential.

Chapter **12**

Pulling Out Even Participation

A few years ago, Joe was in a meeting discussing ideas for planning a future conference for colleagues that study groups and teams. This in-person meeting included people at varying levels of experience within the occupation as well as students learning to become professionals. As the meeting carried on, there were some challenges that needed to be addressed and so ideas were being thrown out as options.

The woman next to Joe tried several times to interject her idea. She then leaned over to Joe and told him her idea, which he thought was really quite good. A minute or so passed, and Joe raised his hand, butted in, and said pointing to his neighbor, "I believe Margie has an idea that we need to hear." All eyes turned to her and she shared her idea.

As the meeting continued, it became clear that this was definitely the best idea and was adopted as the solution to the group's challenge. However, Joe felt both good and bad after this situation. He was happy he was able to be an ally to his colleague and get her ideas heard, but he was sad he needed to do that.

This led to what you will read in this chapter — a discussion of the importance of pulling out even participation from all the people in the meeting. In this chapter, we dig into the science a bit on why a sense of belonging is critical in creating good meetings. We also look at how to manage participation across different meeting formats. And we wrap up by presenting some options for spreading out the responsibility for meeting participation to other attendees.

Ensuring Everyone's Voice is Heard

If you put people on your invite list, we're going to assume that you intend for everyone to share something during the meeting, that their collaboration is required for the purpose for which the meeting was called. Under that assumption, it's on you (and to some degree the attendees) to make sure everyone gets a chance to have their voice heard.

Now, when we say everyone's voice should be heard, we aren't just being literal here. We aren't just speaking about having an adequate audio device for everyone to be heard or making sure mute buttons are off. In fact, if you think about it beyond the technology, our resident psychologist, Joe, asserts that voice is even more than just whether a person is called on to share their idea.

REMEMBER

Voice is the degree to which a person feels as though their ideas and opinions are heard, and whether they are given the opportunity to have those ideas and opinions heard. So, it's both the feeling and the action. This is an important distinction. We've all been in meetings where we didn't feel like our ideas and opinions mattered. Maybe we were given the floor to share them, only to see them promptly dismissed. As a meeting leader, be aware of the environment that you foster. Is it one where ideas can be put forth and be given a true and full hearing, or is it one where people are encouraged to share their ideas, but aren't genuinely listened to or considered?

TIP

Be an advocate of both ensuring people feel free to share their ideas and creating an opportunity for them to do so. Your attendees need to feel it's worth their while to speak up because their voice is valued and then it's up to you to make sure they have a way for it to be heard.

There is a chance that the pendulum will swing too far, and one person feels empowered to really hog the conversation. Remember everyone in the meeting is there because you expect them to contribute. That means everyone. Guard against the possibility that someone will dominate the meeting and do your best to spread participation out.

Sure, there are exceptions to this general rule of even participation. Numerically speaking, a person invited to do a presentation in a meeting that leads to a discussion will speak more words than someone who listens to the presentation and then shares their idea. The key is that within the scope of the meeting's purpose, the participation should be balanced across the attendees.

When people feel excluded or unnecessary in a meeting, they disengage and take their good ideas, their perspective, and their resources with them. At minimum, this is a darn shame. However, it could spell disaster for the accomplishment of the purpose of the meeting, especially if the meeting is leading to a decision. You need everyone's input to come to the best solution. If anyone is sidelined, the quality of your decision is at risk.

As with many of our tips and recommendations, the practice of them differs based on the meeting modality. While there is quite a bit of overlap for pulling out participation, you need to consider some nuances within each and how you can you can use technology tools to aid your efforts. So we break down our advice according to the type of meeting you're having.

UNDERSTANDING ENTITATIVITY

There's a scientific reason for why even participation is such an important thing for all meetings. In a recent study that Joe did with his dear friend Dr. Anita Blanchard from the University of North Carolina at Charlotte, they investigated the concept of entitativity in workplace meetings.

What's *entitativity* you ask? Well, it's the degree to which you feel like the group you are in is indeed, "a group." The groupy-ness of the group. If someone walked by and said, "Are you a group?", how fervently would you say "yes"? Entitativity is all about how much you really identify with the people you are engaging with in conversation. In the case of meetings, it's the degree to which you look around the table, or the computer screen and think "these are my people."

What we found was remarkable! Meetings where people felt more of this entitativity were better, and not just by a little . . . actually better by a lot. There was more participation and the meetings overall were more satisfying and effective. Without burdening you with a bunch of stats, suffice it to say the difference was huge.

This means that when you feel more connected to the people you are meeting with, your meetings appear to go better. You likely care more about those you are with, so you care more about hearing what they think and are more open to their ideas. Entitativity is symptomatic of things like trust and concern for others.

So if you follow the science, the more participation you have by all attendees, the more indicative that is of a group that feels connected. The more a group feels connected, the more likely you are to unlock the potential of your meetings.

When in person

For your in-person meetings, you can often tell when someone has something to share. They may lean in and open their mouth. They may interrupt or jump in when there's a break in the discussion. Some may even use the school-based tactic we all learn in primary school, and raise their hand.

These and other verbal or nonverbal cues are fairly easy to see, recognize, and act upon. But, reacting to these behaviors is not going to ensure even participation among your attendees. In fact, if you just let people do a free-for-all for the floor, you'll get a few people who are good at these behaviors who will likely dominate the meeting and a bunch of others who simply let their more verbose colleagues take over.

TIP

To avoid the possibility of this occurring, we recommend you employ three strategies to provide a more balanced verbal environment:

>> **Set ground rules for participation.** By deciding together with your group how they are to participate, it ensures everyone knows how to get their ideas heard. You can come up with the best participation norms based upon your organization and team culture, but there is one universal truth regardless of what you decide upon. Everyone needs to adhere to the rules. As the meeting leader, you will likely be the one to serve as the chief enforcer, but you will likely need to do less overt enforcement over time as the norms become ingrained in the group dynamic. We go into greater detail on this in Chapter 9.

>> **Pay attention to nonverbal behaviors that indicate someone wants to share something.** We've identified some of these behaviors already (see Chapter 10), but how someone indicates they want to speak varies by individual. You might have a teammate who gets noticeably restless when they have something to say or a colleague who tends to clear their throat in preparation for speaking up. As you get to know your team members, you'll find even more subtle indicators of their interest in sharing an idea. Pay attention to these and call upon people who look like they are ready to jump in.

>> **Call on people by name to bring them into the conversation, even if they haven't strongly indicated they have something to say.** Again, this could be a ground rule that you establish that makes calling on people an understood norm. But, even if you don't identify this as a ground rule for your group, it's sometimes the only way to ensure that everyone gets a moment to share their ideas. However, be sure to legitimize the statement "I have nothing to add." That's a perfectly appropriate response to being called on and takes some of the pressure off of people who may fear being put on the spot. For more on this, see Chapter 9.

If you are in charge of guiding the discussion, it can be hard to keep track of who has talked and who has not. So we recommend making a note of who has spoken and shared ideas during the meeting on a piece of paper in front of you. Check your list periodically and use it as a tool to identify who needs a chance to chime in. You can't have even participation if you aren't tracking participation in some way. Come up with a system that works for you and use it consistently. Over time, you may see trends and know who in your meeting will likely need more prodding than others to speak up.

When virtual

While some of the techniques used for pulling out participation in a face-to-face meeting do work in a virtual one, not all of them do. In a virtual meeting, you can't as easily see the nonverbal behaviors that indicate a desire to participate. Sometimes this is due to the technology itself but sometimes it's due to the choices made by the participants themselves.

Let's tackle the first one — the technology challenge. In a virtual meeting, we are forced to read the room through the screen, so we are limited in our ability to do so by the size of it. You may have recognized this and added an external monitor to increase the amount of space that the gallery view will occupy, in essence, blowing up the size of the faces on your screen. Even with that modification, though, you still need to be a keen observer of the body language of those appearing in the boxes to tell who might have something to add.

If you have maybe three or four people sharing the screen with you, it's relatively easy to work out those nonverbal cues — a subtle lean in or a raised hand. But as soon as you start increasing the number of participants, you increase the level of difficulty. As you add boxes on the screen, you shrink the size of the people appearing in them. Those nonverbal cues become harder and harder to interpret or even notice. And if the number of boxes no longer fit on one screen and you actually need to page through to see the next group of faces, it's nearly impossible. Still, if cameras are on, you have at least some chance of reading the room, even if it's an incomplete picture.

The second and perhaps bigger issue with pulling out participation virtually is when attendees keep their camera off during the meeting. As a meeting leader, you have no way of knowing if someone has something to say unless they use some technology tool to let you know. While we would strongly suggest you encourage the webcam to be on in a meeting where interaction and input is desired, there may be times when people can't use video . . . or won't. (Check out Chapter 5 for guidance on using video when meeting.)

TIP

With this in mind, our advice is two-fold:

» Lean into ground rules you've established for turn taking and establish that you will likely be calling on people by name to make sure no one misses out on an opportunity to have their voices be heard. If multiple people have raised their hand, establish the speaking order by saying something like, "Bob, you go first and then Emily." However, if you'd like to get someone else's opinion on what is being discussed and they haven't proactively raised their hand, feel free to call on that person to get their take.

» Rely upon tech tools to alert you to someone wanting to comment or ask a question. Tech tools available to you in most virtual meetings include the raise hand function (or similar notifications) and the chat. As you set your ground rules, discuss how people can and should use these tools to get into the conversation. We talk more about the importance of allowing for nonverbal participation later in this chapter.

If you are worried about being overwhelmed managing the conversation along with the technology, consider having someone other than you, the meeting leader, help you by monitoring the chat. This is paramount for larger meetings with an active chat box. Make sure you check in with your helper and consider even giving them permission to interrupt you periodically to keep these tech tools attended to properly.

When hybrid

Basically, everything we have said up to this point about pulling out participation in face-to-face and virtual meetings applies for hybrid meetings too. You still have verbal and nonverbal cues for participation, depending upon where your attendees are showing up, in person, or on screen. You still need ground rules to make sure everyone can take part. It's still probably a good plan to have a helper to assist with facilitating the chat and other tech tools.

But there's a big difference that will require you to up your game. Not only do you have to do all the right things for pulling out even participation for both virtual and in-person meetings . . . you have to do them all at once. Doing that is exhausting and challenging. It's just one of the reasons why you might be tempted to just give up on doing a hybrid meeting at all, but you would likely be missing out. Because you've embraced hybrid, you have a unique opportunity to manage the most inclusive form of meeting that allows people to join from wherever they are, presumably where they feel they work best.

REMEMBER

Because people are able to connect from anywhere and may be most comfortable in where they are connecting from, they may also be most likely to share their unfiltered and most useful ideas. Even though the hybrid meeting may initially be hard to handle, take note. The hybrid meeting has the potential to be the most creative meeting type of all modalities. In fact, Joe is deep into the research to confirm this assertion right now.

Validating Both Verbal and Nonverbal Participation

When you think about participation, you might think of just the kind of participation that makes a sound — people literally speaking up, saying words. You'll hear those words and respond, react, pass the participation to someone else, and so on. Their verbal behaviors get acknowledged, in part, because they make noise.

But participation can also make no sound at all but speak loud and clear. People nod their heads up in down in agreement or side to side in disagreement. They roll their eyes when something is silly or absurd. They shrug when they don't know something. The list of subtle and not so subtle nonverbal messages could fill an entire book.

This nonverbal behavior is critical for full communication. In fact, some very early scientific estimates suggested that up to as much as 50 percent of all communication is nonverbal. Joe takes a slightly different perspective. Some interactions can be 100 percent nonverbal, while others may be 0 percent nonverbal, with most interactions falling somewhere in-between.

If this all sounds a bit academic, allow us to provide an example. Have you ever had a nonverbal conversation with a romantic partner? Nothing was said verbally, but you were most definitely communicating. Have you ever had a phone call? Nothing is seen of the nonverbal behaviors that may be occurring on the other end, but, you were also most definitely communicating.

REMEMBER

In a meeting, you want to not only be aware of the nonverbal forms of communication of your attendees but also process what those nonverbal cues mean.

For some more introverted folks, their communication may be limited in words, but their silence and shrugs speak volumes. For some more extroverted folks, their communication may be dominated by words, but their not-so-subtle nonverbal behaviors may communicate additional important information. It's up to you, the meeting leader, to assimilate the verbal and the nonverbal participation to get an accurate read of the message each person is conveying.

A red flag should be raised in your brain if you detect a mismatch between some-one's usual nonverbal and verbal communication and what they are displaying at that moment. Let's say Ellen is normally a very chatty participant and is rarely shy about sharing her opinion. But during this particular meeting, she has been silent with her arms crossed. Even without her voicing her opposition, you can assume she is not on board with the trajectory of the discussion. In this case, you will likely want to ask her to weigh in based upon her nonverbal participation which was out of sync with her usual meeting behavior.

When in person

When in person, with everyone around the table, it's really quite natural to vali-date and acknowledge the verbal and nonverbal participation of those gathered. The one major barrier to this assumption is the room setup.

Take the case of a meeting room set up like a classroom where the leader is at the front of the room and the attendees are occupying seats that all face forward. The meeting leader might be privy to all of the nonverbal communication of the attendees by surveying the room, but no one else will be able to read the body language as well. These nonverbal clues can help everyone to understand how their colleagues are feeling about what is being discussed and can impact verbal participation.

For example, when you see someone nod their head in agreement, you may be more likely to speak up to affirm what is being said. Without a head nod, they may opt to just stay silent. Conversely, those in the back row may miss someone dra-matically rolling their eyes about something that was just said. They may feel like it's not necessary for them to give an opposing view because they assume the silence is indicative of universal agreement. In this rather unique and somewhat unfortunate setup, the meeting leader may need to narrate what they see to help the rest of the room understand the nonverbal communication being displayed by their colleagues.

Given these potential challenges, though, it's best to set up your room so everyone can see everyone else. The classroom setup is an extreme example of meeting room designs that are less than ideal, but the more common one is the conference room with the long, narrow table. It can be really hard for folks on one side of the table to take in the body language of those seated to the right or left of them just a seat or two down. As a meeting leader, give yourself a vantage point that allows you to read as much of the room as possible, so you can be that nonverbal narrator for everyone present.

If your group is large enough that you struggle to monitor nonverbal participation across the group, have a helper assist you with this. They essentially become an advocate for their peers that you aren't able to see as you lead the conversation. Karin was once leading a meeting where there were multiple tables set up in a horseshoe. The theory behind the design was solid; everyone was able to see everyone else. But there were more than 40 people seated at those tables. Even with her head on a swivel, Karin would've likely missed those nonverbal cues and participation. She asked another attendee to be an extra set of eyes and gave her assistant free rein to interrupt her if she saw something that needed to be validated.

When virtual

Virtual meetings present some new challenges and opportunities for acknowledging verbal and nonverbal participation. Yes, provided that cameras are on and the boxes are big enough on the screen, you can read the nonverbal participation of attendees, the head nods, the nodding off, the grins and the grimaces. But it's still not as easy to detect all of these nonverbal cues as it is when you are in the same room. However, technology tools can help level the playing field and provide another option nonverbal participation.

Most platforms have a way for attendees to react to what is being said by displaying emojis or other graphics that visually represent their thoughts. Think about the thumbs up, the clapping hands or the raised hand. As a meeting leader, it's your job to verbally acknowledge their presence on the screen to validate their use. (It also can signal to the individual who clicked on it initially that they can take it off the screen if it doesn't time out automatically.)

Using the chat box also makes for a richer participation environment because it opens up multi-modal communication channels within a meeting. If you encourage your participants to put their comments, questions and reactions into the text thread, you open up another pathway to participate. Those who might be leery of speaking up may find using chat a lower barrier to entry into the conversation, but that's the key. If you encourage people to use chat like this, you need to make sure you don't let those comments and questions languish. Regularly check the chat and incorporate what's relevant into the verbal discussion.

For all of the good that can come out of using chat, you may have seen chat become a distraction and almost a text version of the side conversations that can derail any meeting. You know what we're talking about. Someone announces that it's such and such's birthday and the chat blows up with a continuous string of well wishes and gifs that while comical, can take the meeting too far off track. Or someone cracks a joke in chat and others keep building on it to the point where people are paying more attention to what is being written than the discussion about the topic at hand.

The real issue blooms though when all of these gifs and jokes and seconding of the same sentiment swallow up comments or questions that actually do need to be elevated to the group discussion. The digital noise is too loud. Instead of chat being a second mode of valid participation, it becomes mired in irrelevant content.

If your team has a habit of overusing chat in a nonproductive way, you may need to set some parameters around how you'd like chat to be used. While you don't want to pre-emptively shut down the text conversation, keep an eye on whether it is helping or hurting your cause. If you see chat starting to become a counter-productive technology tool which threatens your ability to accomplish your meeting goal, speak with your team about your concerns. Collaboratively develop some ground rules around its use. Shutting it down without input from your team could turn off the overall participation spigot.

TIP

Allow the technology to support your desire for even participation by acknowledging and verbally validating people's notifications, reactions and comments in chat. This can go a long way to ensuring participation is more even among your many attendees.

When hybrid

Can we just say do it all? That's the challenge of hybrid. In this context you have to validate verbal and nonverbal participation in both the traditional in person environment and in the virtual environment. All these forms of participation need validation as they comprise the entire group's attempt at coming together in a meaningful way.

WARNING

Don't let the two environments create a separation of people into two competing groups. Be on the lookout for proximity bias where the in-person people treat the virtual people as secondary participants in the meeting. You as the meeting leader have an obligation to nip this issue before it becomes a norm.

Hopefully it's not too late, because once the norm of an "in" group (in person) and an "out" group (virtual group) emerges, it's one of the hardest norms to change. We see it all the time in the world we live in where people identify with their group, and it creates friction with other groups. When you are leading a group where you want people to identify with each other together, don't let the duality of the modality create problems.

TIP

Our advice is to heavily emphasize all forms of participation and pull participation out of the virtual attendees. In fact, we recommend over emphasizing the virtual participants so that their lack of in-person interaction doesn't normalize them out of the group. Allow the many methods for participating in hybrid meetings be a source of inclusion rather than a cause for division.

Enlisting the Help of Others to Encourage Participation

As a meeting leader, you might feel overwhelmed by the emphasis on all the things you have to do to ensure even participation among all those in your meetings. It's a lot. Particularly as you transition from in person to virtual to hybrid. It's okay to feel a bit overwhelmed, so long as it motivates you to engage. But perhaps this will make you feel a little better.

REMEMBER

It is not only the responsibility of the meeting leader to pull out even participation during your meetings, but also the responsibility of every attendee in the meeting.

That's right, the burden is not solely upon the meeting leader. If that were the case, it would be truly overwhelming. But, recall that we encourage the setting of ground rules. One of those really ought to be "Participation is required by all attendees and everyone should encourage each other to participate."

REMEMBER

Make it a norm in your meetings that everyone has a responsibility to engage in participation and to help others do so. This is actually both a good idea for making your meetings effective as well as ensuring that you are enacting your organization's diversity, equity, and inclusion policies.

Think back to Joe's story that opened this chapter. Part of the reason he felt bad for calling attention to the fact that Margie had something to share was because it was necessary. Too often the stereotypes and norms of our society infiltrate our meetings. He was painfully aware that women often have a harder time having their voices heard in meetings.

In meetings, women and minorities are often marginalized. They do not get to participate as much as their white male colleagues. Women also get interrupted more often in meetings than their men colleagues. While more organizations have introduced comprehensive diversity, equity, and inclusion initiatives, we acknowledge that there's a lot of ground that still needs to be made up, not just in meeting equity. However, you as a leader can be part of the solution in the meetings you lead by not allowing anyone to be marginalized based on gender, race, social status or any other characteristic that can unjustly stratify participants.

This will require everyone to be each other's allies and advocates. If you collaboratively establish the ground rule that participation is both required and to be encouraged by all, it will quickly become part of the identity of your meeting group.

When in person

When Joe raised everyone's awareness that his colleague had something to say, he was serving as an in-room advocate for his peer, a great way to encourage participation as an attendee. As a meeting leader, work to establish such a norm. What do we mean? Consider setting a ground rule that if an attendee whispers an idea to you during the meeting or if you recall someone in the meeting having shared an idea with you in another setting, bring it up. Help them have their voice heard because it'll make the discussion richer for all involved.

Additionally, as good as you may be as a leader, you will miss things that happen in the in-person meeting. Maybe someone will subtly want to get in the conversation, but their subtlety is lost on you. There's nothing wrong with attendees saying, "Hey Joe, looks like Karin wants to say something." In fact, that's another good norm to help establish.

You can also encourage participation by fostering a collaborative mindset. If you have an idea that another person had previously expressed an interest in, share it and then invite them to comment. This brings others into the conversation and helps you build a coalition of support for the idea. Chances are, you will also be able to improve upon it with the input of your colleagues. Some attendees may feel reluctant to speak up until they have a fully formed thought, but if you create an environment where it's commonplace for colleagues to build upon each other's ideas, you'll stand a better chance of developing a dynamic dialogue with more people participating.

TIP

Establish ground rules that unlock the potential of your attendees to support each other in their participation. Take off the oppressive leader handcuffs and allow others to assist you in leading others to have voice, both in feeling and in action.

When virtual

Much of what works in a face-to-face meeting applies in the fully virtual environment. Like in-person, you want to work towards norms with your group that ensure full participation.

However, the virtual environment introduces some new opportunities to rely on others to help maintain and even out participation.

Assigning a chat monitor

A virtual meeting allows for multi-modal participation via the chat function, which can be very useful or very distracting. The chat can even go fully off topic and pull participants away from the main conversation between individuals as we mentioned earlier in this chapter.

For this and other reasons we invite you to consider assigning a chat monitor. What's that? Well, it's a person in the meeting who keeps an eye on what's going on as people communicate and share thoughts, questions, and ideas in the text-based chat window. The chat monitor can do the following:

» **Track questions as they arise in the chat.** As they do this, they can interject the questions into the conversation as they become relevant. Doing this frees up the meeting leader to focus on the spoken conversation.

» **Respond to questions they know the answer to.** Sometimes people have questions about what's going on in the meeting or related content, and the chat monitor knows the answer. They should go ahead and answer those questions, rather than insert them into the meeting.

» **Keep the chat on topic.** The chat monitor also has the lovely opportunity to be sort of like a hall monitor in high school. When things in the chat run off topic or get too far from the main meeting conversation, the chat monitor should use procedural communication (see Chapter 12) to pull the conversation back to the topic at hand.

» **Share ideas of those who struggle to get their mute buttons off.** Sometimes people are shy or just don't like the sound of their voice. Whatever the reason, sometimes good ideas are placed in the chat that need to be shared with the group for consideration. The chat monitor serves an important role of bringing the ideas to light that might otherwise have never been heard.

Using nonverbal affirmations

In some virtual meeting software systems, you can click a couple times and put a thumbs up on your video square. You can also indicate clapping, celebration with a party hat, or any number of other things. These notifications built into the system used to be a novelty. Before the COVID-19 pandemic, even using them was a surprise in some of the meetings Joe attended. These days, these emoji-like items are often used in meetings.

But what do they do? Well, based on observations and recent data collection, the use of thumbs-up and clapping hands features actually increases other interactions within the meeting. That's right, using those graphic representations of feelings or thoughts increases participation overall. So, a rather simple way to show support and encouragement to others as they share their ideas is to use these tools.

People's comfort and awareness of these tools is not universal. Therefore, if you intend to make this part of your participation encouragement repertoire, make certain your team knows what they are, what they mean, and how to use them. People don't use what they don't understand. Empower them to use these non-verbal affirmations as one more tool in your toolbox to increase participation.

It's worth noting that when it comes to emojis, it is important to stick to the simple and straightforward ones. No one should need an answer key to decipher an emoji message!

When hybrid

How do you enlist the help of others for pulling out participation when hybrid? Easy — just follow best practices for in-person and virtual meetings. Okay, so it's not so easy, and we understand that it's a lot to ask. But hybrid is here to stay, in some form or fashion, and the key to making it work is asking for help.

Adding a moderator

Adding a moderator is a relatively easy way to help deal with the complex communication environment and allow others to help pull out even participation. In this case, a moderator or facilitator takes on the role of managing the communication and participation during the meeting. Putting someone in this position is especially helpful if you, the meeting leader, have to make a key decision as a result of what is said during the meeting itself.

A person in this role keeps the meeting on task. They make sure everyone gets a chance to participate. They likely use a chat monitor or monitor the chat themselves. Further, they track the participation to ensure that everyone gets their voice heard.

In other words, you are sort of outsourcing some of the meeting leader duties so you can pay attention to what people are saying. It does not mean you are no longer responsible for keeping the meeting on the agenda or accomplishing the goal of the meeting. However, it does provide some additional insurance that no one is inadvertently left out.

Make sure you identify what you want the moderator to manage and what you do not want them to do. If you want to maintain control of transitions from topic to topic, then make sure the moderator knows that. Otherwise, they may assume they are to move things forward as they feel best, even if you aren't ready to do so.

Creating in-room allies

One of the biggest issues of hybrid meetings is the in room versus remote attendee groups. If you do nothing to mix that up, you'll artificially create a tiered system within your meetings, with favoritism emerging towards the in- person attendees.

TIP

To prevent a two-tiered system from emerging, deploy in-room allies for each of the remote attendees to give them an advocate who is focused on making sure their thoughts and ideas are shared.

What's an *in-room ally*? It's someone who's assigned to make sure a remote person gets the opportunity to participate. Your meeting composition will dictate whether you need one or multiple people in this role. However, adding this role heightens awareness of the people in the virtual environment.

You can assign the in-room advocate role in advance or name someone at the beginning of the meeting itself. Either way, you are spreading out the responsibility for participation across all attendees no matter where they sit.

Chapter **13**

Delivering Your Messages Effectively

When you need to deliver a presentation during a meeting, how do you typically start? If you're like most business people, you probably open up your slide design software of choice, select your template, and start creating slides. If this is your standard operating procedure, you are likely missing the mark with your audience.

While most meetings should largely be dialogue based, there are times when you are going to be responsible for providing some context for the discussion. While we strongly advocate sending out materials in advance for attendees to review (see Chapter 9), that's not always possible, especially if the topic being discussed is sensitive and needs to be kept under wraps until the live meeting. Maybe it's a personnel matter or a product launch plan that is so secret you can't run the risk of it being leaked.

When these situations arise, you, as the meeting leader, need to be an effective messenger, but for that to happen, you need to focus on two key elements: crafting content that is both memorable and digestible and delivering that content so that it has impact. Too often, business presentations fall short on both.

We could write a book on all of the presentation problems that seep their way into meeting rooms across the entire corporate landscape: presentations that seem to wander about with no defined goal, presenters who speak at breakneck pace because they simply want to get it over with, slide decks with a font so small you'd need binoculars to read what is up on the screen. Rather than focus on the bad, though, we guide you through the good, and give you a combination of frameworks, strategies, and best practices to ensure your presentations enlighten, not lose your audience.

REMEMBER

As a meeting leader, what you do sets the standard for your entire team. They will assess how you put together your slide deck, how you structure your content, and how you talk your way through it. In turn, they will likely attempt to mirror that to reflect the norm you have set by your own actions.

In this chapter, we share a content framework that can be adapted to any presentation you are making. Then focus on delivery techniques that allow your audience to better comprehend what you are saying. We touch on best practices for visual aids that help rather than hinder your presentation, and explain why using humor during a presentation and the meeting as a whole is a valuable tool for team cohesion.

Simplifying Your Content

One of the biggest presentation mistakes we see can be best summed up like this: People try to put ten pounds of content into a five-pound bag.

It's easy to do. After all, you have so much to say! And of course, your audience will want to hear it all!

The reality is that not only does your audience not want to hear it all, they probably can't handle it all either. Information overload may make you, the presenter, feel like you've given their money's worth, but your audience is left feeling like they've been drinking from a firehose. What's worse, if they were thirsty for information before you began, they probably still feel like their thirst has not been quenched. It's hard to take a steady drink when you are being blasted.

As difficult as it may be to hear, the old adage that less is more is absolutely true when it comes to deciding what to include in your content. Your audience has only so much capacity for what you are going to share. Be mindful of that. Be respectful of that. Tell them what they need to hear, not everything you want to say.

TIP

Think about the 50/50 rule when figuring out how much information to include in your presentation. Suppose your presentation is designed to provide context for the discussion that follows. In that case, you want to allot 50 percent of your time to presenting the information and 50 percent of your time for Q&A. Take a look at the timestamps you put on the agenda (see Chapter 9 for more on timestamps). If you've assigned the topic 20 minutes during the meeting, plan for no more than ten minutes of straight presentation time. But don't feel like you need to fill up the full ten minutes either. It's better to have more time for discussion than end up cutting it short.

Analyzing your audience

Cutting a presentation down to size is even harder to do when you are an expert on the topic. Often, you might feel it's your role, even obligation, to share as much information as possible as the voice of authority. However, you are doing your audience a disservice. More information than is necessary can muddy the message.

The first step in determining what to include in your presentation is to analyze who will be receiving it. That determines the tone of and level of detail you need to use. Say you are an IT manager. The way you talk about the latest software release to your team of developers will be very different to the way you talk about the release to business users who don't know the first thing about coding. This speaks to one of the biggest challenges we all face when putting together a presentation — the Curse of Knowledge.

RECOGNIZING THE CURSE OF KNOWLEDGE

Let's say you are on a business trip in a new city and you need to walk to a client's office in the heart of midtown. You figure you will rely upon the directions of your navigation app on your phone, but it's not working well for some reason. You see a police officer on the corner and decide to ask them for help. They are happy to oblige and give you very detailed instructions, citing certain landmarks along the way. The officer thinks they are giving excellent directions. You are completely lost. All you can make sense of is what is in your immediate vicinity. You feel confident you know where to make the first turn, but after that, you will be walking blind.

The police officer in this case has a heavy case of the Curse of Knowledge. They have lived in this city for their entire life and knows it like the back of their hand. You have never set foot in the city before and their very detailed turn-by-turn navigation was completely lost on you. Their frequent asides about landmarks of years past made it even worse ("You know, where the old Such and Such used to be.").

TECHNICAL STUFF

The *Curse of Knowledge* is a cognitive bias that we can have when it comes to relaying information, especially if we are an expert in the field. We suffer from the Curse of Knowledge when we've known something for so long and so well that we can't imagine what it's like to *not* know it. When we speak about it, we tend to leave out a bunch of context that is critical for the less-informed audience to know in order to understand our message.

TIP

To combat your own Curse of Knowledge, try asking yourself these questions:

» **Who is my audience?** Think about the people who will be in the room listening to you. What are their roles? Why is your message important for them to hear?

» **What are their blind spots?** Consider their frame of reference for the topic at hand. What are they likely to know about it but perhaps even more importantly, what do they likely not know about? The gaps revealed by the second question are the ones you need to fill in, especially if their lack of knowledge might be a barrier to their comprehension of your message.

» **What do you want them to learn?** If your audience takes one thing away from your presentation, what would you want that to be? Yes, one thing, and yes, it's incredibly difficult to pinpoint what is basically the key takeaway you want to impart. But it's really important to know what that key takeaway is so you can build your presentation around it.

Asking yourself and answering these three questions before you start crafting your content will allow you to cater your message and your presentation goal to your audience. If you don't do this beforehand, you may end up delivering a highly technical and richly detailed presentation on the latest software update to a roomful of people who can barely find the downloads folder on their desktop. You'll enjoy yourself immensely. Your audience will zone out because it sounds like white noise to them.

REMEMBER

Don't start putting together your presentation until you've carefully considered who will be receiving it. Match your level of detail and tone to your audience in order to have it land with impact.

Structuring your message

You may be someone who agonizes over every word that you say during a presentation. You may even like to write out a full script and labor over whether to use the word "critical" or "essential" in a certain sentence. If so, you may be depressed when we tell you . . . the vast majority of what you say will likely be forgotten.

"What? That can't be true," you protest. But alas, it is. Time and again, research has shown that humans in general are terrible listeners with most people remembering only about half of what they've heard right after a conversation. But it gets worse, multiple studies show people ultimately retain only about 10 percent to 25 percent of what they hear. So you may obsess over each word you choose, but in all likelihood, your audience won't remember the vast majority of them.

Before you decide to just give up on trying to say something of value, there is a way to improve your odds that they remember the good stuff and that's by organizing your content for the ear. If you create a simple structure for your content so they can categorize your content, they are more likely to retain it for the long haul.

Using the Rule of Three

The way we recommend organizing for the ear is by applying a content framework device known as the Rule of Three. You may have heard this principle applied across a variety of fields. Photographers use it when setting up a shot by dividing the field of view into three segments. Interior designers use the Rule of Three when choosing home décor (three *objects des art* rather than two on an end table). Landscapers apply the principles when grouping plants. The eye finds groups of three more appealing.

The Rule of Three has a similar effect in content creation except it makes it more appealing for the *ears* of the audience, rather than the *eyes*. Humans learn best when information is presented in triads. Our brains retain it better. This isn't a modern discovery, rather this device was mentioned by the Classical Greek philosopher and polymath Aristotle in his book *Rhetoric* and has been used throughout history. Here are a just a few examples:

>> Life, Liberty and the Pursuit of Happiness.

>> Veni, Vidi, Vici (I came. I saw. I conquered.)

>> Location, location, location.

REMEMBER

The way we would recommend you apply the Rule of Three for your presentation is to use it to create buckets for your content. Rather than trying to deliver a laundry list of disconnected facts, try to group them in a way where they all fall under one of three categories. However, all three buckets should be supporting your *key takeaway* (your core message that you want your audience to remember above all else).

You can keep your Rule of Three framework generic, which would look something like this:

*Your core message (aka your key takeaway)

    *Supporting point #1

    *Supporting point #2

    *Supporting point #3

Anything that you plan to present would need to fall under one of those supporting point "buckets." Any information that falls outside of those three areas should be trimmed out to keep the message as simple as possible.

Then use your Rule of Three in three different ways (do you see a theme here?):

>> **State it at the beginning.** Tell your audience what you are going to tell them. By giving them a heads up on what you are going to relay, they can create a mental scaffolding for your information and fill it in as you speak.

>> **Present your points in the order.** If you told them you were going to talk about breakfast, lunch, and dinner, don't tell them about dinner, breakfast, lunch. Stick with the order you originally gave them. Then they can follow along and fill in their mental framework with your content as it comes in.

>> **Reiterate it at the end.** To hammer home your key points, remind your audience of what you just shared with them at a high level.

REMEMBER

You might be worried about being too redundant, but repetition is your friend when it comes to making your message stick. Leaning into repeating your key points is a time-honored and effective tool that even spawned its own cliché: Tell them what you're going to tell them. Tell them. Tell them what you told them. It's a cliché that works. Use it.

You can also use some more specific Rule of Three adaptations that might fit your particular situation. For example, when pitching an idea, you might want to try this version:

>> What's the problem?

>> What's our proposed solution?

>> Why? (Why will this work? Why should you care? Why are we the ones to lead this change?)

If you are leading a change management initiative, you could use this variation of the Rule of Three to deliver the news:

» What? (What is happening?)

» So what? (Why should you care?)

» Now what? (What is going to happen next?)

The Rule of Three can also be expanded into the sub bullets within each supporting point bucket. If you were to put it into outline form, it would look like this:

Supporting point #1

    Sub bullet #1

    Sub bullet #2

    Sub bullet #3

Supporting point #2

    Sub bullet #1

    Sub bullet #2

    Sub bullet #3

Supporting point #3

    Sub bullet #1

    Sub bullet #2

    Sub bullet #3

For each additional layer of bullets, try to continue building out the content framework in sets of threes, so it would look something like this:

I. Point #1

    a. Bullet

    b. Bullet

    c. Bullet

        i. Bullet

        ii. Bullet

        iii. Bullet

This technique does provide some flexibility for you. Let's say you planned out a 20-minute presentation but the discussion on the agenda item before it went long. Now, you have only half the time you had planned. You could just cut your presentation in half, sharing only Point 1 and a portion of Point 2. We would suggest you simply cut out a layer of detail. Omit the sub bullets and deliver all three points at a higher level. It maintains the integrity of your message.

Opening in an unexpected way

Today, we face more distractions than ever before. The digital clutter in our brains and on our screens is overwhelming. That's why it's imperative for you, as a presenter, to try to grab the attention of your audience as quickly as possible — to make them put down their phones or look away from their laptops.

If you open like this, "Today I'm going to talk about blah, blah, blah. . ." you aren't going to pull anyone away from anything. If you want to wrest their attention away from whatever distractions they have in their space, try using an unexpected open.

An *unexpected open* can simply be a different approach from the typical way of kicking off a presentation . . . something that makes them pause and pulls them in. When Karin is delivering training, she often likes to use a video montage of news clips from her broadcast journalism career. The vintage video is intriguing enough that her audience usually stops doing what they had been doing . . . even if it's just to marvel at the size of the shoulder pads she used to wear.

An unexpected open does not need to be dramatic, but it does need to go beyond the rudimentary introduction of you and your topic. No one is going to look up from their phones for that. Ask yourself what might be a bit shocking to the ears of that particular audience. Your goal is to get them to wonder, "What did they just say?"

You can ask a provocative question that they likely do not know the answer to . . . but should. That question opens a knowledge gap, and most people don't like when they don't know the answer to something. They'll look to you to fill that gap in by supplying the answer.

Unexpected opens can start with a surprising statistic. Maybe you had a particularly intriguing data point buried in your presentation. Move that stat to the front to get them interested in what you are about to say. Supposed you plan to share some really exciting news about the impressive sales numbers you had over the last quarter, but that golden nugget is buried on slide five. Instead, leverage it at the beginning, saying something like this, "Team, we had a 30 percent growth in gross revenue over the past quarter. Congratulations. Now let me tell you how we got there and how we're planning to keep it going." You've gotten their attention . . . and you're more likely to keep it.

Closing to convince

There is one more piece of presentation real estate that is undervalued — the presentation close. Often the words remembered the most by an audience are the final ones spoken, so why would anyone want those final words to be, "Well, that's all I have. Any questions?" What a wasted opportunity!

Unless your presentation's purpose is purely to inform, when you wrap up a presentation, you want your audience to do something. You want them to take action. Maybe you need their support for an initiative. Maybe you want them to take on new roles. Maybe you need them to allocate resources to your project. Whatever the goal, you need to consider what you need to tell them to get their buy-in. In essence, you want to pull the right emotional trigger to get them to say yes.

Your goal with your close is to get them to care about what you have presented because feelings inspire people to act. An emotional trigger is the motivator that will drive their decision to do so. It could be a financial one, a social one or anything in between. It's up to you to figure out what might inspire action for your particular audience and then plan your final words to reflect that.

Here's an example. Say you are a manager of a sales team that is full of go-getters, but they are drowning in administrative work. You are about to introduce a new software application that will ultimately save them a ton of time, but there's bound to be pushback because learning a new system takes them out of the field. Your goal is to get them to embrace learning the new software, but you know you can't just dictate that from above without creating resentment. Your final words could be something to this effect: "I know learning a new system seems like one more thing on your admin to-do list, but listen to this. Team XYZ in our other division saw a 40 percent reduction in their time spent on busy work and a 20 percent increase in commissions within the first quarter of it being implemented." The emotional trigger for your sales team is financial in nature and your close wisely reflected that.

REMEMBER

The last words you say in a presentation are often the ones people remember above all else. Don't forfeit them by fizzling out at the end. Plan out what you will say and then deliver it with intentionality.

Making your messages memorable

WARNING

Are you someone who loves a good spreadsheet? Do you enjoy rattling off a list of features for a product that you know inside and out? We applaud your enthusiasm but offer you a word of warning. Your data, your facts, your figures alone will not move people to take action. You need to breathe life into them by making the abstract concrete.

When putting together your presentation, go beyond just the facts. To make your message sing, bring it to life. Check out the nearby sidebar, "Breathing Life into Numbers" for an example.

Using stories

Part of many a childhood involves some version of story time. Maybe you were one of those tykes who were brought to a story hour at the local library, or perhaps you recall sitting on the floor in front of your elementary school teacher, captivated by the tale they read to you. Your parents might have nurtured this love of listening to stories as part of a bedtime ritual. You may have taken that early introduction to the joys of a good story into your adult life with a collection of novels lining your bookshelves.

Stories are powerful. They can move us in ways that a straight delivery of facts cannot. So why would you not incorporate them into your business presentations?

BREATHING LIFE INTO NUMBERS

When Karin worked as a broadcast journalist, she would often be given an assignment that began with a number (for example, the exponential increase in the number of homeless people in urban areas in the United States). She could've just reported those numbers, but numbers can be numbing. They're difficult to connect with and they're easily forgotten. Instead, she would seek out a family who was living it and make them the centerpiece of the story.

If you tell people there are more than 500,000 people who are homeless in the U.S., they might acknowledge that sad statistic and move on.

If you introduce the audience to a single mother living out of her car with three little ones, that story sticks with you. In fact, any time Karin did a story in this vein, she was amazed at the offers of help and support that would flood in from viewers who were touched by what they saw.

You may be concerned that a story is superfluous, just fluff that doesn't provide enough substance to warrant being included in your limited time. But consider this: Our brains are programmed to enjoy and engaged with stories. They stick in our heads. We remember them and we even tend to repeat them.

TIP

A well-placed story or anecdote can make all the difference in how much lasting impact your words have. In a business presentation, you can use them in a variety of ways. You can use them at the beginning to draw people in to add a dash of unexpectedness to your open. Most business presentations don't start with a story, which is even more reason to make sure yours do.

You can even consider using a story framework to encapsulate your entire presentation. The typical story structure would look like this:

>> **"Once upon a time. . .":** Establish the setting and characters.

>> **Problem:** Inform your audience of the issue that your characters are confronting.

>> **Resolution:** Describe the actions the characters are taking or are hoping to take to overcome the problem.

>> **Ending:** Wrap it up and/or present next steps.

There are as many storytelling frameworks as there are storytellers, but they all include a beginning, middle, and end (the "Rule of Three" strikes again, as detailed earlier in this chapter). Sometimes a story is just part of the presentation. Sometimes it can provide the entire structure. Communications Guru Nancy Duarte suggests using this story framework in her book the *HBR Guide to Persuasive Presentations* (Harvard Business Review, 2012). She says in order to inspire audience action: Present what is, describe what could be, and then crescendo to a call to action that she calls the "new bliss: how much better their world will be when they adopt your ideas."

REMEMBER

How you tell your story is up to you, but make sure you do stick to the basics. Your story needs to be relevant to the topic at hand. Telling a random story makes no sense and will feel jarringly out of place. By using narrative, you are simply employing another tool to relay your base information beyond just a listing of facts. Stories are tools that light up different neural pathways, so your information can be better absorbed and retained.

Painting a mental picture

Here's a quick exercise for you:

1. **Think about your childhood home.**

2. **Now think about dedication.**

Consider what happened in your mind as you pondered both. When you were prompted to think about your childhood home, you probably started picturing the outside perhaps, maybe mentally wandered inside and took a look around.

Now compare that to what went on in your brain when you were prompted to think about dedication. Did anything immediately come to mind, or did you find it a heavier cognitive lift to even wrap your head around it?

In all likelihood, thinking about where you grew up was likely easier for you to do than thinking about the idea of dedication. Why? Because the first is concrete. You can visualize it. You can literally see it in your mind's eye. The second — dedication — is abstract and requires your brain to fill in the gaps with your own visual representation of what determination might look like. When it comes to putting together a presentation, you want to make it as easy as possible for your audience to connect with what you are saying. Translating abstract concepts into concrete terms is an effective way to do just that.

According to Chip and Dan Heath, the authors of the book *Made to Stick* (Random House, 2007), "memory is like Velcro. The more hooks an idea has, the better it will cling to memory." When you speak in concrete language, you are creating more hooks for your audience to latch on to because they can visualize it. Your words match with an image they can conjure up in their brains. It's easier to remember words that are linked to a picture than just words alone.

Numbers of any sort are ripe for translation into the concrete. If we go back to the homeless population story described earlier in this chapter, you could say there are more than 500,000 Americans who are homeless today . . . or you could say the number of people who are homeless in the United States could fill ten Yankee stadiums. Which is easier for you to visualize?

How you make something concrete is dependent upon your audience. If you are speaking to a group of people who live outside of the United States and have no interest in American baseball, relating a number to the capacity of Yankee stadium may not make sense. However, look for similar opportunities that will resonate with your audience. Maybe you switch Yankee stadium to Wembley for a UK audience or to the Japan National Stadium for an Asia-Pacific audience. Do your homework. Your concrete translation should create common ground, not confuse.

Speaking With Impact

When we ask most people how much they prepare for a presentation, the common answer is "not enough." With so many pressures and demands on your schedule, you might find yourself in the same boat. However, if you want a good general rule, you should plan on one hour of preparation for each minute of presentation. That means you should plan on five hours of preparation for a five-minute presentation.

Even if you do figure out how to carve out that time, you may fall into another trap. You spend almost the entire five hours on creating your slide deck and practically no time actually rehearsing it, giving it voice. You might think simply looking over your slides is enough, but when you get into the actual room, you will likely realize that it is not. Knowing your slides is one thing. Smoothly speaking to them is another. And if you fail on the latter, all of that time spent putting your presentation together will be for naught.

REMEMBER

How you deliver your presentation is equally as important as what you are delivering. Put rehearsal time into your preparation schedule. Even running through it out loud one time before you deliver it to your actual audience can make a big difference because it can help you identify trouble spots. You can then tweak it accordingly, before you do it for real. However, if it's a high-stakes situation, make sure you rehearse it to the point where you feel you can deliver it with confidence. You will be nervous regardless if it's a presentation with a lot riding on it. Putting in the practice time can help you keep your nerves in check.

Using vocal variety to keep attendees' attention

Have you ever found your mind wandering while listening to someone give a presentation? Of course you have, and it's not your fault. Sure, sometimes the content is to blame or perhaps the way it's being packaged, but more often than not, you can blame the speaker who has likely switched into "presenter mode."

By Karin's definition, *presenter mode* manifests in the following ways:

» a flat, unenthusiastic delivery

» a lack of connection between the speaker and the audience

» a disconnect between the words being spoken and the meaning behind the words

When someone is in presenter mode, their focus is on getting through their content, not on how their message is received by the audience. But presenter mode isn't in sync with the speaker's mission.

REMEMBER

Your job as a presenter is to educate your audience about your assigned topic. Your mission is to ensure they comprehend what you are saying, that they "get it." Focus on the audience and their needs, not on simply spitting information at them.

One of the biggest factors in how easily an audience receives your message is your verbal delivery of it and the amount of variation you inject in it. You have three main tools at your disposal: pauses, pacing, and pitch.

Pausing often

Have you ever listened to a speaker whose delivery reminds you of a runaway train? They keep talking and talking and talking, practically nonstop, and you wonder if they will ever come up for air.

They may think they are really giving you your money's worth, but they're actually you a disservice. Your brain needs time to process what is being said and if you don't have any breaks in which to do so, it can be difficult for those words to sink in.

REMEMBER

Pauses are important for you, the speaker, as well as your audience.

As a presenter, you need to pause to satisfy a basic physiological necessity: To breathe. It seems ridiculous to even bring this up, but sometimes we forget to do this in a natural way when we present. We are so set on getting through our content that we let our vocal tone get thinner and thinner before we are forced to take in a gulp of air. When presenting virtually, we tend to do this even more because we don't have those nonverbal signals from our audience that we need to take a break. When presenting remotely, it's harder to detect the eyes of the audience glazing over or the quizzical looks on their faces when they don't understand. Instead, we just put our heads down (sometimes literally, sometimes metaphorically) and go. If you want to have full vocal tone, though, you need to take a moment to let some air into your lungs. It can also help to reduce your nervousness. Breathing through the butterflies is a real thing.

A pause is also important for you when you present because it can replace one of the most annoying verbal crutches around — a filler word, those "um," "uh," and "so" moments that we rely upon as verbal placeholders. They don't have any value for the audience. They are simply a way of not ceding the floor. However, if they are used too often, they start to undercut your authority. They make you sound unsure of yourself. Your audience may even start counting your ums rather than listening to your actual message.

TIP

If you know you tend to use a lot of filler words, self-awareness facilitates change. When you feel yourself about to say one, try to swallow it and substitute silence instead. Your audience may not officially thank you for it, but they will appreciate the pause.

Why? Because they need time to digest your information. A pause gives them space to do that. Plus, it gives your words a bit more gravitas. If you say a key takeaway, for example, and you really want people to think about it, you can almost force them to do that by simply shutting up. Give them a second or two to really consider what you just said before moving on to the next thing. If you don't, all of your words may string together and go in one ear and out the other.

TIP

How long should your pause be? It depends on the purpose, the setting, and the audience. If you have the floor and are not concerned about someone jumping in, feel free to use a longer pause for dramatic impact, especially after a key takeaway. We've seen a speaker pull off what we'd call a "power pause" that lasted almost eight seconds. It was highly effective but hinged on his ability to hold the attention of the audience in a nonverbal way. In this case, the speaker made it very clear with his body language that his pause was just that . . . a temporary hold . . . not an invitation for others to start talking. In fact, during the pause, he made a point of surveying the audience and intensifying his eye contact, as if to say, "Yes, I'm thinking about what I just said too."

If you are speaking virtually, you can't deliver as many nonverbal cues, so a longer pause can be a little tougher to pull off. It's even harder if your audience members are known to jump in as soon as there is a sliver of air time. In this case, still pause, but perhaps don't linger as long as you might if you are presenting in person. Try counting one-thousand-one, one-thousand-two in your head before moving on to your next point.

REMEMBER

If you want your words to land with impact, you need to give your audience time to appreciate them. A pause creates that space for them to consider what you said, ruminate on it, and ultimately digest it.

Pacing with the listener in mind

Have you ever realized you have too much to say and not enough time to say it? If you are like most people you will try to compensate for your lack of planning by turning up the speed of your delivery. What should be a ten-minute presentation will somehow be a five-minute presentation delivered at a breakneck pace.

You might come away feeling very satisfied with yourself. Ha, you got it all in! Your audience might come away feeling overwhelmed by the fusillade of words that were lobbed at them.

When determining how fast or slow to deliver your content, you need to always keep your listener in mind. They can only take in so much information at a time. Put yourself in their shoes and consider how it feels to receive your message for the first time.

Sure, there are certain topics that can be delivered more breezily and at a faster pace, but if you have some complex or dense content to cover, slow it down.

TIP

The denser the content, the more deliberate you need to be in your delivery. Complex topics require more processing on the part of your audience. If you go through it too quickly, you run the risk of them not understanding it at all. Maybe they'll ask you to repeat yourself, but that depends upon their willingness to do so. Depending upon the power dynamic, they may be embarrassed to ask you to go through it again. Give them their best shot to get it the first time through by delivering at a pace that they can handle.

Changing your pitch to emphasize the critical words

Think back to your college days. Did you ever have one of those professors who had a habit of droning on and on in a monotone, where every sentence sounded like every other sentence? You may have done your best to actually listen, really *listen*, to what they said, but it was an exercise in futility.

Listening to someone speak without changing their inflection or pitch is nearly impossible to do for any period of time. Steady tone becomes white noise. Our brains are hard-wired to pick up change in the environment, and if nothing changes, we simply tune out.

Everyone has a different vocal range. That's how high your voice goes and how low it goes. It's not like one is better range is better than another; it's just how we are created. What is important, though, is that you seek to hit the highs and lows of your own vocal range, so you can vocally highlight what is important for your audience to hear.

How do you appropriately inject that pitch variety into your delivery? One of the easiest ways to do this is by using your presentation notes. In your text, try to identify the critical words or phrases in a bullet or a sentence. Don't go overboard, maybe look for a word or two in each key point. Once you've found them, underline them. Here's a quick example:

Pick your <u>pace</u> with the <u>listener</u> in mind.

The words "pace" and "listener" are the most important words in that sentence. They are the meaning words, the ones that hold the essence of the thought.

When you glance down at your notes while you are presenting, you'll see those underline words and will likely emphasize them, often by raising your pitch.

WARNING

In tonal languages, our advice about changing your pitch may be totally off base. In fact, in languages such as Mandarin, a single word can have several different meanings depending upon different tonal inflections. If the language in which you are presenting is a tonal language, rely upon changes in pace and pauses to better enhance comprehension for your audience rather than changes in pitch.

Minding your body language

We communicate not just with our words and our tone of voice. We communicate with our entire bodies. If we try to muzzle any aspect of that, it'll have an overall detrimental effect on our ability to communicate effectively and authentically.

REMEMBER

Your body language should be natural and not contrived when you present. If you focus on your message, your body will respond appropriately and organically to what you are saying. When you are talking to a friend about what you had for dinner last night, you don't say, "I had chicken for my entrée." (I'm going to now lift my right hand.) "And I had a chocolate torte for dessert." (Now I'm going to lift my left hand.) That doesn't happen. If you are relaxed and not holding yourself stiff, your body language will complement your verbal delivery. The less you think about what your hands are doing, the better off you will be.

MOVING WITH MEANING IN PERSON

One of the best ways to get any nervousness energy out of your body is to move. That's why you see some speakers pacing up on stage as if they are tigers in a cage. The perpetual and apparently aimless pacing can be distracting to your audience.

TIP

However, staying in one place the entire time, especially if you have a larger room, seems like a waste of space. Instead, we suggest you move with meaning. Change to a different location in the room when transitioning to a new concept within your presentation. For example, after you are done speaking to slide one, shift to the other side of the room as you start to speak to slide two. It adds some dynamism to your presentation by switching things up visually for your audience, but it also gives you an opportunity to wake up Jane who has zoned out on the other side of the room. If you are delivering a key takeaway, though, stay planted. You want people to focus on what you are saying and not be distracted by any extra movement.

LETTING YOUR HANDS DO THE TALKING

When Karin teaches any presentation class, she always begins with participants delivering a baseline speech which allows each person to get a sense of where they are in their skill set, so they know what they need to work on to improve. Even though there might be some common challenges, everyone usually has their own individual quirks. Never, though, had Karin seen an entire class exhibit the same odd behavior before.

Each speaker took to the stage and delivered their entire presentation with their hands cemented to their sides. Not just at the beginning but for the entire performance. It was almost as if someone had taken an inflatable inner tube, put it over their head and trapped their arms to the sides of their body. Now a few folks did try to break their arms free with a slight flapping of their hands at the wrist, but that was it.

After the tenth person displayed the same odd behavior, Karin asked what was up. The response from one of the class participants, "That's the ready position." (Imagine lots of nods from fellow classmates.)

Karin's response, "Ready for what?"

Come to find out, this client had used a different communications trainer for many years who had taught that any gestures when presenting were distracting. The result? A bunch of speakers who insisted upon gluing their appendages to their sides which was awkward for them and certainly for their audience.

ENGAGING WITH GOOD EYE CONTACT

If you want to build trust and believability, establishing good eye contact with your audience is one of the best ways to do it. By looking people in the eye, you are connecting with them as individuals which makes them feel seen and draws them in.

Be careful to make your eye contact genuine. Don't do what Karin calls "eye grazing" where you don't really look people in the eye but rather look just above their heads and sweep across the room, back and forth. Seek eye connection where you hold an individual's gaze for a thought or sentence before moving on to the next person.

FRAMING YOUR BODY LANGUAGE VIRTUALLY

When presenting virtually, you are confined to a much smaller space, whatever happens to be showing on the screen. While you can stand when presenting, you can't exactly move from one side of the frame to the other. You also don't want to pick up your webcam and move around. It's liable to give your audience motion sickness.

Your body language on camera will be focused on your facial expressions and your gestures, rather than your movement from one part of the room to the other. As with any presentation, you want your gestures to be organic and not something that you plan out or they'll come across as fake.

WARNING

If you are a hand talker, by all means, allow yourself to be one during your virtual presentation, but we have one caveat. If you are framed so that you are just seen from the shoulders up on the screen, make sure you don't have your hands flying around in front of your face. Instead, allow yourself to talk with your hands, but try to keep those gestures a little lower. If your hands pop into the frame periodically, that's not a big deal. In fact, it can make you appear more authentic.

LOOKING AT THE CAMERA WHEN PRESENTING

One of the toughest things to do, but one of the most important for any virtual presenter, is to look at the camera when speaking. It feels so unnatural to look at a piece of glass, especially if you have the faces of your audience in view on the screen. Your natural human impulses will push you to look at the gallery view because it feels like you are making good eye contact with your audience. But to your audience, it feels like just the opposite.

If you don't look at the camera when you speak, you will appear to be looking somewhere else to your audience. For example, if you are using your laptop webcam that's embedded at the top of your screen, you will appear to be looking down, just about chest level of each person who is watching you on the other side.

Think about this way. What if you were talking to someone in person and instead of them looking you in the eye, they look just below your chin. How would that make you feel? Not so great, right? Perhaps you'd even wonder if you have crumbs from lunch stuck to your face?

REMEMBER

Not looking people in the eye makes people feel uncomfortable. Looking people in the eye makes them feel connected. Before you start protesting about how you can't see your audience, remember this. You don't want to be staring at them. We break gaze all the time when we talk to people face to face. Do so when speaking to the camera as well. In those split seconds when you look away, you can quickly see if someone is nodding, smiling, or frowning.

KNOWING WHERE YOUR AUDIENCE IS WHEN HYBRID

Eye contact becomes even trickier when your audience is both in person and virtual, but it's important to pay an equal amount of attention to both. That means spending time returning the gaze of folks in the same room with you as well as looking at the camera to engage with the remote attendees.

The camera is the in-room representation of the faces of your virtual audience. If you don't look at the camera at all and only look at the in-person audience, the remote attendees will feel like they're on the outside looking in.

Invite them in to the action by engaging with the lens. You don't want anyone to feel left out, and you want everyone to feel like they are included. For your in-person audience, it's a given. For your remote audience, the extra effort you make by speaking directly to them through the camera will be much appreciated and go a long way in enhancing meeting equity.

Using Visual Aids

Think about the term "visual aids." If you break it down into its two components, it seems pretty self-explanatory. So why are so many visual aids not visual and why do so many visual aids hurt the presentation rather than help it?

Entire books have been written on how to make solid slide decks, so we encourage you to seek out one of the many well-written and researched options on the market. What we are going to share with you here are some essential best practices for how you design slides and how you interact with them.

Creating complementary slides

Try this challenge. Open up the last slide deck you created. No cheating. Pick the last one you made. What do you see? Lots of white backgrounds with black text? A wall of words or numbers? Maybe fonts so small that you need a magnifying glass to read them? If you answered yes to any of these questions, your slides would not pass The Glance Test.

The term *The Glance Test* was coined by Nancy Duarte, the author of the book *slide:ology* (O'Reilly Media, 2008), who says your slides should be as easy to consume as billboards. When you are driving down the highway, you can't afford to look away from the road for longer than a few seconds. That means whatever appears on those giant road-side signs needs to be simple enough to be understood at a glance. The same holds true for slide design.

To follow The Glance Test, people should be able to get the gist of your slide in three to five seconds. More often than not, though, slides are teleprompters and not billboards, appearing more like a plain word-processing document that has been pasted into a slide template.

REMEMBER

Your visual aids serve an important role. With the majority of the world being primarily visual learners, your slides can help reinforce your verbal message. They give your audience one more way to relate to and remember your message. The problem occurs when your visual starts fighting with your verbal.

When you share a slide that has a lot of text on it, your audience has a choice: to listen to you or to start reading. They can't do both unless the words on the screen match what you are saying. If they are forced to make a choice, the majority of the time, they will read and tune you out. The more text you have on a slide, the more likely your slides will hijack the attention of your audience.

TIP

Here's what you can do to make sure your slides help and don't hinder your presentation:

>> Pare down the text. The only words on the slide should be the critical ones.

>> Opt for bullets over full sentences and try to have no more than three bullets on one slide.

>> Use animations to reveal only one section at a time to keep people from reading ahead. Only show the bullet that are you are addressing in that moment.

>> Keep the "visual" in visual aids by using images and graphics to add visual appeal. Pictures are more memorable than words.

WARNING

The number of slides you use isn't as important as what you have on each slide. Don't be worried about having a longer deck so long as each slide on its own follows The Glance Test. Don't try to limit your number of slides at the expense of good design. Cramming three slides worth of content onto one slide isn't improving your presentation.

Interacting with visual aids

When delivering a presentation, always remember where the value is coming from — you, the speaker. Sometimes, though, that gets lost when the visual aids steal too much of the show, not because they deserve the attention but because they're placed in a position of power by the presenter themselves.

Your slides help you share your information, tell your story, maybe even move your audience to action, but you are the one primarily bringing the value. Some-time we forget that fact, especially when we present virtually.

Use your visual aids to support your verbal message, not supplant it.

When in person

You'll find a wide range of opinions on how you should interact with your slides when presenting to an audience in the same room. Some communication experts will suggest you never look at your slides and just allow the audience to take them in as they please. Perhaps in a TED talk, this advice holds up.

We suggest you think of yourself as a tour guide, directing your audience through the information you need them to hear and understand. There are times when they can best learn that information from by watching and listening to you. You are the main and perhaps only conduit for them to receive that information. There will also be times when your slides are the best conduit for your content — such as a slide with a graph showing a slip in revenue over the past few weeks. It makes much more sense for your audience to look at the graph as you are talking through the data than for them to watch your face as you are tossing out numbers.

The way you interact with your slides should be in response to this question: Where do you want them to get their information? If your slide helps your audi-ence to better understand what you are saying, then prompt them to look at the screen and join them by looking at the screen as well. But if you are the key con-duit of the information, by all means, ignore your visual aids and look at your audience. That will signal to them that they should be paying attention to you, not the screen.

A quick word about the ubiquitous laser pointer. Some presenters love that blazing red ball of light that they can zap from here to there on the screen. While the laser pointer is designed to focus the audience's attention on a certain area of the slide, unless the presenter has a very steady hand, that ball of light bounces around so much that it's distracting. As much as we love technology, we are pretty old school in our preference for using a physical gesture to indicate where to look on the screen. Better yet, use a gesture as well as a verbal cue to guide their gaze. ("If you take a look at the top lefthand corner of the screen. . ." accompanied by a gesture indicating the same instruction.)

When virtual

Blame the video collaboration platforms for messing with the power dynamic of presenters and their slides. When virtual, slide decks tend to suck up most of the screen time which diminishes the impact and value of the person behind the slides.

Why does this happen?

Even with years of practice, most people are still not fully comfortable with the technology used to share their slide deck with their fellow meeting attendees. If they manage to share the content that they want to share at all without switching between their desktop, their email app and their search engine window, they often consider that a small victory. So when Karin suggests that the best way to keep an audience engaged throughout a virtual presentation is to move in and out of sharing their screen, they give an emphatic "no thank you."

However, mastering this tech skill can make all the difference to whether your audience stays with you for your entire presentation or proceeds to do some online shopping.

The typical virtual presentation scenario looks something like this:

>> The presenter introduces themselves and the topic.

>> The presenter shares the slide deck (on the first attempt if they're lucky).

>> The presenter stays in a little box while the slides dominate the screen for the duration.

This is the in-room equivalent of facing your audience as you introduce yourself and then almost immediately turning your back on them for the rest of your presentation. Heck, you wouldn't even glance over your shoulder to see if someone has fallen asleep. This would be totally unacceptable in an in-person presentation but happens all of the time in virtual ones.

TIP

If you are presenting remotely, think what the virtual equivalent would be for the way you would typically interact with your slides in-person. You would probably spend the majority of your time looking into the faces of your audience but also turn to look at your slides when talking through data points or something of that nature that are represented on the screen. Here's how you translate that in-person interaction to a virtual one:

>> If you are speaking to something that is specifically on the slide, share that slide on the screen.

>> If you are speaking about something that is not referenced on the slide, stop sharing your screen and allow just you to be on camera.

Keep this in mind. At first, your slide may be helping you impart information, but there will come a time when it is no longer being absorbed by your audience and is just a resting spot for their eyes. Take that resting spot away.

By moving in and out of screen share, you are changing up their virtual environment. It automatically reengages them, especially if the audience has their cameras on and when you stop sharing your screen, the gallery view returns of which they are a part.

TIP

Don't let your slides dominate your virtual presentation for too long or you will lose your audience. It gives them license to check out. Instead, regularly alternate between sharing slides and having just attendees on the screen. If they know they could pop back up on the screen at any time, they are more likely to stay engaged and less likely to multitask.

When hybrid

Interacting with slides during a hybrid presentation should mirror the same principles as those for a purely virtual presentation. The difference is that it's harder to remember to do so especially if you are presenting from an in-person position.

Imagine this scenario. You are conducting a presentation during a hybrid meeting where you will be in the physical conference room with four other people while three other attendees are joining remotely. You are sharing your slides through the meeting platform which is being projected onto the monitor in the physical conference room.

For the in-room attendees, the setup is working great. They can see you because you are right in front of them. They can see your slides on the monitor. They can even see the faces of their remote colleagues.

Now consider the remote attendees' experience. Due to the platform's setup, their screens are almost completely occupied by the slides, and you, the speaker, share the same size little box on their screen as the boxes that contain the faces of the other virtual attendees. They can sort of see your gestures. They really can't see your facial expressions.

You can feel confident that your in-person attendees are receiving your message in full. Your virtual attendees? Not so much.

So what should you do?

For a hybrid presentation, you need to enhance your "presence" as a presenter for all audiences by minimizing how much screen time your slides are given. If your slide is critical to you telling your story, then by all means, keep it up on the screen, but if it's not, take it down. Overusing slide share during a hybrid meeting can make your remote attendees feel marginalized.

Engaging in Humor During Your Meetings

You may have been told a tried-and-true way to kick off a presentation is to start with a joke. Not if you aren't a funny person!

Good comedic timing is not innate for most of us, and you certainly don't need it to be a solid presenter, regardless of the kind of meeting you are presenting in. However, injecting a bit of levity into your presentation or meeting is an excellent idea, provided that it's the right kind of humor.

Laughing and joking in meetings is normally a very good thing. For people to be able to joke together, it suggests they like and trust each other enough that they are comfortable to do it.

TIP

Humor is a good thing when it brings people together, when it helps strengthen rather than harm relationships. Use humor with care and it can help build a better group or team.

The challenge here is that humor in meetings can also have a not so good side. While certain forms of humor will lead to people laughing together and building stronger relationships, other forms of humor lead to people laughing *at* others, harming relationships and reducing overall trust within the team.

TECHNICAL
STUFF

When Joe worked with Dr. Nale Lehmann-Willenbrock on a study focused on dis-covering the effects of humor in meetings, the teams in the study were German engineering teams. Using some fancy analyses strategies called sequential analy-sis, they discovered that sequences of positive humor increased the effectiveness of the meeting. In fact, they found that humor even appeared to make the teams perform better overall. They concluded that there's something special about humor among team members. Likely positive humor that is shared among coworkers is symptomatic of a positive work culture and environment. Those things make working harder together a meaningful thing to do. It's always easier to work with friends, and people don't usually joke around with people they don't like.

However, it's hard to tell what will be both humorous and appropriate for a certain group. For example, the engineering teams that they studied would joke about specific pieces of equipment operating in unusual manner. It's like saying to someone, "Remember Machine 27 on Line 8?" and the team busting up, laughing their heads off. While neither Nale nor Joe understood what was funny about statements like that, the behavior they observed (uproarious laughter) told the story. These coworkers liked each other and had a long history together.

Not all humor is created equal and you must be careful how you use it. There are different types of humor and they cause very different reactions among people. In fact, there are two types that we want to discuss in greater detail here: affiliative humor and aggressive humor:

>> Affiliative humor is like the story we just described about German engineers. Jokes or humorous statements that everyone in the meeting understand and likely find funny, and appropriately funny. This kind of humor builds affiliation. That is, it makes people feel all warm and fuzzy inside about the people they are meeting with.

You might use affiliative humor by telling a funny story about something that happened to most or all of the team members in the meeting. By laughing over the shared experience, you're building camaraderie among your coworkers. Think of it as "remember the time when we. . ." followed by rolling laughter by everyone in the meeting.

Affiliative humor can be inside jokes, but the insiders must be most or all of the group in the meeting in order for it to have the desired effect. This form of humor is generally positive and puts people at ease. Joe's been known to try to engage in this type of humor at the beginning of meetings with long-standing teams. It becomes a form of pre-meeting talk that really launches off the meeting in a good way.

>> Aggressive humor is negative or derogatory in nature. There usually is a target of the joke who is being put down. We, as a society, enjoy this type of humor quite a bit, particularly in the television shows and movies we watch. While aggressive humor typically does not have a negative effect on those who witness it, it certainly can on the person who is the butt of the joke and can harm the connections that person has with the rest of the group.

For example, reminding a team member of a mistake they made that was embarrassing will often get a laugh, but it will also make that person feel really bad. In fact, it may make them relive the experience again in their minds, ruminating, and not engaging in the meeting.

All evidence suggests that aggressive humor harms trust and cohesion in groups and teams and should not be used in meetings. In fact, we argue that it should rarely be used in general.

However, you will see people use it as a method of lowering the status of a coworker who they do not like or just want to get ahead of. It is an unfortunate tool that can be used to harm people's standing in the group or organization, and some people do use it to their advantage. It is often associated with Machiavellian forms of leadership.

Encouraging affiliative humor

The best way to encourage affiliative humor is to use it. That's right, crack a joke from time to time. As you get to know the people you work with, you'll learn what they consider humorous, you'll have experiences together that might be funny to share time and again, and you can use this to your and your team's advantage.

As you use this form of humor in your meetings, people will get used to a greater level of levity in your meetings, and begin to use this as well. As the trust builds among peers and coworkers, overall performance will improve across the team because people will help each other. They will care about each other's feelings, and they will want to see each other succeed.

WARNING

Even affiliative humor can get lost in translation. And timing is everything with jokes. Some meetings may have a very serious purpose and joviality will undermine the formal nature of the situation. Read your surroundings and use affiliative humor with care. When someone's future with the company is on the line, humor in all its forms may not be appropriate for that meeting.

Squelching aggressive humor

WARNING

Aggressive humor is generally bad. It's symptomatic of an unhealthy group, team, or organizational climate and culture. If you see this in many of your meetings, it's time to squelch it and fast.

But, how do you do that?

Many of the tactics we've discussed for establishing and enabling good behavior (see Chapters 11 and 12) can be used here too:

>> **Engage in the good to edge out the bad.** Engage in affiliative humor when appropriate and encourage others to do likewise. If you're busy laughing together, you are less likely to laugh at others.

>> **Set a ground rule.** In fact, general professionalism expectations likely already support not using put down or aggressive humor. You should collaboratively establish a formal ground rule for your meetings that joking is cool so long as it's positive and supportive. Humor at the expense of others, particularly those in the room must be avoided.

>> **Build a psychologically safe environment where power and politics are not part of the collaborative equation.** Essentially, try to harbor a "safe space" mentality in meetings where people can share openly without worry of repercussion for their ideas, no matter how crazy.

At the same time, avoid creating a meeting environment where it's "us" against "them." The more people perceive that someone has power over them, the more office politics come into play, creating a breeding ground for aggressive humor that pokes at "the powers that be."

Chapter **14**

Stifling Bad Meeting Behaviors

L et's face it. People are not always good in meetings. They engage in monologues that reduce participation from others. They run off topic and down the rabbit hole. They may criticize others both inside and outside the meeting. Some may express resignation at the issues being discussed or let their mind wander when they feel there's nothing that can be done to solve a particular problem. They may multitask to try to catch up on the "real work" they have to do, or they may try to be the center of attention.

These and other bad meeting behaviors are all too common in most workplace meetings. The science is clear: They derail meetings and make it extremely difficult to get anything good out of a meeting. In other words, bad meeting behaviors make meetings bad.

Although we are certain you can think of many examples of times when you witnessed bad behavior in meetings, an example from Joe's experience is both humorous and sad. Check out the nearby sidebar to find out more!

SETTING A BAD EXAMPLE

"Earlier in my career, I was invited to a meeting with the executive team for a large non-profit organization. They wanted to chat about how to more fully engage their volunteer workforce, and my expertise in that area was what led them to me. As a good meeting scientist, I arrived early with the intent of engaging in some pre-meeting small talk, feel out the situation, and get an idea of some of the potential insights I might share with them.

The conversations were light, and I was informed we were waiting for the executive director to arrive. A few minutes past the start time, the executive director came into the room and indicated he'd had back-to-back meetings all day and could use a minute to find the restroom. Everyone was fine with that, obviously, and we continued to chat about local events and a little about volunteer engagement.

Ten minutes later, the executive director walked back in, on the phone and put a hand up indicating "five more minutes." Fifteen minutes later, the executive director came in and sat down. We were now 30 minutes into the 60 minute scheduled time.

We started with introductions and as I explained who I was, the executive director looked at one of the other leaders in the room, and said something like "Where did you get this guy? Do we need an egg-head from the university?" I reminded him that I was invited to this meeting and that they were currently receiving free consulting from me. It seemed to appease him for a moment.

With introductions done, he asked me, "So how do we fix our volunteer problem?" I then asked him and the rest of the attendees to tell me more about the problems they were having. The executive director threw his hands up in the air, indicating this was a waste of his time. Five minutes later, he got up and left the room."

If you've read the sidebar (go on — you'll enjoy it!), you might be thinking, "I didn't know Joe also studied volunteer engagement." Okay, maybe not. You're probably thinking that this executive director was rude. You'd be right. You'd also be right to assume that it wasn't long before this director was asked to move on. Sadly, his interactions with some of the volunteers were a major source of the problem.

All of that aside, though, let's focus on the bad meeting behaviors that were all too apparent. There was lateness, complaining, resignation, and even leaving the meeting early. All of these translate into bad behaviors that derail the meeting. We've been in many a meeting where all of these behaviors happened, but what was unusual about this situation was they were all displayed by one person. Most of the time, the bad meeting behaviors are more evenly distributed across attendees and leaders.

If a set of these behaviors are exhibited by only a single person, there may be more developmental guidance needed and perhaps some coaching for that person. However, when the set of behaviors is shown by a number of people in the same meeting, a different set of tactics and strategies are needed. In fact, much of the research in meeting science suggests there is a *social contagion* effect (if someone else is doing it, I'll do it too, for good or ill) of good and bad behavior. So, usually if you have one person engaging in bad meeting behavior, others will start doing similarly.

WARNING

If you do not take bad meeting behaviors seriously and work to eliminate them, no meeting you run will be as effective as it ought to be. However, eliminating bad meeting behaviors can be a delicate process and sometimes requires performance review efforts and coaching.

Intervening When Dysfunctional Communication Occurs

As bad meeting behaviors cause bad meetings, you have to intervene when such behaviors occur. Making that decision means you have to recognize the potential for conflict that doing so may cause. Welcome to working with and managing people!

Unfortunately, conflict is not something that can always be avoided. However, it can be managed more effectively. For example, let's suppose you have a person who is notorious for arriving late to every meeting. One option may be to call attention to their tardiness in front of everyone in the meeting. Depending upon the nature of your relationship with them and your team, this may be a viable option. It may, however, not be an option as it's basically public shaming someone to change their behavior.

Yes, public shaming is effective at changing behavior, but it's not typically viewed as a kind way to change behavior and can result in both open conflict and hurt feelings. Thus, we often recommend more subtle approaches.

Instead of calling out the bad behavior openly in front of all their colleagues, taking the person aside, pointing out the issue, and discussing it quietly together is typically much better practice.

TIP

Use this general tip when it comes to correction: Know your people and learn how they respond to correction. As you do so, you can customize your intervention into their bad meeting behavior accordingly.

Identifying bad meeting behaviors

Overall, we recommend intervening when dysfunctional communication and bad meeting behaviors occur. But, you might be asking yourself, what constitutes bad meeting behavior. In fact, some of the behaviors that are actually bad meeting behaviors might surprise you and you might find yourself thinking, "Geez, I gotta stop doing that myself!". It's okay, Joe and Karin both have been known to engage in some of these behaviors in their meetings, and so we recognize that we are all works in progress.

In our books *Suddenly Virtual* (John Wiley & Sons, Inc., 2021), we provided the following checklist of bad meeting behaviors that attendees are known to engage in. We reproduce the checklist here and also encourage you, if you have a lot of virtual meetings, to consider checking out that book for even more guidance on bad meeting behaviors and all things related to virtual meetings.

Counter-Productive Meeting Behavior

1.	Meeting attendees engage in long monologues that do not move the discussion forward.	[ ] Yes	[ ] No
2.	Meeting attendees go off the topic (e.g., talking about TV programs or other spare time activities).	[ ] Yes	[ ] No
3.	Meeting attendees heavily criticize others in the meeting or others not present in the meeting.	[ ] Yes	[ ] No
4.	Meeting attendees use sarcasm to criticize others.	[ ] Yes	[ ] No
5.	Meeting attendees express resignation.	[ ] Yes	[ ] No
6.	Meeting attendees complain about things during the meeting.	[ ] Yes	[ ] No
7.	Meeting attendees use random sayings or empty phrases.	[ ] Yes	[ ] No
8.	Meeting attendees express little interest in trying out new ideas or procedures.	[ ] Yes	[ ] No
9.	Meeting attendees explain why everything has to stay the way it is.	[ ] Yes	[ ] No
10.	Meeting attendees shift responsibility to others or to management.	[ ] Yes	[ ] No
11.	Meeting attendees point out their work experience/expertise to show that they are superior.	[ ] Yes	[ ] No
12.	Meeting attendees occasionally leave the meeting.	[ ] Yes	[ ] No
13.	Meeting attendees arrive late to meetings.	[ ] Yes	[ ] No

14.	Meeting attendees leave the meeting early without giving a reason.	[ ] Yes	[ ] No
15.	Meeting attendees occupy themselves with things unrelated to the meeting (e.g., texting, emailing, etc.).	[ ] Yes	[ ] No
16.	Meeting attendees seem to let their minds wander during the meeting.	[ ] Yes	[ ] No
17.	Meeting attendees rarely participate in the meeting.	[ ] Yes	[ ] No
18.	Meeting attendees show obvious disinterest in the topics that are discussed.	[ ] Yes	[ ] No
19.	Meeting attendees express disinterest with their facial expression.	[ ] Yes	[ ] No
20.	Meeting attendees interrupt others.	[ ] Yes	[ ] No
21.	Meeting attendees try to be the center of attention in meetings.	[ ] Yes	[ ] No
22.	Meeting attendees are not interested in the views of the others.	[ ] Yes	[ ] No
23.	Meeting attendees make fun of other meeting attendees.	[ ] Yes	[ ] No
24.	Meeting attendees deliberately try to show up other meeting attendees.	[ ] Yes	[ ] No
25.	Meeting attendees intimidate other meeting attendees.	[ ] Yes	[ ] No
	TOTAL YES		

As you can see, there's quite a few different bad behaviors that people can and do engage in. Even though the checklist references bad meeting behavior on the part of attendees, the checklist can be modified to apply to the actions of supervisors, meeting leaders, or bosses. The key here is that our checklist provides you with a bit of a diagnostic tool to identify the behaviors you need to work on in your meetings among the people you meet with.

If, by chance, you don't see some bad behavior on this list, remember that humans are creative little critters and they'll find ways of disrupting meetings that they don't personally find meaningful. And those ways will be varied and often creative. For example, one colleague of Joe's would often bring their lunch to a non-lunch meeting. Now, most people can eat in a relatively subtle manner. But, not this person. They were loud. Their food often had a strong smell to it. And they never brought enough for everyone. That is a bad behavior that did not make the checklist, but does make the list of possible derailing behaviors.

It's important to identify the behaviors before intervening and then make a plan on how to intervene. Some behaviors require immediate, real-time intervention while others do not. Because meeting and group cultures differ, we don't make too many assumptions about which behaviors require immediate intervention. However, we would say that anything that amounts to abusive or bullying behavior cannot be tolerated and often requires immediate action (and sometimes HR involvement).

Stopping bad behavior without derailing the meeting

In many cases, bad behavior can be stopped without disrupting the meeting to a great degree. We talk about our favorite method for this in Chapter 11, procedural communication which helps you to keep the meeting on track.

In that chapter, we use the example of the monologuer that needs to be shut down so the meeting can move forward. They get onto their favorite topic and go on and on and on. Procedural communication, or statements that pull people back to the key steps in the meeting process, is a great way to stop bad behaviors related to communication. These include the following, as listed on our checklist earlier in this chapter:

» Monologue behavior

» Complaining behavior

» All forms of criticizing others

» Interrupting behavior

» Making fun of others

» Intimidating behavior

These forms of communication rarely have a place in meetings and procedural communication is a kind way in the meeting to stop those behaviors in their tracks. This is particularly true because these behaviors pretty much never contribute to the purpose of the meeting. Because of that, pulling people back to the purpose in a logical fashion stops the bad behavior, usually.

Start practicing with the different procedural communication statements right now and make it standard in all your meetings. It will immediately begin to reduce many of the most problematic communication behaviors that drain the effectiveness out of meetings.

Another key recommendation for stopping bad behavior without derailing the meeting is establishing meeting etiquette ground rules. We talk about ground rules throughout the book, but all of those focus on good behaviors (such as having an agenda, starting on time, and encouraging participation).

Ground rules can also include rules about what not to do during a meeting, and what bad behaviors are unacceptable. You can even consider including what sanctions fall upon those who break the ground rules. For example, late participants have to bring coffee for everyone at the next meeting.

TIP

Most meeting ground rules documents should err on the positive side, encouraging good meeting behavior. However, identifying a few bad meeting behaviors that you pledge to avoid can also be helpful, especially if you've noticed certain practices that you know are problematic. By codifying what you want to do and what you don't want to do in your meetings, you run a better chance of having your good meeting behavior crowd out the bad.

TIP

TACKLING A SERIAL INTERRUPTER

A quick word about the serial interrupter — this is one of the most common bad meeting behaviors we are asked about at all levels of the enterprise. It's especially tricky when the person who loves to interrupt is the senior person in the room, but it is no less frustrating. What do you do when someone has a habit of butting in and throws you off your stride?

It's all about controlling the conversation as best you can depending upon the power dynamic in the room. If you are running the meeting and someone insists upon trying to hijack the conversation by talking about what they want to talk about, it's totally within your rights to use procedural communication to redirect the meeting to what is on the agenda (see Chapter 11). Don't completely ignore what they brought up, but table it for now to protect the integrity of the meeting topic. If your interrupter is rambling on, use their tactic to rein them in. Interrupt the interrupter by saying something like, "Lisa, I get what you're saying here but let's take this up at another time. We really need to stick with what's on the agenda here."

If the serial interrupter is someone senior to you, it can a bit trickier. You don't want to offend them or hurt your career prospects. However, our advice is to acknowledge what they are saying or asking you about, and look for an opportunity to get back on track as soon as possible. Let's say they want you to talk about something while you are presenting slide 2 that you plan to address on slide 5. Let them know that you appreciate them bringing that up and you plan to talk about that in depth in just a few minutes if they are okay with you finishing up your thought. Being respectful goes a long way and will usually allow you to satisfy their curiosity while also maintaining control of the meeting.

Keeping Counterproductive Meeting Behaviors At Bay

As any behavioral psychologist will tell you, the best way to stop a behavior is for it to never happen in the first place. Once it's happened, it gets harder to get rid of, particularly if the person feels the alternative is less satisfying. For example, showing up late is often more comfortable for people because it takes the pressure off of arriving on time. So it makes sense that the easier option is what people do all too frequently.

TECHNICAL STUFF

Many years ago, B.F. Skinner, a behaviorist within the area of psychology, first described the concept of *operant conditioning*. He believed that it is not necessary to look at the internal thoughts, feelings, or motivations of people to understand and explain their behavior. Rather, all you have to do is see what they do. Specifically, he said that people do what they do in response to the pattern of rewards and punishments they receive for their actions.

What does this look like? Well, for Skinner, it looked like a box with a button that controlled a food pellet door for a rat. Depending upon how many button presses it took to open the door, the rat would press the button frantically or more lazily. Some would argue that the modern-day escape room is nothing more than a Skinner Box for humans. Press the right button enough times and you get rewarded by getting out.

In other words, people will do things if they believe they will be rewarded for doing that thing and people will not do things that they believe will earn them a punishment. There's all sorts of variations on this theme, but the bottom line is that people like to be rewarded and don't like to be punished.

Whether you realize it or not, you already use operant conditioning in your life. We all do. We do things all day, every day, in order to receive something in response, a reward shall we say. For example, we flip the light switch in our bedroom in the morning and are rewarded with light, so long as we've paid our electric bill and were rewarded with electricity.

In terms of meetings, we share ideas in the hope that others will agree with us, which is rewarding, and support us as we move forward with our team. We show up on time to a meeting because we don't want to be publicly embarrassed again or we don't have the cash on hand to buy everyone their favorite coffee.

The point of all this is to provide a meaningful explanation for why people do what they do that still applies today. We disagree with Skinner in the belief that people's thoughts and feelings and motivations do not matter. However, we agree that an awful lot of behaviors can be explained by the outcomes people experience.

TIP

Use rewards and punishments to keep good behavior in meetings happening and keep bad behavior in meetings from ever happening. Take a page out of behavioral psychology and your favorite parenting book, and realize that people will do an awful lot for a piece of candy or to avoid a terrible task.

Using good meeting behavior to edge out bad behavior

One of our favorite recommendations around keeping bad behavior from happening in the first place is emphasizing and engaging in good behavior. That might be why so much of this book is devoted to all the good behaviors we want everyone to know about and engage in during all their meetings. And here's why. . .

REMEMBER

People have a finite amount of time, energy, and resources. If they use all those resources doing the good behaviors that you want them to do, they won't have any time, energy, or resources left to do that bad behavior.

That's right. Keep everyone busy doing exactly what will unlock the potential for your meetings. Keep them participating and helping other participate. Keep them intently listening to others and adding to their ideas. Keep them actively monitoring the chat in the virtual meeting or being an in-room ally during a hybrid meeting (check out Chapter 12 for more on these roles). If you give people roles and responsibilities, and you hold them accountable to that, then they just run out of time to do the bad stuff.

For example, if someone has to monitor the chat and summarize comments, including identifying questions that arise, how will they also check their email? When they are busy doing something you've asked them to do, they can't do things you have not asked them to do. There's no time for multitasking because they have plenty to keep them busy in the meeting itself.

When Karin designs any sort of training, she always keeps that in mind. Throughout any session, she intentionally inserts opportunities for participants to "do" things. If people are passively listening for too long, they will at minimum mentally tune out and at maximum completely disengage and do something else. (Obviously, this is easier to do if you are attending remotely and can hide behind a black box.) What participants must "do" runs the gamut. It may be simply answering a poll. It could be answering a question in chat. Often, it's opening up the floor for full discussion of something related to what was just presented. The idea is to minimize the passive downtime and make the session active for all. However, sometimes things don't go as planned as you can read in nearby sidebar on perils and pitfalls.

KNOWING THE PERILS AND PITFALLS OF BREAKOUT ROOMS

If you are running a virtual meeting, you may like to use breakout rooms to break up a larger meeting into a more intimate setting with smaller groups. This is also a way to get people to "do" something because it almost forces engagement. If you are in a breakout room with just a few people, you would come across as rude if you didn't take part in the discussion. However, do know that there may be some folks who may have no problem blowing off their colleagues and doing something else that they consider more important.

For example, Karin was leading a session with some of the most senior leaders of a global company. At one point, she put them in breakout rooms to work on an assignment in pairs. She decided to drop in on the various groups to see if they needed any help. For the most part, everyone was on task and appreciated the chance to work one on one with a peer, but when she entered one of the breakout rooms, she was shocked. One of the participants was muted and on the phone on a totally unrelated call while their partner was sitting there looking lost. When the person on the phone realized Karin had entered the room, they did eventually get off the call and offered a quick apology. However, Karin is pretty sure that the phone call would have continued had she not appeared unexpectedly to offer some guidance if needed. Apparently, the guidance they needed was to actually do what they were supposed to do . . . and these folks were at the highest level of the enterprise.

Breakout rooms can be viewed by some as a chance to throw meeting etiquette out the window and allow bad meeting behaviors to flourish. Think back to primary school when the teacher needed to briefly leave the classroom. Without supervision, it didn't take long for the behavior of the students to quickly devolve. Now granted, you are leading a team of adults and should not feel the need to check up on your direct reports, but do make sure you have some way to hold people accountable.

In the case of a breakout room, consider assigning a task and then make them aware that they will be required to report back once they return to the main session. Popping into breakout rooms to check on the progress of each group is also a way to ensure everyone is following through as directed.

One of the trickiest bad meeting behaviors to snuff out is meeting lateness where people show up to a session after its scheduled start time. Meeting lateness is a bit unique because the behavior itself is sometimes rewarding. Maybe they were able to squeeze in that one extra task, and they found great pleasure in crossing it off their mental to-do list. The problem is what they found personally rewarding had a very negative impact on the rest of the people waiting for them to arrive. (In general, people hate when others are late for a meeting. See Chapter 10 to discover more about this.) However, do know you need to work a little harder to break the meeting lateness habit by taking away the benefit of showing up late.

We suggest using social pressure to motivate the behavioral change. Most people will stop arriving late if the majority of folks are on time and the meeting has started when they walk in. If they are the last one into the room, most will even apologize. In this case, the good behavior of others narrows the lateness down to the last straggler who will feel immense social pressure to comply. That social pressure in essence is the punishment.

Most bad behaviors are not deliberate. People don't walk into a meeting thinking, "How can I make this a terrible experience for everyone?" Well, at least we hope people aren't thinking like that. Sticking with lateness, sometimes people are late for legitimate reasons. For example, if you schedule a 9 a.m. meeting and someone is consistently late, they may be dropping off kids at school and the traffic causes their lateness. It's also good to be careful not to assume that a bad behavior is deliberate or malicious. Sometimes it's completely out of their control or they may not even realize it's a bad behavior. Talk to the repeat offender about what might be causing it and show some empathy in finding a solution if necessary.

Rewarding good behavior and reining in bad behavior

A few years ago on a popular TV sitcom called "The Big Bang Theory," Sheldon attempted to use operant conditioning to train Leonard's girlfriend Penny to stop engaging in what Sheldon considered bad behavior. Leonard said something like "You can't use operant conditioning to train my girlfriend to stop doing things you find annoying." Sheldon's response was something like, "Actually, it appears that I can."

The same applies to meetings. You can (and in many cases should) reward good behavior and punish bad behavior. You probably already do this in your meetings. For example, you reward people by paying attention to their nonverbal cues and calling on them to share their thoughts. You punish people by giving them a sour look when you catch them texting during the meeting.

We recommend thinking through how best to reward good meeting behavior and how best to sanction bad meeting behavior. There's no one-size-fits-all approach. Match both to the culture of your team and organization.

Let's give you an example. You might think it would be fun to buy a bunch of candy and toss each person a piece after they share an idea. For some teams, this might be a perfect way to inject some levity into the proceedings and actually pull out participation (especially if your team has a collective sweet tooth). But food rewards are rife with potential pitfalls — allergies, medical conditions, lifestyle choices. Yikes!

There also will be contextual factors that make some rewards inappropriate. Candy being passed out to a team that works directly with hazardous chemicals while they are still in their protective gear is probably a bad tactic.

The point is that groups are different. For one group, candy may be the way to go while for another it might be inappropriate. People are also different. One person may be strongly motivated by one type of reward while others might find that reward less desirable.

The key is to get to know your people and your groups. Identify what rewards would motivate them and use them for the benefit of the entire team. Remember, if you can get people to do more of the good behavior, the bad behavior will be crowded out, making for a better and more productive experience for everyone. Technically the same applies for punishments, but you will likely run into some barriers. Punishments are harder to implement due to HR policies and general professionalism practices.

Motivating people to engage in good behaviors has the potential to essentially solve the bad behavior problem as well.

BAD IS STRONGER THAN GOOD

That's right. Meeting science and other social science research confirms that bad behaviors have a greater impact than good behaviors. One bad behavior can completely derail a meeting, even when there are many good behaviors that were occurring throughout the meeting. We know from our research that the negative impact of bad meeting behavior frequently outweighs the positive impact of good behavior on meeting satisfaction and outcomes. Put differently, you have to engage in a *lot* of good behaviors to compensate for the bad.

For example, when someone monologues for five minutes of a 25-minute meeting, the entire agenda is affected. This means that some topics simply won't now get the time they need to be considered by the team. Further, if the monologue is relevant to others in the meeting, it might change how they will respond or react to the next things on the agenda. Ultimately, that one monologue changed the entire experience of the meeting, making it different in ways both expected and unexpected. All the procedural communication in the world won't fully be able to overcome whatever was stated during that verbal binge.

But, it's not a hopeless situation just yet! The key is to recognize that eliminating bad behaviors is just as, if not more important as encouraging good behaviors. And if you can get enough good behavior happening, the bad behaviors will become fewer and fewer.

4

Making a Meeting Worthwhile — What to do after a Meeting

If there's ever a time when you don't want to let down your guard, it's at this point along the meeting continuum. What you do after a meeting can make or break the effectiveness of your meeting overall. That's why we've devoted this entire part to addressing what steps are critical at this stage.

In this part, you discover why follow-up is so important after the meeting adjourns and how best to do this depending upon the meeting format you used. We also highlight the value of creating a feedback loop, so you can find out what is working and what is not in your meetings.

Remember, if you don't measure it, it didn't happen . . . and that includes what happens in your meetings!

Chapter **15**

Following Up Effectively

Congratulations! You've managed to conduct a productive and effectively managed meeting. You can pat yourself on the back for setting yourself up for success by making sure you had an agenda that actually was shaped by participant feedback. You even assigned prework so when everyone gathered for the actual event, you jumped right in to the discussion at a higher level of understanding. The conversation was well-balanced with input from everyone in attendance. You started and ended on time, and when you brought it to a close, everyone felt like a lot had been accomplished, including the goal of the meeting itself.

You might think you are good to go and want to move on to the next item on your to-do list. Not so fast! There's this concept called a *meeting continuum* which means there are things that have to be done before, during, and after a meeting, and it's that last one that tends to trip people up.

All of that good work done up to this point will have no lasting impact if you don't take action after the meeting is adjourned. Human beings have very short attention spans, and as great as the session went, much of the progress made within it will be lost unless you have some way of recording it and following up on it appropriately.

REMEMBER

What you do after your meeting matters as much as what you do before and during the session. Don't let all of your hard work up to this point go down the drain. Put as much effort into your follow up as you invested so far.

That's why we devote this chapter to following up effectively after your meeting. In this chapter we discuss what needs to occur as you wrap up the meeting itself before you walk out the literal or virtual door. We give you some ideas on how to make sure everyone has access to the pertinent information afterward, and we talk about ways to manage those quick clarifications, so you don't end up with another meeting on your calendar.

Creating and Recording an Action Plan

Were you ever in a meeting that sort of just fizzled out rather than came to a fulfilling close? Maybe you wrapped up discussion of the final item on the list and then the leader said something like this, "Well, that's all that we have on our agenda today. Thanks everybody." Maybe a few folks exchanged some furtive glances, wondering "Is that it?" while others skipped out of the room as soon as they were given license to leave.

Discussion for the sake of discussion might be enjoyable but is likely pointless if your meeting was designed with a purpose and goal in mind. How can you be sure you've accomplished your goal if you haven't acknowledged that you've done so far? What's more, how will people know what comes next if they are unsure what decisions were actually made?

REMEMBER

Proper follow up for any meeting begins at the close of the session itself. You might think attendees will organically understand the decisions that were made and will take it upon themselves to figure out what needs to happen as a result, but that assumption leaves a lot to chance. The better practice is to be explicit with this information and not leave any of it to individual interpretation.

With this in mind, don't let anyone leave until you've completed the following:

>> Summarized the decisions that were made

>> Listed the action items that stem from them

>> Delegated who is responsible for each action item

TIP

Many teams make it a practice to do all of the above throughout the meeting rather than at the very end. In fact, meeting science indicates this to be the preferred way. Either way, make sure you have accomplished all three at some point during the meeting before adjourning.

Let's take a look at each of these in a bit more detail.

Summarizing decisions made

Wouldn't it be nice if every decision that we made began with "We have decided to . . .?" That way, it would be crystal clear where the consensus landed. Unfortunately, we typically don't use direct language like that, and sometimes our final decisions get muddied by the verbiage around it. That's why it's important for you, as the meeting leader, to add clarity for your team, so everyone knows what was decided and what next steps need to be taken.

Hopefully, you've been keeping track of the decisions made throughout the meeting or assigned someone to do so for you (see Chapter 10 for more on this). Either way, begin the process by revisiting the notes that highlight the key takeaways. Explicitly state each decision made and make sure everyone gathered agrees with how you verbalized it. Not everyone hears things the same way and that can lead to confusion going forward. You might think the decision was to stop working on a particular project entirely while others in the group interpreted that as putting the work on hold for now.

TIP

Don't assume that everyone understands a decision in the way you do. As you go through each decision made throughout the course of the meeting, ask if your explanation jibes with everyone else's. If not, don't rehash the discussion, but do probe for additional clarity to find out where the disconnect lies.

At the end of this reiteration of decisions, you will have a concise summary of what you agreed to do, but you will also have a common understanding of what those decisions are. This sets the stage for natural progression — figuring out the next steps that are informed by that decision.

Listing action items

Like the decisions themselves, you may have been jotting down throughout the meeting various action items that need to happen. If so, your job is relatively easy here. Simply go back through your notes or ask your assigned minutes keeper to repeat the items that need to be added to the collective to-do list. If you haven't determined those action items along the way, you may have to do it at the end. This will no doubt extend the length of your meeting, but it's absolutely necessary to ensure your team knows how to proceed.

REMEMBER

Regardless of process, make sure you build adequate time to do this step. Making decisions with meaningful next steps is great. But, if those next steps aren't assigned to people as action items, then all too often nothing happens, and the next meeting is a repeat of the previous.

The action items should be as a specific as possible and with a finite end point:

>> **Here's an example of a poorly designed action item:** "Learn more about client A's supply chain."

>> **Here's how a well-designed version would look:** "Find out what suppliers client A uses and report back at our next team meeting on February 5."

The first version of the action item is too vague and doesn't give enough guidance. The poor person assigned the task could end up doing exhaustive research into what they thought was the right stuff, only to find out they had completely missed the mark. Also notice that there's no deadline for the action item to be completed by. If you don't set an end point for when the information needs to be produced, you can't expect for it to be available when you want it to be. The second version of the action item asks for specific information and sets a date for when it needs to be ready to present. Holding people accountable in this way ensures the action items get done.

Delegating responsibilities

Determining who needs to take responsibility for each action item is just as important as figuring out what those steps are. That's why you need to clearly express who is assigned to do what and by when.

You may find it obvious who should be delegated to take on a certain task. Maybe it falls specifically under their job duties, or they have the contacts or connections to follow through best. The challenge is when there isn't an obvious choice for a particular task that needs to be done. In that case, you can take two paths: Ask for a volunteer or assign it to them proactively.

TIP

Most teams have someone who is always willing to step up, almost to their own detriment. They're the folks who are gifted the coffee cup saying, "Stop me before a volunteer again." If you ask for someone to volunteer for a task and you see the same hands go up every time, perhaps pick one of those people to take it on. However, reserve the right to ask someone else to do it if you think they might be uniquely suited for the job or they have a tendency to let others pick up the slack. The best teams have full engagement from everyone. If you need to orchestrate that by assigning an action item to someone who is a little checked out, we encourage you to do so.

As we mentioned before, your action items should be specific with a deadline, but you may want a progress report before the due date. If that's the case, let the person responsible for that action item know. Your team doesn't want to disappoint. Help them out by setting clear expectations for how you want the task completed.

Further, just letting people know that they are welcome to ask you questions or to check-in with you on progress before the deadline can help ensure the action item is accomplished in the way you want.

WARNING

If someone is new to the team, you need to be even more explicit in how you word your action items because they might be reluctant to ask for clarification. They may still feel like they are proving themselves to the team and don't want to appear to be in the dark. They may waste a lot of time and energy on a task that was not quite what you had in mind. Remove the ambiguity for them and be as clear as possible in what you are asking them to do. You can also relieve some of their anxiety by letting them know you understand they are new and may need some additional guidance. Provide a psychological safety net for them that normalizes the need to ask for help.

Making the Meeting Materials Accessible

Are you someone who lives by lists? You have a lot of company if you do. In fact, most people love (and rely upon) lists to keep themselves organized and perhaps more importantly to ensure they get done what they need to get done.

When it comes to meetings, you and your attendees can also benefit from having everything in writing. In most cases, this means documenting it in digital form so it's accessible to all, regardless of where people are located.

TECHNICAL STUFF

The most successful remote only companies have a strong documentation culture. For example, one company even has an ever-evolving on-line handbook that includes everything employees need to know about every aspect of the business. In fact, their Head of Remote once said, "If it's not in the handbook, it doesn't exist." This extreme affection for digitally documenting everything may not make sense in your organization, but there's a lot to be learned from this orientation. In general, in a fully virtual environment organizations likely need all of their employees to have access to information from anywhere in the world.

WARNING

If you are operating in a fully virtual or hybrid work model, you need to carefully consider how you are recording your follow up information from a meeting. You can't just pass out pages of written minutes or make sure no one erases the notes from the whiteboard in the conference room. If you are relying upon non-connected modes of transmitting information, you are keeping that information from those who aren't in the physical office. That breeds a two-tiered system where those in the office have better access to information than those who are not, and that in turn will breed hostility and resentment.

Make certain to set up a method for sharing information from your meetings that is inclusive of all participants, including those in person and remote.

Determining where to store meeting information

Even if you have assigned someone to record the minutes of the meeting and they are writing everything down by hand, ask them to transcribe them into a version that can be stored and distributed digitally. For people like Karin who have a habit of writing in chicken scratch that only she can read, the process of transcribing the handwritten notes into a shareable document can help to refine the narrative to truly reflect what occurred.

Then, that information needs to be disseminated to all key stakeholders, including the meeting attendees themselves and might also include others who need to know what happened but did not need to be a part of the conversation. In fact, making it a habit to carefully document what happened in the meeting can help you curate the invite list. If someone was originally on the list of attendees but their only role was to be a spectator, you can safely give them back their time by assuring them that they'll receive the minutes of the meeting afterward. If you make this a habit, you might be surprised by how many people thank you for both letting them out of the meeting and including them in what's going on.

TECHNICAL STUFF

One practice that really took hold during the pandemic was recording meetings in their entirety. While this wouldn't apply to face-to-face meetings, any fully virtual or hybrid meeting would have this option provided that it conforms with the policies of the organization and passes legal muster for recording consent. We've worked with companies where every meeting that involves a video collaboration platform is recording and stored in their enterprise video repository. Attendees are given a quick heads up that the meeting is being recorded and then asked to acknowledge the fact by clicking a button on a pop-up window. You can also opt out of the meeting if you are not comfortable having the conversation recorded.

Meeting recordings have a lot of value for those in the meeting as well as for interested parties who either couldn't attend live or simply need to be kept in the loop. Not only can they watch it at a time that's convenient for them, but they can also watch it in 1.5 speed or even 2X speed.

The idea of picking up the viewing pace does rub Karin wrong. She spends much of her time helping speakers to slow down their delivery, so their audience can easily digest the information. However, in this case, efficiency trumps communication best practices. If the goal is to get the general gist of what happened, watching the meeting in double time works. If the goal is to fully digest the information in a way where it'll sink in, take the time to watch it in normal speed.

Whether slowed down or sped up, video recordings of meetings can now be stored and sent out almost as easily as a document.

Sending out minutes

The most traditional method of sending out follow up information is via email. In fact, this is still the default way of communication for the majority of businesses (as evidenced by the 200 emails that seem to drop at 9 a.m. every day in Karin and Joe's inboxes). But the digital clutter that accumulates in them can quickly overwhelm the emails that truly need attention. If you are planning to send it out via email, use the different settings in your email provider to indicate or flag that the contents are important.

For internal dissemination, we are seeing an ever-growing trend to use collaboration hubs to both store and send out post-meeting information. The hubs (such as Slack and Microsoft Teams) allow information to be categorized and stored in threads or channels on the platform which can be accessed by the team or even the entire enterprise if appropriate. This cuts down on the digital noise that might interfere with the message being received and makes it easily searchable in an archivable form.

REMEMBER

You want to send out the information as soon as possible after the meeting. What's the point of sitting on it, especially if you want people to immediately get to work on their assigned action items? Now that doesn't mean you want to send out without ensuring its accuracy. If you have someone else prepping the minutes for you, take the time to look them over and correct anything that needs to be tweaked. If you are sending out the meeting information yourself, make sure it's a good reflection of what happened. Highlight the action items assigned and who is responsible for each. Send it out as soon after the meeting as possible, so you have a written form of accountability.

Being Available for Quick Clarification

As a meeting leader, you never want to be the first one to leave the room. The meeting may have officially adjourned, and the majority of folks may have high-tailed it out of there, but you need to stick around. Why? Because you may have some people on your team who want to talk to you about something out of earshot of the rest of the attendees.

While this may sound ominous, it's usually not. Sometimes you may just need to give a bit more context around what is being asked of them for a particular action item. Sometimes they have something they want to discuss with you that may have been tangentially related to the meeting topic, but not directly related. Rather than occupying meeting time, they chose to wait until after the session to bring it up with you individually.

TIP

Regardless of the reason, create that window of opportunity for your team to come to you in a less formal way. For one thing, those quick chats afterward can keep you from having to do what no one wants to do . . . add another meeting to the calendar. If you can avoid that by staying behind an extra few minutes, that's a tradeoff worth making.

However, do account for that in how you are scheduling yourself. Give yourself some pad on either side of a meeting. As we talk about in Chapter 10, plan on arriving several minutes before your meeting for setup and small talk. Plan on staying at least a few minutes after your scheduled meeting time to have these quick clarification conversations.

Holding a brief follow up

When meeting face to face, you have a whole host of ways to do a brief follow up. Sometimes it's a matter of hanging around after the meeting breaks up so you can address any comments or concerns of those who linger for that purpose. Sometimes it only requires a walk down the hall and popping your head into someone's office as a quick check in. It could look something like this:

> You: "Hey Jack, are you okay with spearheading that initiative with Client B?"
>
> Jack: "Sure. I've got some pretty solid contacts there."
>
> You: "I thought that was the case. If you need any help strategizing the initial approach, let me know."

That 30-second conversation potentially saved you from a thirty-minute meeting. In this day and age of the meeting-ization of our workday, too often, people just default to grabbing an open calendar slot with a meeting invitation. Train yourself to not be that person. Even if you can't do a quick face-to-face followup, pick up the phone. A five-minute phone call is preferable to another meeting on the calendar.

Following up when virtual

If you just wrapped up a virtual meeting, the same policy holds true. Don't immediately click that "end meeting" button on the platform after you officially dismiss the group. If you click on it before everyone else is ready to go, it almost feels like you are throwing them out of the room. It's super abrupt. Give everyone a chance to do whatever goodbye ritual that they have. For some, that means typing in some parting words in the chat. For others, it means a hearty wave. Both of these rituals are important for their transition to whatever comes next in their day. If you take that away from them, it can leave your attendees feeling unfulfilled.

TIP

By keeping the meeting link open, you also may find the virtual equivalent of the person lingering behind in the physical conference room — you know, that one person who doesn't log off when everyone else does. That's the person who needs to talk to you one-on-one and their behavior (not clicking "leave" on their screen) is a dead giveaway that they have something to address with you. Be open to it and use that time as you would in person. It's a shortcut to a conversation that might take up more time if it is not had right after the session.

Following up when hybrid

Keeping the meeting link open beyond the official end time is even more important in a hybrid meeting. Why? Because it helps to remove any concerns for the remote attendees that they might be missing the "meeting after the meeting." You know what we're talking about. The scheduled session draws to a close, but the conversation keeps going — often an extension of what just occurred. If you close the virtual meeting link before all of the in-person attendees leave the physical conference room, they may feel like they are missing out. You may protest and say, "They aren't missing anything. There wasn't any meeting after the meeting. People just started talking about where they were headed for lunch." But your remote attendees don't know that for sure, and that doubt can infiltrate their sense of belonging.

REMEMBER

Leaders leave last. One way to level the playing field in a hybrid meeting is to make sure everyone has equal access to opportunity and information regardless of location. By keeping the link open until everyone has left, you are doing your part to create meeting parity.

When wrapping up a hybrid meeting, make it clear that you plan to stay behind for anyone who wants a quick clarification or needs to ask a question. Let them know you will be available for both the in-person attendees as well as the remote ones. If everyone leaves the physical conference room and no faces are left on the gallery view except for your own, then you can feel free to close the meeting link.

Thinking about one-on-ones

Throughout much of this book, we focus on group and team meetings and making the most of them. However, sometimes the most valuable kind of meeting you can have are the ones where it's just you and one member of your team. This is especially true when you are leading a virtual team and you don't have those moments of serendipity where you bump into someone in the break room.

If you follow up your virtual team meetings with quick one-on-ones with individuals, you can get a better read of how people are doing, what is working for them and what is not . . . including how they feel you are running your meetings.

In a dispersed team, those more intimate conversations can lay the groundwork for better team cohesion and a stronger sense of belonging for each person on the team. Don't underestimate their value. Make it a part of your regular follow up routine or implement open office hours when anyone can join you in your virtual meeting room for any reason at all. In order to avoid someone barging in on a private conversation you may be having with someone else, make sure you have set up a waiting room in your meeting platform settings. It forces people to hang out in a virtual lobby before being you manually let them into your virtual office. Consider advertising your open office hours after any meeting you have. Establish that practice as a norm, so your team knows they have a set outlet for one-on-one discussion with you.

Chapter **16**

Evaluating Your Meeting Effectiveness

T he most neglected best practice for meetings is evaluation. Joe kind of gets on a soap box about this one. And here's why. Take a look at your calendar. If you're a mid-level manager or higher in your organization, you likely spend upwards of 75 percent of your worktime on meeting-related activities. In fact, you might even describe yourself as a person who goes to meetings, with a bunch of other things you try to get done despite your meeting schedule. If that's you, you're not alone!

Now, ask yourself this question: When was the last time you were asked to evaluate your own or other's meetings? Some of you will probably be able to answer "yesterday" or "a few minutes ago." However, the vast majority of you, upwards of 90 percent of you, will probably say "I can't remember the last time I was asked."

Let's put these two facts together:

» 75 percent of worktime spent on meetings

» Most of the time no one asks for feedback on their meetings.

That means that probably the thing we do most goes unevaluated and unmeasured. Is that a good way to run an organization? Never evaluating truly how people are doing with the work, work that is gobbling up a huge percentage of people's time?

Taken a step further, think about your last performance review. Did your boss ask you about your meetings? Did they get your take on how you felt your meetings were going? Did they ask if you were a good meeting leader, and if so, how you were able to evaluate your skill in this area? Did they ask if you are a good meeting attendee, and how you know that to be the case? Based upon our conversations with leaders across the world, few if any performance appraisal processes include anything about meetings.

Once again, let's think about this a bit. Most of our time is spent in meetings. Most of the time we don't evaluate the meetings in real time. And, we don't ask about them during performance review or hold people accountable in a formal way whatsoever. Then why would we expect them to be good? Why would we expect any meeting to be good if we don't expect anyone to be held accountable for their actions, good or bad? If we don't reward the good behavior and sanction the bad behavior, people will sort of just "meh" their way through their meetings.

TIP

Don't wait for your organization to get with the program. Start evaluating your meeting effectiveness immediately, and use that feedback to make changes suggested throughout this book. In time, you'll be running effective meetings and most of the things you are asked about in your performance appraisal setting will be better than ever. How? Because 75 percent of your time will be more effective than it was before!

In this chapter, we share with you how to gather valuable intel on the effectiveness of your meetings. We look at the different methods you can use to solicit feedback and how to interpret what you receive. We wrap up by helping you put feedback into action so your meetings can continue to improve over time.

Soliciting Feedback

How much do you like tests? You might be surprised that some people do like tests. But, that's not the common attitude. What's more common is the feeling of *evaluation apprehension*. Most people have this challenge. We don't like to be evaluated. We don't like being put under a microscope and observed. It's not a fun thing. But, it is a necessary thing.

As an educator, Joe sees this all the time. Students nearly universally do not like to take tests. They do not like to be evaluated. However, how else can we see if they know that they have learned the material? Okay, yes, we could do observations or just call each person into the office for a chat about the class, but it would still be an evaluation. It just might feel a little bit different, until someone wises up and realizes, "Dr. Allen's actually testing us when we go to his office!" Suddenly, the stream of people voluntarily coming into my office might seize up.

Karin sees it during her on-camera training sessions. Part of the evaluation process involves doing a video presentation and then watching it back for immediate critiquing. No one likes it. In fact, most people hate it. But almost universally, people begrudgingly acknowledge it's valuable because you can't fix what you don't know is broken. It takes actually seeing the problem to diagnose it and solve it.

This is all to say, we know that soliciting feedback about your meetings will be uncomfortable. It's often said, "Don't ask a question for which you do not want the answer." And maybe you don't really want to know how good or bad your meetings are. But, how do you make them better if you don't know where you stand?

REMEMBER

It's okay to feel a bit of uneasiness when you ask for feedback about your meetings. That's normal. You're only human and you're not perfect. We often ask for feedback about our meetings, and it's not all sunshine and roses. We all have room for improvement. The key is overcoming the fear and embracing the opportunity to be better.

Creating a process for gathering feedback

Alright, assuming we've convinced you that you need to ask for feedback, now you need to figure out how to do that. There's a lot of different ways to do this. In fact, there's entire graduate programs about the various processes of gathering data and feedback. Not everyone can or should program a survey and blast it out. It's a science. So, we're going to give you a few tips on how you might proceed with designing a process for gathering feedback about your meetings.

Here are two points to ponder when it comes to feedback:

>> **Do you want the feedback to be anonymous or not?** Logistically speaking, if you are asking for feedback on a specific meeting of your team of seven people, it's close to impossible to get truly anonymous feedback, even with an online survey tool. So, in some cases, anonymity is not going to be possible. But, if you solicit feedback over a time period for all your meetings across all the people you meet with, the pool of respondents is much deeper and your feedback could take on a layer of anonymity.

>> **Do you want the feedback to be global or specific?** In other words, do you want people to tell you how your meetings are in general, or do you want the feedback to be more granular and focused on just one particular type of meeting? That specificity will determine who you need to ask for feedback from and what you might be able to do with the information.

Global feedback would help you identify things you might want to change about all of your meetings, whereas specific feedback would help you identify things you might want to change about that particular type of meeting. You have to decide what you want to know.

With these two bigger issues in mind, you now have to decide how you're going to get that feedback. Our advice is to keep whatever process you want to use short and sweet. You do not want to burden yourself or others with so much evaluation and feedback work that they come to resent your meetings merely because you keep pestering them to tell you how things went.

Imagine setting up a system that sends a 15-minute survey to your colleagues after every meeting you lead. Take a look at your calendar. That's a lot of meetings and a lot of emails. How much would your colleagues love you if you did that for a week or month or year? Yeah, you get the idea, not very much!

Here are three potential processes for gathering feedback from attendees. There are other options, but these are a good place to start:

>> **Ask them at the end of a meeting.** In a completely "not anonymous" way, you can ask people what they think right as the meeting ends. You can ask everyone or you can target a couple people. Get their immediate reactions to the experience. Ask them, "What did you like about this meeting?" and "What do you think I could do better to make the meeting more effective?" Since most best practices for effective meetings are fairly intuitive, this can be a fruitful and easy way to start getting insights into your own meetings.

This is the least effective way of getting unbiased and nonsubjective feedback. Due to *social desirability bias* (the pressure to do or say what is acceptable to the people in the room, particularly, in this case, the meeting leader), you are not likely to get fully accurate information. So, it's worth a try, but we recommend using the next two options here if you are really serious about getting meaningful feedback and changing your meetings for the better.

>> **Ask them in a quick email or text message.** Instead of cornering people after a meeting, perhaps when they are running to their next meeting, asking for feedback via email gives them a chance to respond on their own time. It also allows them some thinking time, to reflect on how best to answer your question. This can lead to a bit of filtering (for example, "How do I tell Joe his

meetings suck without it coming back to bite me?"), but also to more thought-ful answering (such as, "Here's a polite way to tell him starting late is killing productivity.").

>> **Use survey technology.** Yes, we as a society are over-surveyed. We can't walk into a retail establishment without being asked to complete a survey upon checkout. It's annoying. So, we get it if your reaction to this option is "Dear God, not another survey!" However, survey tools have gotten better and you can make this as short or as long as you need it to be. It can be as easy as swipe left if the meeting was good or swipe right if the meeting was bad. Perhaps if they swipe right, you ask them why it was bad. But keep it simple.

There are a number of different companies that specialize in this form of automated feedback, with fancy dashboards and so forth. We aren't here to recommend a specific vendor or company, as much as some of our friends might like that. Instead, we do want you to recognize the economies of scale that these tools offer as well as the ease in gathering and analyzing the data.

If you are just interested in feedback for yourself, these three options are a good place to start. However, if you are a leader in a large organization that needs help changing the meeting culture, you probably need to assess where things stand across the enterprise. And that will take more planning and effort (and expertise in measurement or software) than you have time to curate yourself. So, hire some experts!

Choosing what to measure

Once you've decided to solicit feedback, you have to decide what you are going to measure. As a *psychometrician* (a scientist who builds measures and tests), Joe would want you to make sure you use validated, reliable, and *legally defensible scales* (meaning that it would hold up in court because of its basis in scientifically sound and ethically proven methods). However, that really only applies to when using the survey technology mentioned previously. The more informal feedback processes probably aren't going to include psychological scales assessing meet-ing satisfaction and effectiveness. Instead, you'll ask your coworker, "What did you think about that meeting?" That's probably sufficient for those informal processes.

Deciding on global or specific feedback

However, if you want data that can drive sustained change and give you an idea of how you have improved over time, you probably need to consider using survey technology and what questions and scales to include. And this brings us back to something we mentioned but did not define previously, global versus specific feedback:

>> Global feedback helps you identify things you might want to change about all of your meetings.

>> Specific feedback helps you identify things you might want to change about that specific type of meeting.

You have to decide what you want to know and then gather the questions that will get you answers. If you want to measure meeting satisfaction or effectiveness for a specific meeting, consider using a slider scale from 0 to 10 with the question reading something like: "On a scale from 0 to 10, how satisfying was the meeting you just attended." For effectiveness, you'd ask the same question by just switching out "satisfying" with "effective."

In contrast, if you want to ask about meetings in general, how satisfying and effective they are, we'd recommend the following scale:

>> **Meeting satisfaction:** Please indicate your level of agreement with the follow words or phrases concerning the meeting you just experienced.

- Unpleasant

- Satisfying

- Enjoyable

- Annoying

These items should be rated on a five-point scale of agreement (strongly disagree, disagree, neither agree nor disagree, agree, strongly agree).

>> **Meeting effectiveness.** Please rate how the meeting you just experienced was in:

- achieving your own work goals.

- achieving colleagues' work goals.

- providing you with an opportunity to acquire useful information.

These items should be rated on a five-point scale for effectiveness (extremely ineffective, ineffective, neutral, effective, extremely effective).

In both cases, higher ratings mean more satisfaction with or effectiveness of the meeting overall. Also notice that the satisfaction measure includes some negatively worded items. This helps give you an idea of the overall feeling people have in the meetings. The good and the bad.

If you use these kinds of measures, you're going to want to use a survey. However, the good news, you'll be using valid, reliable, and legally defensible scales that Joe and many other meeting scientists have used for years.

Measuring meeting satisfaction and effectiveness

TIP

To get a general understanding of how things are going with a specific meeting or for your meetings in general, we recommend measuring both meeting satisfaction and effectiveness. However, these don't tell you specific things to change, just whether or not change is needed at all (which in most cases, it is).

While it's good to know that change is called for, it is just as important (if not more so) to know what specific aspects of the meeting are ripe for revision or tweaking. Shape your questions to uncover insights into those elements of the meeting that can potentially be changed for next time. Maybe you want to know if a presentation in a certain meeting was delivered in a way that was effective or was considered good? Maybe you want to know if people liked the social interaction you facilitated at the beginning of your last few meetings. More informal feedback options, like asking people for their thoughts, suit this quite well.

You could also take the after-action review approach. *After-action reviews* are a form of debrief meeting where you go over what went well, what didn't go well, and what you would do differently in the future when engaging in similar activities. Firefighters, military, and commercial pilots are just a few industries and groups that use this type of meeting all the time.

Rather than a formal 60-minute debrief meeting, consider simply asking the same questions in a less formal way (maybe use the last five minutes of the meeting to do this). What went right? What went wrong? What should I do differently in the future? Those questions are a great way to get specific feedback without too much effort.

If you've decided you're going to use survey technology, you've chosen to automate the collection of the information. That means you can then ask about a lot of specific things you're trying to do or know you should be doing. We won't list all those things here, but a quick glance through this book should give you ample things to ask about specifically in this more concise and quick format (such as your use of an agenda, whether the meeting had a purpose, or if they felt they could participate easily).

Using the Feedback

It's better to not ask, than to ask and then do nothing with the information. Don't ask people for feedback unless you plan to do something with it. Don't be like those big chain stores that send out automated surveys after every purchase without ever revealing how your responses made a difference. Use the feedback and then let people know what actions you took as a result.

So, you've rightfully decided to gather all that data because you do want to use it, and the feedback is waiting for you to mine it. What do you do? Well, hopefully you learn from it. If you've established a psychologically safe work environment (as discussed in Chapter 9), your team or whomever you solicited feedback from will have provided you with meaningful information. They felt safe to give you candid responses in service to all of your future meetings which will surely be better.

Here's what steps to take next:

1. **Take a deep breath and read through all the feedback, the good and the bad.** Take adequate time to celebrate the good things you are doing. Most people, including you, are doing some good things in their meetings, and it's important to note those and keep doing them.

2. **Note the things they suggest you change.** Please keep in mind that some recommendations will be garbage. For example, someone might suggest that your meetings would be better if you held them at the pub down the street. Although that might be true, doing so might not be in line with company standards for professionalism, and beer at 9 a.m. is not usually a good idea for most people.

   As you note the things they suggest you change, pay attention to the things that are actually good advice. Maybe even things you thought you were doing that they point out you apparently aren't. Time to ramp up your efforts there. Sometimes people don't notice the good things you are doing, so in those cases, you should emphasize those good practices in the future.

3. **Decide what recommendations you are going to follow and which you are not, and consider why.** It's typically not possible to make all the changes at once, and we'd not recommend you do that. If you do, then you won't necessarily know what's made the difference in your meetings. Think about if you're trying to find out what in your diet is upsetting your stomach. If you eliminate potential triggers all at once, it'll be hard to diagnose what was the source of the problem. Instead, you add one thing back at a time and see how it feels. The same holds true for meetings. Select one or maybe just a few things to work on at time and see if they move the needle.

REMEMBER

No one is perfect and most of the people giving you feedback could also improve their meetings. Take their feedback seriously and do what you can to improve your meetings. But, never be discouraged by those comments or feedback that are not particularly useful or helpful. Change what you can change, and don't worry about the things you cannot (or shouldn't) change.

Sharing the results

If you ask people for feedback, you owe it to them to share the results. Particularly if you do a larger-scale survey among your organization about meetings in general, you have to tell people what you heard. In this case, you likely have anonymous or mostly anonymous results, and so sharing the results is more about sharing the trends. For example, you might talk about how satisfying or effective meetings are in the organization in general. Or you might talk about trends in specific good or bad meeting behaviors. The point is, you share the results.

If you receive more informal feedback from just a few people, thank them personally one-on-one, and in the team meeting, thank them generally for their feedback. Then tell your team what you would like to do to make the meetings better. By doing so, you are getting their input and buy-in. That's essential to producing real improvement, because often times the solutions lead to changes in ground rules or norms in your group meetings.

WARNING

Honor people's requests for confidentiality. If you know who's provided feedback, it's generally good practice to keep that knowledge to yourself. There may be cases where you'll want to let everyone know who gave you such a good idea. Before you share that, you must ask the person who suggested it if you have their permission to let the team know who was the source. Honor their wishes. Don't share their connection to the change you'd like to make unless they say it's okay to do so.

Implementing changes based on feedback

Even though we warn against this, you will likely be tempted to do everything at once. That is, once feedback comes in, you may be jazzed about doing all the good things that are recommended. This would be folly to implement a wholesale change approach because:

» It might be a heavy lift to implement everything all at once.

» You might not be able to maintain such a change long term without help.

> » If you implement multiple changes to how you meet all at once, and you solicit feedback on meeting satisfaction or effectiveness again, how do you know which thing made the difference, good or bad? You won't know. And then you won't exactly know how to proceed.

TIP

Experiment with the recommended changes. Make one change and see how it goes. Get some more feedback, and if things are getting better, make the next change. This is the ideal manner of making changes for most folks.

MAKING MORE THAN ONE CHANGE AT A TIME

We'll provide one caveat here with a bit of a story. Joe was working with a client a few years ago, and was asked to do some observations. The leader wanted expert feedback on their meetings, which they believed were quite good and could be a template for others.

Unfortunately, they were wrong. Using Joe's checklists of good and bad meeting practices, he's never seen a meeting observation have so many bad practices and so few good practices at the same time, before or since. It was so bad that he really wasn't sure how best to approach this leader who clearly had a bit of a blind spot around his meetings.

Joe tactfully gave him their feedback and made suggestions for changes, but instead of saying, "Try one, see how it goes, and then add something else," he advised him to implement five things immediately.

This is all to say that sometimes, some meeting leaders are going to make wholesale updates to how they run their meetings. Obvious best practices that need to be followed may need to be implemented in bulk. But, for the vast majority of folks, likely including you, a slow and study addition of new approaches and changes overtime will lead to a steady increase in the effectiveness of your meetings.

5

The Part of Tens

IN THIS PART . . .

If you are looking for a quick and easy way to level up your meetings with some top ten lists of to-dos, you've come to the right place!

In this part, we seek to empower and inspire you with "news you can use" to improve your meetings right away. We put some words in your mouth that you can say when your meeting is going off the rails. We help you discover the many places you can meet, some physical and some meta-physical. We also share some of our top tricks for enhancing participation that you can try out in your next meeting.

Chapter **17**

Ten Things to Say to Move a Meeting Along

E ven though you may be a meeting's official leader, there will be times when you'll feel like your meeting has a mind of its own.

You carefully laid out a plan for a productive dialogue that will get you to your ultimate goal, to make a decision on a key business initiative. But somehow, 30 minutes in, you haven't even made it past agenda item number one, and there are ten on the list. What's even worse, the meeting's lively conversation isn't even tangentially related to what you had planned to discuss.

How did this happen?

Meetings are made up of people, and no matter how much planning you put into them, personalities of those in attendance can often heavily influence what happens during the proceedings. Sometimes, those personalities can hijack your meeting and make it less effective than you want it to be.

In Chapter 11, we talk about procedural communication (things you can say to allow you to accomplish a meeting goal). Sometimes those statements are designed to wrest control back from meeting members who take things off track. Sometimes those statements serve as reminders to everyone in attendance that the meeting has an agenda and you plan to stick to it.

While you might know the intent of what you want to say, sometimes it can be hard to find the exact words. This chapter supplies some phrasing and verbiage that you can try out when your next meeting requires a bit of intervention.

Killing Them with Kindness . . . and Moving On

When trying to regain control over a meeting that is going astray, your default position should always be to be polite. Unless you enjoy being dictatorial in your leadership style, you should always try to be respectful when, in essence, butting in and bringing it back to the topic at hand.

If you find someone is going on and on and on about a topic that is no longer relevant or has been exhausted to within an inch of its life, trying saying something like this:

"Thank you! Our next topic is. . ."

You might want to add a bit more color to your comments after you say thanks, but don't go on to long. The idea is to acknowledge and briefly appreciate what has been said and then quickly transition to the next item on the agenda.

Rephrasing for Clarity

Do you have someone on your team who thinks out loud? They verbally process how they are feeling about something before they truly know. The result? A lot of talking in circles which can seem aimless at times.

While we know this is a communication preference for some, especially those who enjoy hearing the sound of their own voice, it can eat up a substantial amount of meeting time. One way to help speed up their thought process is to serve as a paraphraser for them. As they are bobbing and weaving their way through their feelings and thoughts, try to find the common theme, the key takeaway, and say something like this:

"What I think Joe is trying to say is. . ."

REMEMBER

Not only does your paraphrase cull their thoughts into their critical essence but it also allows you to take the baton away from them and hand it to someone else to build upon their thoughts.

Closing the Door

Sometimes a discussion just needs to end. That's when it's upon you to make it clear that you are moving on, in no uncertain terms. In your most diplomatic tone of voice, try saying this:

"The next thing on the agenda is. . ."

If the group doesn't take the hint after as blunt a statement as that, you may need to be more forceful in your approach. Say why you are shutting down discussion on the topic and then open up dialogue on the next agenda item by inviting someone to speak to it directly. It might sound something like this:

"Thanks for everyone's input but we need to move on. Julie, I'd like to get your thoughts on the next thing on our agenda."

TIP

Make sure the person you ask to speak first isn't one of the people who has been prolonging the discussion on the previous item. The idea is to firmly close the door on one thing and open the door to another.

Creating Order out of Chaos

Conversations can always run off course, but sometimes the new paths they take can be valuable. If that's the case, don't just abandon them altogether. Instead, provide structure. Let's say there are two new ideas on the table that are worth exploring, try saying something like this:

"Great thoughts! I think we should talk about this first and that second."

REMEMBER

By creating a discussion order, you allowing the conversation to focus on one thing at a time. Just like multitasking leads to lower productivity (although people like to think the opposite) multi-conversation topics leads to less effective communication.

Naming the Elephant in the Room

As the meeting leader, it's ultimately your job to keep the meeting on track, and that means being on the lookout for when your meeting has gone seriously off the rails. Rabbit holes can be fun to wander down for a bit, but it won't take long for them to feel more like bottomless pits. Pull everyone out of them by saying something like this:

"I think we've gone a bit astray. What about. . ."

Not only have you stated what is probably obvious to more than just you, but you've also pivoted the conversation to something more productive.

REMEMBER

Some people might be just as annoyed as you are by the wandering dialogue that has nothing to do with the meeting topic, but they may not want to speak up. That's definitely your job as the meeting's leader . . . and they'll thank you for it.

Being a Timekeeper

If you have followed best practices, you probably created timestamps for each agenda item (if not, check out Chapter 9). Timestamps aren't just for show or even simply aspirational. With a few exceptions, they should be your guardrails for how much time to devote to a certain topic. Your meeting design requires you to execute on it. Any extra time spent on one item will cheat the planned discussion time for another. Use this as your motivation when you say something like this:

"To keep us within time, we need to transition to our next discussion item."

REMEMBER

It's not personal. It's the agenda. Really . . . you were enjoying the prolonged and well-traveled pontifications of your team member (or not).

Protecting the Wellness of Your Team

As Joe found in his research, we need five minutes to recover from a good meeting and 17 minutes to recover from a bad one (find out more in Chapter 14), but sometimes it's hard to eke out even a minute to find the bathroom.

While some organizations have developed ways to build in buffers between meetings, many have not. Here's where you can make a difference. You can create buffer time for your team by not letting your meetings go long (see Chapter 8 for more on this). Try saying something like this:

"We need to wrap up so we have time to recover and get to our next task."

TIP

Your team may not realize just how hard it is to task switch, to flip from focusing on one thing to devoting brain power to another. But they will reap the benefits when they're actually given time to decompress and ramp up for what comes next.

WARNING

The feelings created by bad meetings can bleed into the next meeting too. Give your people time to process them. Otherwise, they may enter the next meeting with a less than stellar attitude and their fellow attendees will have no idea why.

Scheduling a New Conversation

As hard as you try, your agenda may not include everything that needs to be discussed. During the course of the conversation, there may be something brought up that absolutely deserves attention. However, it may not be a topic that can be tackled right at that moment. In this situation, we suggest saying something like this:

"That's an important thing to address but it deserves a longer discussion than we can do here. Let's set up a different time to talk about it."

REMEMBER

If you use this line, you have to actually mean it and follow through. You can even schedule that meeting to discuss it while you are in the current one. That way, it doesn't sound like you are simply blowing off the conversation. Rather, you demonstrate that you value the discussion and want to prioritize tackling it adequately.

Putting it in the Parking Lot

There will be times when you truly don't want to talk about a topic. Not now, not ever. Think about those complaints that people love to bring up over and over again, but there is no way that they will ever be addressed in a way that will satisfy the complainer. What we suggest is, in the nicest possible way, to put the kibosh on it quickly by saying something along the lines of:

"Let's table that for now."

Most people will know that this is code for "stop talking about this." Not everyone will be thrilled that you pulled this one out (especially the complainer who may feel like they haven't been "heard" . . . even though the reason why you are tabling it is because everyone has "heard it" umpteen times).

The feelings of a few disgruntled people can't trump the needs of the group as a whole. If the comments being made are not productive or attached to the purpose of the meeting, table away.

Using Team Code Words

In elementary school, teachers often come up with code words or phrases that their students immediately understand are associated with a certain desired action. A teacher may say "Give me five" when they want students to quiet down and raise their hands to demonstrate they are paying attention.

You may want to come up with some code words for your team when your meeting starts to bog down and you want to get it moving forward again. Exactly what you say will depend upon your own personality and the culture of your team and organization. One of Joe's all-time favorites that he tends to use most often is:

"Meanwhile, back at the ranch. . ."

When Joe says that phrase, his team usually laughs but simultaneously recognizes what he means. The meeting is getting off track and it needs to get back on.

Be very aware of your tone when saying any of these statements. You can make any of these innocuous comments sound condescending if you don't deliver them with respect. Yes, your job as a meeting leader is to keep your meeting from getting out of control and ensuring you accomplish the meeting goal. However, you will find it much easier to do both if you treat your team with respect. Being an autocratic taskmaster is no way to lead a team.

Chapter **18**

Ten Alternatives to Meeting in a Conference Room

I bet at least some of you reading this book thought this chapter might be ten ways to do something other than a meeting. For example, we could've listed ten different asynchronous communication options that you could use instead of meeting face-to-face, virtually, or hybrid. And, frankly, that might be a useful thing to do in a book that's not about meetings, but in a book that's about how to make asynchronous communication work.

Instead, this chapter is all about alternative locations. Options of places you could meet, connect, and engage with each other that are not the conference room. Sometimes the old standard conference room becomes stale. We get used to operating a certain way and we get into patterns that may or may not be effective. These patterns are actually cued up by the environments we are in.

That means that in the conference room, we fall into our own patterns of behavior, and it's hard to break out of them. People expect you to sit in a specific spot and to behave the same way, maybe regardless of what the purpose is for the meeting. ("Jim's the guy we can't get to shut up, so that's what Jim does in every meeting in the conference room.")

TIP

One way to break out of the problematic patterns that emerge in the conference room is to get out of the conference room. Meet somewhere else. Meet somewhere unique and different for the team, so the environment isn't cueing the bad behaviors.

Standing in the Conference Room

Alright, you're probably thinking, "Now wait just a minute, you said get out of the conference room!" And yes, we will talk about nine more alternatives to meeting in the conference room. However, at the core of our recommendation (and why this chapter exists) is the goal of breaking your meetings out of the behavioral rut.

In a classic study of workplace meetings from 1999, Dr. Allen Bluedorn and colleagues found that stand-up meetings (where people literally stand) are just as effective as sit-down meetings. The bonus here is that they are shorter! That's right, stand up and meet, and your meeting will be shorter and just as good.

TIP

As an alternative to the conference room, remove the chairs and stand. You'll be glad you did because you'll meet more efficiently and effectively.

Gathering Around the Water Cooler

Consider meeting at the place where people naturally gather in the office. If there's a water cooler and people often congregate there throughout the day, commandeer the location for your meeting.

Again, from the idea that cues of the environment change our behavior, if people are more comfortable "spilling the tea" around the water cooler, then they might be more open, honest, and less filtered if you meet there.

What's that you say? You don't have a watercooler! Well, where does casual conversation between coworkers occur? If you are in the office, there's probably a place where quick chats happen. Could be a workroom or a breakroom. Could be at the copy machine. Could be anywhere.

Meet there!

WARNING

Just keep in mind, that you still need to maintain documentation of your meeting (meeting minutes), so make sure your choice of location won't make this too difficult to accomplish.

Meeting in Someone's Office

The conference room is a pretty formal setting. Not everything needs that level of formality. Further, some meetings only need a few people because they are sensitive issues (such as a performance review). These kinds of meetings might best be done in someone's office.

In this case, it likely requires that the office have several chairs and a door. A cubicle might do it for non-sensitive meeting topics, but it's probably not the best option.

Also, meeting in someone's office could also be the virtual office. Sometimes you just need a small meeting with a few people, and not everyone's in the office. So, by "meet in someone's office" it could be their home office via virtual means.

Doing an Offsite, Onsite

Another alternative is simply to meet in a different location in the building or on the campus of your offices. That is, you do the equivalent of an offsite, onsite. You don't ask people to go anywhere too far, just another floor in the building or another building on campus.

Again, the idea here is that you are breaking up the routines. This also allows you to see the resources that other departments have, which might be worth finding out as well. Maybe their conference room has nicer technology allowing for a better hybrid meeting. That's worth noting and knowing.

TIP Take a local field trip. Try using the conference room in another department. Who knows, you might find a room with more comfortable chairs. Or you might learn that you have a pretty nice space where you are. The point is, break out of the rut of the same place every time.

Taking it Outside

Weather permitting, take the meeting outside. Some offices are next to a greenspace or have a garden in the office suite area. Sometimes you'll catch a colleague using these spaces for a quiet lunch. Most of the time, they go empty, except for the occasional bird or squirrel. Why not use them?

By taking it outside, you definitely break the routine. But, you might also get some other added benefits. As nice as the fluorescent lighting is in most offices, sunshine is actually very good for people. Get into the sun. Let people soak up some vitamin D while discussing the quarterly earnings report.

TIP

Meeting outside reminds people that business can be done in the great outdoors and perhaps we should do it there a bit more. And, when we say weather permitting, use your judgment. Depending on the disposition of your team, you might be able to meet outside rain or shine!

Walking and Talking

For this one, you have to consider both the weather and the footwear. Depending upon dress code or personal choices, doing a walking meeting might inadvertently exclude someone or make someone more uncomfortable (for example, try walking a mile in heels).

However, barring weather or footwear issues, a walking meeting is a great way to get the benefits of the outdoors, break up the routine, and even do a standing meeting. People probably aren't looking to walk too far and when you circle back to the office, the meeting has a nice opportunity to break up.

We know this alternative may not work for everyone, but if you can make it work, it might be a nice change of pace. However, this option is difficult if you have remote participants.

Heading to a Coffee Shop

Rather than sending someone to pick up coffee for the team, consider having everyone go together to the coffee shop. Most coffee shops have WiFi, so pulling up documents will be easy. You'll be able to both refresh and get the meeting done.

In fact, going to the coffee shop has all the benefits of the other alternatives, plus the added bonus of increasing energy with a caffeine boost. After a few sips of their coffee, people will be feeling a bit more energized and be ready to engage more fully in the discussion.

Coffee isn't for everyone, but everyone likes a break from the norm. Just make sure the shop has a juice or water option so everyone can get a beverage. Then enjoy the benefits of a reinvigorated group discussing the important items on your agenda.

Going to a Restaurant

Breaking bread together has been a tried and true way to help connect individuals together since people started interacting. Take your agenda and go to a local restaurant. Hopefully you have options close to the office that everyone enjoys.

The social atmosphere of a lunch meeting allows for people to be filled physically so they can share their ideas more openly. In fact, you may even consider including things on the agenda that you might not normally talk about in your conference room meetings. People will be less filtered and good ideas (and bad ones) will be free-flowing.

Thus, you get the benefits of getting away from routines, getting a meal in, and getting people in a comfortable space to allow for social bonding that doesn't happen easily in the sterile conference room.

Holding a Virtual Reality Meeting

If you insert the word "reality" in between the words "virtual" and "meeting," you get another option that can transform your meeting space . . . literally.

Meeting in virtual reality rooms is now available via a few different virtual reality technology firms and allows you to meet virtually anywhere. And we mean *anywhere.* Perhaps you want to meet in the Jedi Council room, or on a cliff over-looking the ocean, or in the Louvre, or on top of Mount Everest, or in a board room, or anywhere else. You can probably do that.

The other advantage to the virtual reality meeting is that it's more flexible for the remote attendees. Unlike some of the other options we've mentioned, this one is naturally suited for the virtual and hybrid situations. Instead of turning on the camera, you pick put on your goggles and pick your avatar.

REMEMBER

In the flexible work environments we now work in, finding ways to break out of the norm have already occurred. But, sinking back into them is not a good option, in part because not everyone is even present. Virtual reality allows for the novelty and inclusion of remote attendees at the same time. So it is worth a try.

However, be mindful of the tech proficiency of your group. If they struggle with basic technology, pushing them into what is considered cutting-edge by even the most forward-thinking folks may diminish the value of the exercise.

Heading Down to the Railroad Tracks

One of Joe's favorite experiences studying meetings came when he worked with a rail company and met with rail workers right next to the railroad tracks. Yes, they did have to wait for the occasional train to pass, but the conversations were just as interesting and meaningful as one might experience in any conference room the world over.

For these workers, next to the tracks was their office. That's where they meet. And it works for them. In fact, meeting in a conference room would be a huge switch for them, and actually be the way for them to break out of their behavioral norms.

Let's return to our main tip here. The goal is to meet somewhere other than where you meet normally to break out of the negative behavioral norms that may have emerged in meetings past. In fact, maybe an agenda item while standing next to the tracks could be how to permanently end the counterproductive meeting behaviors.

TIP

Our point is that people can potentially meet anywhere. However, not everyone can meet well anywhere. The key is to apply the best practices described in this book while using the alternative locations as a means to break out of norms and establish new more positive and effective ones.

Chapter **19**

Ten Ways to Bolster Participation

I f you want your meetings to get high marks in terms of satisfaction and effectiveness, focus your efforts on pulling out even participation amongst attendees. Almost everyone likes to feel like they've been seen and heard. (We say "almost" because we acknowledge there are indeed those who would rather just hide in the corner, literally and figuratively.)

Barring those exceptions though, the road to a productive meeting is paved with active participation by those who are gathered for it. We talk quite a bit about participation in Part 3 of this book, especially in Chapters 10, 11, and 12. This chapter is designed to give you our top ten ways to get everyone engaged in the meeting in a meaningful way . . . yes, even those who want to hide in the corner.

Assigning Agenda Items to Other Attendees

Here's one way to drag that person from the shadows into the spotlight. If you make that individual responsible for a particular topic on the agenda, they can't exactly take on a passive role. Now, this shouldn't be punitive. You don't want them to feel singled out. However, if there is a certain discussion topic they might have particular interest in or have specific knowledge about, by all means, empower them to lead the conversation about it.

TIP

A meeting is designed to be collaborative. Leverage the very nature of the meeting by spreading out the responsibility for the content to others who will be attending. Empower people to take the lead on various agenda items. Just make sure you give them plenty of advance notice so they can prepare adequately to do so.

Setting and Sticking to Ground Rules

What does good participation look like? It's a meeting where everyone has an opportunity to have their voice heard. However, the typical meeting is usually dominated by the loudest and longest-winded. One way to even things out is to set participation ground rules.

TIP

Try adopting a turn-taking policy that states how everyone can get into the conversation queue. In a fully face-to-face meeting, this isn't as necessary because conversations have a more natural rhythm when everyone is sharing the same space. There's no need to adjust for audio lag or wonky WiFi.

But if you're virtual or hybrid, using a more formal turn-taking policy is essential. When you are fully virtual, it can be hard for people to know when it's their turn to talk unless they are given the floor proactively ("Julie, did you have something you wanted to say. . ."). When hybrid, you run the risk of the in-person attendees talking the entire time and not letting the virtual attendees get a word in at all.

Come up with your participation ground rules as a team and reiterate them at the top of any meeting until they become routine.

Making Multitasking a No-no

One of the best ways to screw up a meeting is to allow people to multitask while in them. We've said it once (see Chapter 5) and we'll say it again. Multitasking is a myth. It doesn't work. Don't do it in your meetings or guess what, you'll have to add another meeting to your calendar because the one you "sort of" attended didn't get the job done.

As the meeting leader, don't be afraid to put your foot down about this. Set the expectation that you want their full, undivided attention to what is being discussed. If you've done your job right, the meeting has a purpose and that purpose requires the collaboration of everyone on the invite list. That means if the attendees are there, their input is essential.

TIP

If you notice someone doing other work during the meeting, feel free to call them out. You don't have to do it in a nasty way that embarrasses them (even though they should be embarrassed by their lack of respect for the proceedings). You can be overt by asking them to close their laptop if you are meeting in person. If it's a virtual or hybrid meeting, you can remind remote participants that it is obvious when they are doing something other than being engaged in the meeting. You don't need an eye tracker to see when people are typing or reading when they should be listening to what's going on in the meeting.

You can also indirectly bring them to attention by doing this. Ask them a question related to what is currently being discussed. If they've been doing other work, they likely will not be able to provide a sufficient answer . . . or if they're really checked out, they may not have even heard the question. Either way, you've hopefully made your point. Multitasking should have no place in a good meeting.

Getting People to do Stuff . . . Regularly

Meetings should not be spectator sports, but if your meeting consists of a series of people delivering long presentations without any discussion in between, you are asking for trouble. It's an even bigger problem if you have virtual attendees who are constantly at risk of checking out because they're fighting even more distractions (the constant pinging of incoming messages, the dog barking, the kids fighting in the other room, the UPS driver ringing the doorbell. . .).

Your job is to use every tool of engagement you can muster and give people something to do throughout your meeting. In its most basic form, that can be simply opening up group discussion. If you are using a virtual meeting platform, you have even more options at your disposal. You can launch polls to get a quick snapshot of opinions. You can send people into breakout rooms to do a quick brainstorm and then ask them to report back once they return to the main session. You can use virtual whiteboarding or collaborate on a coauthoring document platform.

REMEMBER

Your virtual attendees will want to take a passive observer position. It's how we've been conditioned to work with screens. We watch television and we watch movies on screens. Move them off the passive observer default by giving them activities that require their engagement.

Reading the Room

TIP

In professional poker, the best players know to look for a *tell*, a physical or verbal action that gives away how strong or weak a player's hand is. In a meeting, you want to look for the nonverbal tells of your participants, body language or actions that might indicate they have something to share.

When meeting in person, that can mean a sharp intake of breath that happens before someone speaks. If you hear that, you want to make space for that person to chime in. You can do that by either calling on them or using your body language to indicate they have the floor.

When attendees are virtual, it's a little harder to read the nonverbal cues, but there are still some pretty typical signs. For example, if someone leans towards the camera, that's usually a precursor to them wanting to offer their input or ask a question. If someone unmutes themselves, that's also a subtle sign that they would like to join the conversation. Be quick to respond to those signs and proactively call on them by name in a way that's nonthreatening. ("Emily, I see that you've unmuted yourself. Was there something you wanted to add?") If you misread the sign, no problem. Hopefully you've established that it's perfectly okay to say, "Nope, just unmuted myself by accident."

Cold Calling with Good Intention

We've already mentioned the idea of calling upon people by name, but this alludes to a specific strategy that we employ to ensure everyone's voice is heard. There will be people who are naturally more extroverted and are eager to speak up in your meeting. There will also be people who are more measured in their approach and won't speak up unless they are called upon to do so. As a meeting leader, you'll start to recognize who falls into each category on your team, but both categories require a different approach.

Cold calling with good intention is designed to create an opportunity for your less verbose team members to have their opinion be heard. You don't want your decisions to be based only upon the thoughts of the loudest individuals on your team. You want to access the input of everyone.

Fostering a Speak-up Environment

One of the things we warn about in Chapter 9 is the importance of establishing psychological safety in meetings where you hope to encourage a speak up culture. If you suddenly start calling on people (like the cold calling with good intention we just mentioned) without explaining why you are doing this, you may end up terrifying certain members of your team who are more introverted and cautious in sharing their opinions.

TIP

Don't just start doing this out of the blue without discussing it with your team and explaining your motivation for doing so. Establish as a norm that you may call on people who haven't raised their hand but make it clear why you feel like this is a good idea. Let your team know that you value everyone's opinion and participation, and you don't want to overlook anyone. It's not because you want to put people on the spot. If you let people know it's okay to say "pass," then your cold calling won't feel like an attack but rather an effort to be inclusive.

Using Chat

One way to lower the barrier to entry for participation is to validate the use of chat as an equally important way of providing input. For those who are reluctant to speak up unless they have a fully formed thought that they've vetted well in their own minds, chat provides a platform to get their thoughts out there, using the exact wording they desire.

For global participants who are non-native speakers of the language being used during the meeting, chat is a less intimidating way to share their thoughts. They don't have to worry about trying to access the vocabulary in the moment and can take more time to shape their sentences.

TIP

If you are encouraging the use of chat, that demands you actually look at it and incorporate whatever thoughts are being shared in text form into the verbal dialogue. If appropriate, feel free to bring the author into the discussion by asking them to expand upon what they wrote in chat.

Be mindful of *chat abuse* (the misuse of the chat function to troll people's comments in the meeting or to have long sidebar conversations). It's okay to point those out and discourage such behavior.

Encouraging Webcam Use for All Remote Attendees

We feel so strongly about the use of video for virtual attendees that we spend an entire chapter on it (see Chapter 5). However, keeping the webcam on is worthy of appearing on this list because it is critical for participation.

If remote attendees want to fade into the background, they can easily do so by keeping their video off. As a meeting leader, you are much more apt to call on people who have the most "presence" in the room. Those who are represented both visually and auditorily will garner more attention than those who are a black box.

Your remote attendees need to do you and themselves a favor by establishing their presence as fully as possible. Turn that webcam on.

Asking for Help

The success of any meeting is a shared burden between the meeting leader and attendees. Ensuring even participation is also the responsibility of both.

Create an environment where your attendees regularly encourage their colleagues to speak up by praising or affirming their ideas or even by taking it upon themselves to ask for their peers' opinions.

TIP

If you are running a hybrid meeting, you can go a step further. Assign in-room allies for the remote attendees. Those in-room allies actively look for opportunities to bring their remote counterparts into the conversation by advocating for their voices to be heard. If you'd like to learn more about in-room allies, check out Chapter 12.

Index

buffers, building between meetings, 58

business hours, 101

C

calling on people, in meetings, 135–139, 188

cameras. *See also* video

　downside of being on, 64–67

　for hybrid meetings, 55

　looking at when presenting, 219

　for virtual meetings, 109–110

chairs, for hybrid meetings, 55

challenging conversations, 96

changing

　agendas, 124

　for internal/external participants, 98–99

　pitch for emphasis, 216–217

chat, using, 281

chat abuse, 281

chat box, 193

chat monitors, assigning, 196–197

Cheat Sheet (website), 3–4

China, lateness in, 77

choosing

　communication styles for meetings, 20–24

　equipment, 107–110

　length of meetings, 114–116

　meeting formality, 25–26

　meeting format, 46–53, 96–101

　meeting space, 53–56

　physical rooms for meetings, 53–56

　sets, 66

　software, 105–107

　what to evaluate for feedback, 257–259

clarifying

　being available for quick, 249–252

　meeting goal/purpose, 118–122, 159

　rephrasing for, 266–267

closing discussions, 267

closings, convincing, 209

code words, 270

coffee shop meetings, 274–275

cold calling with good intention, 40, 137, 280

collaboration

　meeting for, 92

　planning for, 26–27

collaborative communication style, 23

comments, paraphrasing, 179–180

committee meetings, 13

communication

　driving productive dialogue using strategies for, 172–176

　dysfunctional, 231–235

　patterns in, 28–30

　procedural, 37

　selecting style of for meetings, 20–24

complementary slides, creating, 220–221

complexity, of meetings, 14–17

conference rooms, alternatives to, 271–276

consequences, defining, 42–43

content, simplifying, 202–213

conversation flow

　about, 167–168

　active listening, 178–179

　driving discussion, 176–181

　driving productive dialogue using communication strategies, 172–176

　keeping meeting on track, 168–171

　leading discussion until moment of decision, 184

　making statements, 174–175

　managing, 167–184

　managing brainstorming sessions, 181–184

　monitoring time spent on topics, 170–171

　monologuing, 172

　paraphrasing comments, 179–180

　probing for deeper dialogue, 180–181

　procedural communication, 172–174

　repeating questions, 179–180

　sticking to agendas, 169–170

　transitioning between topics, 175–176

conversation queue, 160–163

convincing closings, 209

counterproductive behaviors, preventing, 236–240

Covid-19 pandemic

　meeting complexity and, 15

　meeting statistics during, 8–9

creating

　action plans, 244–247

　buffers between meetings, 58

　complementary slides, 220–221

　in-room allies, 198

　meeting space, 102–111

　order out of chaos, 267

creative problem-solving approach, 22, 29

cultural diversity, maintaining in behavior, 78–79

cultural expectations
  about, 75–76
  allowing for cultural tolerance of silence, 79–81
  cultural diversity in behavior, 78–79
  norms about lateness, 76–78

cultural stereotypes, 74–75

cultural tolerance, of silence, 79–81

culture norms, integrating in meetings, 27–31

Curse of Knowledge, 203–204

D

debrief meetings, 13, 121

decisions
  leading discussion until moment of, 184
  summarizing, 245

defining consequences/expectations, 42–43

delegating responsibilities, 246–247

delivering messages, 201–228

designing
  for hybrid meetings, 55–56
  for before the meeting, 35–36
  for during the meeting, 36–37
  meetings to match goals, 95–116
  rooms for face-to-face meetings, 54

determining
  amount of pre-work, 126–129
  meeting needs, 89–94

developing meeting culture, 30–31

dialogue
  driving using communication strategies, 172–176
  probing for deeper, 180–181

discussions
  closing, 267
  driving, 176–181
  facilitating productive, 38–41
  leading until moment of decision, 184

displaying emojis, 193

distractions, managing, 65

drafting agendas, 118–124

dress code, for virtual meetings, 149

driving
  discussion, 176–181
  productive dialogue using communication strategies, 172–176

Duarte, Nancy (author)
  HBR Guide to Persuasive Presentations, 211
  slide:ology, 220

dysfunctional communication, intervening in, 231–235

E

early arrival, 146–148

effectiveness
  about, 253–254
  evaluating, 253–262
  improving for meetings, 7–18
  soliciting feedback, 254–259
  using feedback, 260–262

efficiency, patterns in, 28–30

email, asking for feedback via, 256–257

emojis, displaying, 193

emphasis, hanging pitch for, 216–217

encouraging
  affiliative humor, 227
  participation, 195–199
  webcam use for remote meetings, 282

engaging, in humor during meetings, 225–228

entitativity, 187

environment, normalizing differences in, 83–84

equipment, selecting, 107–110

establishing participation expectations, 130–135

evaluating
  meeting effectiveness, 253–262
  satisfaction, 259

expectations
  about, 117–118
  adjusting agenda, 124
  assigning work before meetings, 125–126
  asynchronous work, 126
  calling on individuals in meetings, 135–139
  clarifying meeting goal/purpose, 118–122
  defining, 42–43
  drafting agendas, 118–124
  establishing for participation, 130–135
  participation ground rules, 129–139
  pre-sharing agenda with attendees, 123–124
  pre-work, 124–129
  rightsizing list of agenda items, 122–123
  setting, 117–139
  soliciting feedback, 124
  synchronous work, 126

external participants, adjusting for, 98–99

external stakeholders, 12

eye contact, 218

F

face-to-face meetings. *See* in-person meetings

facilitating productive discussions, 38–41

fear of missing out (FOMO), 28

feedback
  choosing what to measure, 257–259
  implementing changes based on, 261–262
  process for gathering, 255–257
  sharing results from, 261
  soliciting, 124, 254–259
  using, 260–262

50/50 rule, 202–203

filler words, 214–215

Finland, lateness in, 77

follow-up
  about, 243–244
  accountability and, 44
  after hybrid meetings, 251
  after one-on-one meetings, 252
  after virtual meetings, 251
  being available for quick clarification, 249–252
  brief, 250
  creating action plans, 244–247
  delegating responsibilities, 246–247
  listing action items, 245–246
  making meeting materials accessible, 247–249
  recording action plans, 244–247
  summarizing decisions, 245

FOMO (fear of missing out), 28

formality, managing for meetings, 24–27

fostering speak-up environments, 281

framing body language for virtual meetings, 218–219

frequency, of pausing when speaking, 214–215

Friedmann, Susan (author)
  Meeting and Event Planning For Dummies, 13

full meeting continuum
  about, 33–34
  facilitating productive discussions, 38–41
  holding people accountable, 41–44
  meeting scaffolding, 34–37
  procedural communication, 37

G

generating
  action plans, 244–247
  buffers between meetings, 58
  complementary slides, 220–221
  in-room allies, 198
  meeting space, 102–111
  order out of chaos, 267

geographic locations, recognizing, 99–100

Germany
  about, 73–74
  cultural expectations in, 75–76
  lateness in, 77

The Glance Test, 220–221

global feedback, 256, 257–259

global participants
  about, 73–74
  accounting for setting, 81–85
  allowing for differences in video use, 84–85
  cultural diversity in behavior, 78–79
  cultural expectations, 75–81
  cultural stereotypes, 74–75
  cultural tolerance of silence, 79–81
  normalizing differences in environment, 83–84
  norms about lateness, 76–78
  time zones, 82–83

globalization, meeting complexity and, 14

goals
  clarifying, 118–122, 159
  designing meetings to match, 95–116

grace period, for lateness, 77–78

ground rules
  for bad behavior, 235
  setting for participation, 40–41, 278

groups, running effective, 17–18

H

hands, talking with your, 218, 219

HBR Guide to Persuasive Presentations (Duarte), 211

Heath, Chip (author)
  Made to Stick, 212

Heath, Dan (author)
  Made to Stick, 212

help, asking for, 282

hide self-view function, 64
HR decisions, meeting for, 120
humor, engaging in during meetings, 225–228
hybrid meetings
  about, 51–53
  activating participation in, 165–166
  audience location in, 220
  calling on people in, 138–139
  checking technology for, 152
  designing for, 55–56
  determining amount of pre-work for, 128–129
  early arrival for, 147
  encouraging participation in, 198–199
  ensuring voices are heard in, 190–191
  establishing participation expectations for, 134–135
  follow-up after, 251
  getting into conversation queue in, 162–163
  interacting with visual aids in, 224–225
  length of, 57
  managing brainstorming sessions in, 183–184
  pre-meeting talk for, 157–158
  presenting slides in, 107
  selecting equipment for, 110–111
  selecting length of, 116
  selecting software for, 106–107
  taking turns in, 39
  using video in, 59–71
hybrid work model, 45–46

I

icons, explained, 3
identifying
  bad meeting behaviors, 232–234
  main structures of meeting communication, 21–23
impact, speaking with, 213–220
implementing changes based on feedback, 261–262
improving
  effectiveness of meetings, 7–18
  participation, 277–282
inclusion rule, 29
informing, without deciding, 93–94
in-person meetings
  about, 46–48
  activating participation in, 164
  active listening in, 179

calling on people in, 135–136
checking technology for, 149–150
designing rooms for, 54
determining amount of pre-work for, 127
early arrival for, 147
encouraging participation in, 196
enhancing environment for, 104
ensuring voices are heard in, 188–189
establishing participation expectations for, 130–132
getting into conversation queue in, 161
interacting with visual aids in, 222
length of, 57
managing brainstorming sessions in, 182
moving with meaning in, 217
nonverbal behaviors in, 188
pre-meeting talk for, 155–156
selecting length of, 115
taking turns in, 39
in-room allies, creating, 198
integrating culture norms in meetings, 27–31
interacting, with visual aids, 221–225
internal participants, adjusting for, 98–99
internal stakeholders, 12
internet connections, for hybrid meetings, 56
intervening, in dysfunctional communication, 231–235
inviting people, to meetings, 112–113
Iran, lateness in, 77
Italy, lateness in, 77

J

Japan, cultural expectations in, 76
job satisfaction, relationship with meetings, 10

K

Keith, Elise, 8–9

L

last-minute nature, of virtual meetings, 50–51
lateness
  normalizing, 28
  norms about, 76–78
leading discussions, until moment of decision, 184
Lehmann-Willenbrock, Nale, 173, 225

length
  of meetings, 30, 57–58, 265–270
  of pauses, 215
  selecting for meetings, 114–116
lighting
  for face-to-face meetings, 54
  for meeting space, 102
  for virtual meetings, 109
listening, active, 178–179
listing action items, 245–246
long-term strategy, meeting for, 120
Lucid Meetings, 8–9

M

Made to Stick (Heath and Heath), 212
managing
  attendees' attention using vocal variety, 213–217
  brainstorming sessions, 181–184
  conversation flow, 167–184
  cultural diversity in behavior, 78–79
  distractions, 65
  formality of meetings, 24–27
  serial interrupters, 235
  technology, 64–65
  time spent on topics, 170–171
materials
  accessibility of, 247–249
  physical manipulation of, 96
meaning, moving with, 217
media richness theory, 61
Meeting and Event Planning For Dummies (Friedmann), 13
meeting format
  about, 45–46
  expectations of, 99
  hybrid, 51–53
  in-person, 46–48
  selecting, 46–53, 96–101
  selecting meeting space, 53–56
  selecting physical rooms, 53–56
  setting up virtual space, 56
  timing, 57–58
  virtual, 49–51
meeting goal, matching with meeting style, 19–31
meeting practitioners, 176
meeting preparatory talk, 154

meeting scaffolding
  about, 34–35
  before the meeting, 35–36
  during the meeting, 36–37
meeting size, video and, 67–68
meeting space
  creating, 102–111
  selecting, 53–56
meeting style, matching with meeting goal, 19–31
meetings. *See also* hybrid meetings; in-person meetings; virtual meetings
  ad hoc, 46
  "all hands," 121
  assigning work before, 125–126
  building buffers between, 58
  calling on people in, 135–139, 188
  for collaboration, 92
  committee, 13
  complexity of, 14–17
  debrief, 13, 121
  designing to match goals, 95–116
  determining need for, 89–94
  engaging in humor during, 225–228
  evaluating effectiveness of, 253–262
  importance of, 8–9
  improving effectiveness of, 7–18
  integrating culture norms in, 27–31
  inviting people to, 112–113
  keeping on track, 168–171
  length of, 265–270
  managing formality of, 24–27
  most common types of, 12–13
  moving along, 265–270
  one-on-one, 13–14, 252
  preventing bad behaviors in, 229–240
  project team, 13
  project updates, 121
  for promotion decisions, 120
  with purpose, 91
  for Quarterly Business Reviews (QBRs), 120
  relationship with job satisfaction, 10
  restaurant, 275
  scheduling, 112–116
  selecting length of, 114–116
  for services development discussions, 120
  setting tone just before, 145–158

performance pressure, 40

personal production value, 148

pitch, changing for emphasis, 216–217

planning

   for collaboration, 26–27

   for hybrid meetings, 53

policies, setting for video, 68–72

positioning, for meeting space, 102

power seats, 103

pre-meeting talk, 153–158

presenting

   looking at camera when, 219

   slides in hybrid meetings, 107

preventing

   bad behaviors in meetings, 229–240

   counterproductive behaviors, 236–240

   multitasking during meetings, 62–63, 278–279

pre-work

   about, 124–125

   assigning work before meetings, 125–126

   determining amount of, 126–129

procedural communication, 37, 172–174

product development discussions, meeting for, 120

project team meetings, 13

project updates, 121

promotion decisions, meeting for, 120

protecting wellness of team, 268–269

proximity bias, 134

psychological safety, 138

purpose

   clarifying, 118–122, 159

   meeting with, 91

Q

Quarterly Business Reviews (QBRs), 120

questions, repeating, 179–180

R

reading the room, 280

recognizing

   geographic locations, 99–100

   meeting culture, 30–31

recording action plans, 244–247

reducing aggressive humor, 227–228

Reed, Karin M. (author)

   Suddenly Hybrid: Managing the Modern Meeting, 16, 71, 97

   Suddenly Virtual: Making Remote Meetings Work, 16, 97, 232–233

refreshments

   for face-to-face meetings, 54

   for meeting space, 102

reining in bad behavior, 239–240

reiterating participation ground rules, 160–166

relationships, using video based on, 68

Remember icon, 3

repeating questions, 179–180

rephrasing, for clarity, 266–267

responsibilities, delegating, 246–247

restaurant meetings, 275

rewarding good behavior, 239–240

rich medium, 96

Rogelberg, Steven, 10

room, reading the, 280

round-robin approach, 21–22, 29, 38

Rule of Three, 205–208

running effective groups/teams, 17–18

S

satisfaction, measuring, 259

Saudi Arabia, lateness in, 77

scheduling

   meetings, 112–116

   new conversations, 269

science-based practice, 8

seating

   for meeting space, 102

   power seats, 103

selecting

   communication styles for meetings, 20–24

   equipment, 107–110

   length of meetings, 114–116

   meeting formality, 25–26

   meeting format, 46–53, 96–101

   meeting space, 53–56

   physical rooms for meetings, 53–56

   sets, 66

   software, 105–107

   what to evaluate for feedback, 257–259

U

Ukraine, lateness in, 77
unexpected opens, 208–209
United Kingdom, cultural expectations in, 76
United States
  cultural expectations in, 75
  grace period, for lateness, 77–78
  lateness in, 77
urgency, of meetings, 48

V

validating verbal/nonverbal participation, 191–194
verbal participation, validating, 191–194
video
  allowing for differences in use of, 84–85
  benefits of using, 67–68
  for hybrid meetings, 55
  potential for overload of, 63–68
  setting policies for, 68–72
  using in virtual or hybrid meetings, 59–71
  value of, 60–63
video culture, of organizations, 69–70
virtual backgrounds, 66
virtual dress code, 149
virtual meetings
  about, 49–51
  activating participation in, 164–165
  calling on people in, 136–138
  checking technology for, 150–151
  determining amount of pre-work for, 127–128
  early arrival for, 147
  encouraging participation in, 196–198
  encouraging webcam use during, 282
  ensuring voices are heard in, 189–190
  establishing participation expectations for, 133–134
  follow-up after, 251
  framing body language in, 218–219
  getting into conversation queue in, 161–162
  interacting with visual aids in, 222–224
  length of, 57
  managing brainstorming sessions in, 182–183
  nonverbal behaviors in, 189
  pre-meeting talk for, 156–157
  selecting equipment for, 108–110
  selecting length of, 115–116
  selecting software for, 105–106
  setting up for, 56
  taking turns in, 39
  technology in, 189
  using video in, 59–71
virtual reality meetings, 275–276
virtual space, effectiveness of, 104–111
virtual whiteboards, 133
visual aids
  about, 220
  creating complementary slides, 220–221
  interacting with, 221–225
vocal variety, maintaining attendees' attention using, 213–217
voice, 186–191

W

walking meetings, 274
Warning icon, 3
watching yourself speak, 64
water cooler meetings, 272
webcams, encouraging use of during remote meetings, 282
work talk, 154
workday schedules, 101
work-family conflict, 101

Z

Zoom fatigue, 60

About the Authors

Joseph A. Allen, Ph.D., is a professor of Industrial and Organizational Psychology at the University of Utah. Before he completed his doctorate in Organizational Science at the University of North Carolina at Charlotte (UNCC) in 2010, he received his Master of Arts degree in I/O Psychology at the UNCC in 2008 and his Bachelor of Science degree in Psychology from the Brigham Young University in 2005. His research focuses on three major areas of inquiry including the study of workplace meetings, organizational community engagement, and occupational safety and health. He has more than 200 publications in academic outlets, and has published several books including *Suddenly Virtual: Making Remote Meetings Work* and *Suddenly Hybrid: Managing the Modern Meeting*. He has presented over 300 papers/posters at regional and national conferences and given more than 100 invited presentations on his research. He serves as a reviewer for various journals and is an editorial board member for the Journal of Business and Psychology, Group and Organization Management, and the European Journal of Work and Organizational Psychology. He directs the Center for Meeting Effectiveness housed in the Rocky Mountain Center for Occupational and Environmental Health. Dr. Allen has consulted for more than 400 non-profit and for-profit organizations, *and his* recent work can be found at www.joeallen.org.

Karin M. Reed is an Emmy award-winning journalist and CEO of Speaker Dynamics (https://speakerdynamics.com), an executive communications training firm featured in Forbes. Karin has been teaching business professionals how to be effective communicators across all platforms for nearly a decade — whether the audience is in the same room or the other side of a camera lens. A three-time author, she has been quoted as a thought leader by various prestigious publications, including Inc. Magazine, Fast Company and Business Insider and was named an "Author who Inspires Us" by McKinsey and Company.

Dedication

Writing a book is a commitment, but not just for the authors. In our case, it also requires the endless support of our families who are willing to let us disappear into the process for countless hours . . . and at all hours of the day and night. For that, we are forever grateful.

Authors' Acknowledgments

A few years ago, Joe and Karin experienced a collision of their expertise precipitated by the COVID-19 pandemic. Joe has been studying meetings for decades. Karin has been helping clients to communicate effectively across all platforms, including video, for nearly as long. When video became a larger part of meetings as a whole, a prolific collaboration occurred. Joe and Karin managed to write three books in just about three years. This feat would not have been possible without their strong friendship and mutual respect for what each brought to the table. It made the writing process not only manageable but enjoyable.

We'd both like to thank our amazing technical editor, Nale Lehmann-Willenbrock, and our development editor, Daniel Mersey, for their efforts to help us make this book an amazing read for our readers.

Karin would like to additionally thank her thousands of clients who have entrusted her to help them problem solve any communication conundrums that they have encountered. Many of their experiences inform her writing and her current training practice. What a gift!

Joe would like to also thank his many students and professional collaborators for their help in establishing the science of meetings, upon which the recommendations, practices, and procedures in this book are based. Without their tireless help and assistance, none of the many academic articles, book chapters, and books would not exist. Truly meaningful!

Publisher's Acknowledgments

Acquisitions Editor: Tracy Boggier

Development Editor: Daniel Mersey

Technical Editor: Nale Lehmann-Willenbrock

Managing Editor: Kristie Pyles

Production Editor: Saikarthick Kumarasamy

Cover Image: © Andrey_Popov/Shutterstock